God's town
LIVERPOOL
& her Parish since 1207

God's town
LIVERPOOL
& her Parish since 1207

CRISPIN
PAILING

First published in 2019
by Palatine Books,
Carnegie House,
Chatsworth Road
Lancaster LA1 4SL
www.palatinebooks.com

British Library Cataloguing-in-Publication data
A catalogue record for this book is available from the
British Library

Paperback ISBN 13: 978-1-910837-27-6

Designed and typeset by Carnegie Book Production
www.carnegiebookproduction.com

Printed and bound by Jellyfish Solutions

In Memoriam

Sir William Gladstone Bt K.G.

Contents

Foreword

This learned and engaging book sets out to correct what its author sees as history's failure to appreciate how central the Church has been to life in the great city of Liverpool. I am exceptionally proud, albeit in the most cursory way, to be associated with the book and even more proud to be able to write this foreword.

Like many of the best books, this is a labour of love; by its author – the Rector of Liverpool – who has written late into the night for countless months to complete it and by my late father – Sir William Gladstone, Bt, K.G. – who both encouraged and sponsored its author. It may be a labour of love but it is also a work based on deep scholarly knowledge and conviction and it is that combination of love and expertise that makes it such a valuable project.

I am sure that my father would be happy with the results. This project was of great interest to him; he was a man of deep religious conviction and an historian. So this book is the perfect combination of some of his strongest interests.

The Gladstone connection to the church and to Liverpool is strong and my father felt it keenly. My great, great grandfather, William Gladstone, four times Prime Minister, was born in Rodney Street (his father was MP for the city) and his politics were always informed by his strong religious beliefs.

I well remember how excited my father was when Crispin embarked on this project. They both spent many happy afternoons talking – in their gentle scholarly way – about countless subjects, many of which have – in one way or another – found their way into the pages of this book. I am sure my father would have loved reading it and equally sure that he would have found very little within its pages to quibble about which would have been both unusual for him and testament to the depth of knowledge and passion contained within its pages.

Sir Charles Gladstone
Hawarden Castle

Introduction

There are many histories of Liverpool, and many prisms through which the city has been seen. Very often the ecclesiastical history of a city is seen as a peripheral matter, but in Liverpool the parish has had an unusually strong connection with the city as a whole. There are many reasons for this, but it is significant that whereas other cities are littered with historic churches and parishes, Liverpool only ever had one parish and, until the eighteenth century, one church. The Parish Church of Liverpool is therefore the oldest surviving institution in the city, and the thesis of this book is that the relationship between the parish and the city has been unusually close in a way which is not usually apparent in other places in the country. If this were a history of a particular church, then there are many details which could be included which I have not mentioned, but this is essentially an account of a relationship between parish and city.

The origins of the book lie in an exhibition which I put together for the narthex of the church in the spring of 2018. This was not the first history exhibition in the church, but the installation of a permanent display was a response to the ever-increasing visitor numbers. I should like to argue that the growing numbers are a result of our work as a church, but whilst that may in part be true, the most significant increase in visitors is a result of the resurgence of Liverpool as a destination. Just as in the early days of the church, many of our visitors now arrive by sea: when a cruise ship arrives in Liverpool, the Parish Church is the first open heritage building which her passengers encounter. And although the church is today dwarfed by the buildings around us, the Parish Church is still marked on maritime navigation charts which now appear electronically on the bridge of every ship which approaches the port.

There are a couple of small details of explanation required. The first is minor, that before 1752 any date between 1 January and the beginning of the next year on 25 March I have noted with both the Julian and Gregorian calendar years. So, for example, I refer to the consecration of the Chapel of St Nicholas in February 1361/2. The other point of explanation is the dedication to Our Lady and St Nicholas: as we see in Chapter 1, the first chapel was dedicated to St Mary, and the second, adjacent chapel was dedicated to St Nicholas. Until the Reformation, they co-existed, and it is slightly unclear in which building the various chantries had their altars. With the closure of St Mary's in 1548 the other chapel effortlessly took on the dedication of Our Lady and St Nicholas. Throughout the following five hundred years the full dedication has commonly been used, but either through protestant sentiment or for ease of articulation it has equally been known just as St Nicholas: the use of designation is completely random. I have followed this randomness in using both terms at various points, often reflecting the language used in contemporary sources, but the meaning should always be clear.

There are very many organisations to thank across the city, including the City Archives, National Museums Liverpool, the *Liverpool Echo*, the Athenaeum, the University of Liverpool and many others. Most of all, my thanks go to many friends within these institutions who have helped me at various points. They are too numerous to name, as are all those at Liverpool Parish Church who have aided me on my way, but my gratitude is sincere.

It was when I was putting together the exhibition that the Patron of the Parish, Sir William Gladstone, suggested to me that it was time to develop this into a book, and that if I would write it then he would provide some of the necessary support. Willie – as he was known to us all – was tremendous in his friendship of a number of rectors, and he was also a fine historian himself. In the week after we hatched our plan he wrote to me twice about it, and so it was a shock that he died just nine days later, on Maundy Thursday 2018. Since then, I have been grateful for the continuing support and friendship of his son, Charlie Gladstone, who continues the relationship between the Gladstone family and the Parish of Liverpool which began on 29 April 1800 when Charlie's great great great grandfather, John Gladstone (later the first baronet) married Anne MacKenzie Robertson in the Parish Church of Liverpool (St Peter's). It is with sadness and gratitude that I dedicate this book to John Gladstone's great great grandson, William Gladstone.

CHAPTER ONE

A Medieval Chapel

Liverpool

Very few things start from nothing, but despite the Charter of King John in 1207 which formally founded the township of Liverpool, there is barely any trace of a settlement earlier, except a brief mention of Liuerpul in a charter in the last decade of the twelfth century.[1] The districts of West Derby and of Walton-on-the-Hill were already in existence when the strategic possibilities of the inlet on the banks of the Mersey were first noticed, and the foundation by King John afforded tremendous military advantages for transporting troops to wage war in Ireland, not to mention the possibilities of seaborne access into Wales and Scotland. A charter granting the status of a borough meant that Liverpool was, from the beginning, independent from West Derby and Walton, as well as from Chester, which was well established and with a significant Abbey Church which had already been in existence for a number of centuries.

There is no record of the foundation of the chapel in Liverpool, but it is difficult to imagine that, as soon as the original seven streets were cut, there was not also a chapel. The streets separated out the burgages (portions of land) which the first citizens (burgesses) acquired and on which they promptly paid tax, firstly to the Crown, and then later to the Earl of Chester, who acquired the rights to the town from Henry

1

A copy by W. Herdman in the 1870s, supposedly of the earliest view of Liverpool from the twelfth century. Although Herdman registers doubt about the authenticity, he accepts it on the strength of the learned collections of papers in which he found copies. In fact there can be little genuine about the picture, not least because the church resembles the Chapel of St Nicholas, rather than the later images which survive of the Chapel of St Mary.
From W. Herdman, Pictorial Relics of Ancient Liverpool, *1878*

III in 1233. It was the Earl of Chester who laid the foundations of the castle in the 1230s, which included a chapel.[2] But such a chapel was commonly for the garrison and the noble family inhabiting a castle, and the evidence of a town chapel which appears shortly afterwards might imply that the chapel was already in existence. The Earls of Chester had a short tenure in Liverpool and were supplanted by Edmund of Lancaster, a son of Henry III, whose short but intense dominance over the town led the burgesses to a complaint before a royal enquiry in 1292, after which Edmund quietly forgot about Liverpool.[3] Sixty years later, Edmund's grandson, Henry 1st Duke of Lancaster re-established the family connection by the founding of a chantry, and the connection between the chapel and the Dukes of Lancaster continues to the present day.

The First Chapel

By the middle of the thirteenth century the written record of the chapel begins. The first mention of the chapel is in a property conveyance from the 1250s.[4] One of the witnesses to the document was Richard 'capellanus' (chaplain), who was also the scribe of a number of contemporary title deeds. The document itself is a conveyance of land from Ranulph de Mor to his daughter Margery and his son-in-law John Gernet. Only a lifetime interest is given if Margery fails to produce an heir. Amidst the description of property is a reference to a quarter burgage by the chapel ('jacent iux capellam') and a further reference to a half burgage by the chapel. No dedication of the chapel is given but it is this which became known as the Chapel of St Mary del Quay. The description of the parcel of land is 'a fourth part of one burgage lying next to the chapel and next to the land of William of Chnouslee [Knowsley].' The Knowsley family lands lay adjacent to the river, which helps to identify the chapel. The dating of this document is complex, but would seem to be in the 1250s. There is another property conveyance[5] in the same bundle which is witnessed by both Ranulph de Mor and John Gernet and which can be dated more precisely because it transfers

MS containing the first written reference to the chapel *c.*1250s.
Liverpool Record Office, Liverpool Libraries

property owned by Robert de Ferrers, son of William de Ferrers, formerly Earl of Derby. William died in 1254 and Robert surrendered his lands to his son, Edmund Crouchback, in 1257. We can say nothing more precise than that Ranulph de Mor and John Gernet were active in the 1250s, and the references to the chapel will date from around this time. John Elton, writing in 1902, makes an error in giving the date of William de Ferrers' death as 1252. He tries to go further and say that the document referring to the chapel *must* be before 1257, but there is no good reason to draw this conclusion.[6] Elton's dating, though, took on a revered status in later histories of Liverpool. There was sufficient doubt in 1956 that a letter was published in the *Daily Post* inviting comments on the proposal that the following year would be the seven hundredth anniversary of the foundation of a church on the site. In the absence of any response or challenge, an anniversary festival took place.[7]

There is one further document from the bundle of Moore Manuscripts worthy of mention: another undated, though obviously later, manuscript recording an agreement between John Gernet and Ranulph de Mor by which John Gernet and his wife Margery return to Ranulph and his wife Agnes one burgage and ten selions which they had previously been given. But, in a reversal of the previous conveyance, Ranulph and Agnes are only given a lifetime interest in the property. An early twentieth-century cataloguer of the Moore Manuscripts has annotated the index slip which is kept with the manuscript with the comment: "A curious indenture," which indeed it is. But at least we know the scribe, who is named as Richard, scriptor, capellanus.[8]

Although the written record of the chapel is faint, references to Chapel Street begin to appear in the thirteenth and fourteenth centuries. The first is in a grant of property dated 26 June 1294 from John del Mor. The next is in a grant from John, son of Alan de Liverpoll, and dated 9 October 1317.[9] Thereafter the references are plentiful.

The First Chantries

We cannot know the nature of the foundation of the chapel – Elton claims it is monastic, though offers no evidence[10] – or the terms on which the chaplain had his income, but the first chantries appeared in the fourteenth century. The first was the Chantry at the Altar of St John, which the King's Commissioners at the Reformation record as having been founded by John Liverpole to pray for the souls of his ancestors. This appears to date from the 1320s.[11]

The next foundation dates from the 1350s, when land was given to support a priest for the Altar of St Mary. The evidence is retrospective: in the Rent Rolls of a later Duke of Lancaster, John of Gaunt (1340–99) there is a reference to the grant of 12 shillings to the chapel from Liverpool rents from Henry, sometime Duke of Lancaster (*c.* 1310–61).[12] Two centuries later, in the report on the chantries from the King's Commissioners in 1548, the chantry of the High Altar (St Mary) at the chapel is described as the foundation of Henry, Duke of Lancaster, to commemorate the souls of his ancestors.[13] Further evidence of the gift of land to support the chantry is in the Patent Rolls of Edward III, which confirm the gift of land made by Henry, Duke of Lancaster which were worth £10 a year, and dedicated "to celebrate divine service every day, for the Souls of all the faithful deceased, in the Chapel of the Blessed Mary and Saint Nicholas, of Liverpull, according to the Mayor and Commonalty aforesaid."[14] Of note here is that the foundation of the chantry is supposedly not on the initiative of the Duke of Lancaster, but the "Mayor and Commonalty" which presumably requested the financial aid to provide for a priest.

The New Chapel of St Nicholas

It was around the time of the foundation of the first chantry that plans were made for a new chapel. Clearly, as the town grew, the Chapel of St Mary was of insufficient size: eighteenth-century engravings of the Chapel of St Nicholas show a small building at the west end which is identified as the old Chapel of St Mary, and it is obvious that the growing town needed somewhere larger. The land for the new chapel may have come from the Duke of Lancaster,[15] and, as we have seen, the grant of land to provide the income for a priest certainly did come from him, and the Patent Rolls of 1355 imply that there is already a single place of worship, dedicated to Our Lady and St Nicholas. Until the Reformation, there remains some confusion about the dedication. Given that the new chapel was not consecrated until 1361, the reference in 1355 to the Chapel of the Blessed Mary and Saint Nicholas suggests that the old chapel had already acquired the joint dedication, though, as we shall see, the lack of clarity remains throughout the following century. The other conclusion we could draw is that the new chapel was built on to the old one. This is the assertion of John Brownbill, writing in 1914, who thought that the Chapel of St Nicholas was a north aisle, and that each chantry foundation necessitated further building.[16] Whilst this resolves the early evidence of a joint dedication of the new chapel, the evidence at the Reformation is that there were two distinct buildings, one of which was bought by the town and became the school.

As the chapel was built, the need for a burial ground became more urgent. The prevalence of the Black Death (plague) of 1361/2 across England is well documented, and it seems likely that the burial ground of the parish church in Walton was all that was available. The Earl of Ulster was on his way to Ireland and stationed in Liverpool when he saw the pressing need for burial space in the town.[17] Ulster then petitioned the Bishop of Lichfield and Coventry (in whose Diocese the town then stood) for a burial ground in Liverpool itself. Temporary permission was given in a Licence of September 1361 to inter victims of the plague in a burial ground at the Chapel of St Nicholas: "Licence to the burgesses of the town of Litherpole granted in consideration of the plague, which is specially bad there, at the instance of Leonill, Earl of Ulster, for burial in the cemetery of the Chapel of St Nicholas in the said town until Christmas next Saving the rights of the parish church."[18]

Although the reference to the burial ground is for the Chapel of St Nicholas only, it would still be another six months until the new chapel was consecrated in February 1361/2.[19] The evidence from the previous decade of the two dedications together makes it too difficult to separate the two buildings at this stage. Even the High Altar Chantry of St Mary appears as much connected with the new building as the old chapel and we can speculate that the chantry was quickly established in

Extract from Second Register of Bishop Robert Stretton, granting permission for burials at St Nicholas' Chapel, September 1361.
Reproduced courtesy of Staffordshire Record Office (B/A/1/5 Folio 44a)

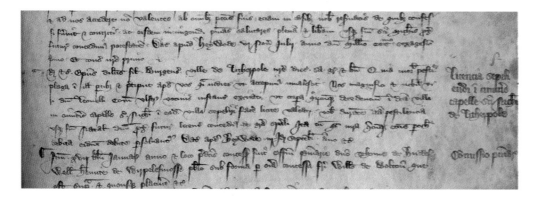

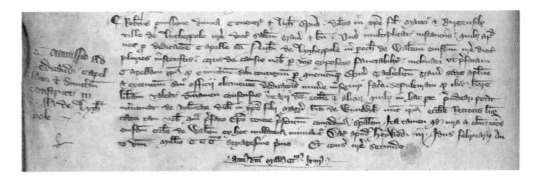

Extract from Second Register of Bishop Robert Stretton, with a commission for the
dedication of St Nicholas' Chapel, February 1361/2
Reproduced courtesy of Staffordshire Record Office (B/A/1/5 Folio 45b)

the new chapel. The consecration of the new chapel took place on the
authority of a further licence in February 1361/2, allowing any passing
"Catholic bishop" to perform the ceremony. The same licence allowed
for the temporary permission for burials from the previous September
to become permanent.[20]

There is no direct evidence to help us understand the physical
appearance of the new chapel, although we can trace back some of
the details from later centuries. We know that the original building
enjoyed later additions, such as the 'out-aisle' added at the end of the
seventeenth century, and the spire built in 1746. The first picture of
the chapel is incidental in a copy of a plan of town defences of 1644,
but it is visible in more detail in the larger picture of Liverpool in
1680 by an unknown artist,[21] and appears to show a square tower with
buttresses, and a nave with a single aisle and south porch. The chapel
will, of course, have grown piecemeal, as money became available, and
although the north side is not visible in the painting of 1680, at some
point a north aisle was added to the original nave. Later, in 1697, a
further 'out-aisle' was added to the north aisle with a capacity in that
first building of perhaps just 250 people.[22] At some point a tower was
built, but it was only in 1433 that the will of Margery Fyche (who
stipulated burial in the churchyard) gave one heifer for a belfry for
the Chapel of St Nicholas, which may have been the construction
of the entire tower, or just an addition to it.[23] We could speculate
whether the entrance was ever on the north side of the building,
because in the eighteenth century the font – traditionally near the

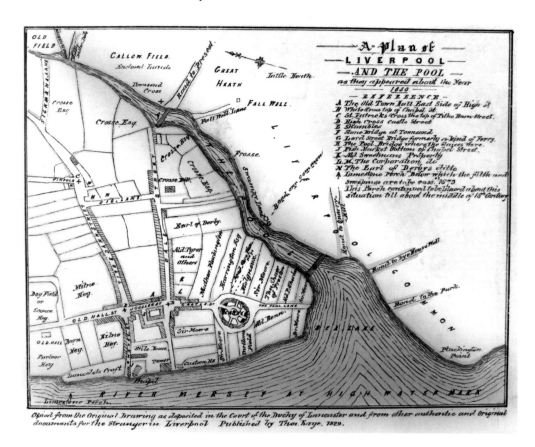

Map of Liverpool in 1650 (copy published in 1829) Until the seventeenth century, maps of Liverpool still focused on the original 'seven streets' laid out in the thirteeenth century: High St, Chapel St, Water St (Bank St), Castle St, Dale St, Tithebarn St, Old Hall St.
Courtesy of the Athenaeum, Liverpool

entrance to a church – was situated in the north west corner of the chapel.[24] Subsequent additions, as well as the rebuilding of the church in 1775 and again in 1952 have wiped away virtually every trace of the medieval building. All that remains are pieces of dressed stone, presumably from the medieval tower which collapsed in 1810. They were re-used in the foundations of the new tower built in 1815, now visible in the current boiler cellar.[25] Intriguingly, there is a contemporary reference to fragments of an earlier building being found when digging the foundations of the new tower, though no comment is made about what was done with these remains.[26]

Property and Chantries

The first chantry founded specifically for the new chapel was that of the Altar of St Nicholas, possibly established in the 1360s. The benefactor is named as John [of Gaunt], sometime Duke of Lancaster, and the purpose was to celebrate Mass for his soul and for his ancestors.[27]

Property deeds and other legal papers continue to be the main source of information about the chapel until the end of the fifteenth century. Alongside the gradual acquisition of land by the chapel and the chantries, we catch fleeting references to the chaplains by name. For example, in a document of 1416 we learn that the chaplains were Thomas of Caton and Henry of Bretherton.[28] In 1466, half a century later, two documents mention William Amot as chaplain, and ten years later another reference is to Richard Twathes.[29]

At the same time, the chantry lands steadily increased. For example, in a deed of 1411 in which Nicolas de Lyverpull was disposing of the estate of William de Penereth, it is noted that some land had already been given to the chantry of the Blessed Mary of Lyverpull, to celebrate for the soul of William de Penereth.[30] Similarly, in 1465 there is a grant of land in Garston from Charles and Elena Gelybrond to the Mayor and Commonalty of Liverpool for the support of a chaplain to serve at one of the altars.[31]

Income and Favour

Although we cannot always separate the activities taking place in the two chapels, and they are often named as one chapel or foundation, there was clearly no desire to reduce the role of the older chapel. An enterprising spirit led to an application to higher ecclesiastical authorities for support. The first was to Rome, and on 25 June 1456 Pope Calixtus III issued a papal bull granting an indulgence and remission of sins to those who visited or worshipped in the Chapel of St Mary, or contributed to the building or the maintenance of the priests.

> *To all Christ's faithful who shall see these presents. Confirmation of the indulgences and remissions which the late John cardinal bishop of St. Rufina's and by papal dispensation archbishop of Canterbury, William archbishop of York and very many bishops of England, having regard to the devotion of the people who flock*

Calixtus III (1378–1458), who pledged indulgencies for those who contributed towards or prayed in the Chapel of St Mary
Oil on guadameci, Juan de Juanes, 1568, held in Valencia Cathedral, via Wikimedia Commons).

to the chapel of St. Mary de Key situate within the cemetery of the chapel of Lyverpolle in the [united] dioceses of Coventry and Lichfield, and to the miracles which God was working therein by the merits of the same Virgin, have granted to all faithful who pray there, or who make an offering for the repair of the said chapel, or for the maintenance of the priests who celebrate [divine offices] therein, or for the adornment of divine worship in the same; with relaxation hereby of five years and five quarantines of enjoined penance to all who, being penitent and having confessed, visit the said chapel on the feasts of St. Mary and Whitsuntide and the octaves thereof and give alms for such conservation, repair and maintenance, or for such adornment, these presents to hold good for ever. The pope's will is that if any other indulgence have been granted by him to the same chapel, in perpetuity or for a certain time not yet elapsed, the present letters shall be null and void.[32]

An almost identical document dated 14 December 1459 was then procured from John, Bishop of Lichfield, who granted an indulgence of forty days to those who gave money for the chapel or for the chaplains.[33]

Another attraction to draw pilgrims with their votive offerings to the chapel was a statue of St Nicholas outside the Chapel of St Mary, where sailors made offerings before they went to sea. The written record of this is no earlier than the eighteenth century, but is consistent. William Enfield's *History of Leverpool* from 1774 refers to the statue which formerly stood outside the church, but a manuscript of Sir John Prestwich's *History of Liverpool*, which remained unpublished at his death in 1795, quotes earlier sources describing the statue.[34] There is a further reference to the statue, though perhaps also derivative of eighteenth-century descriptions, in Herman Melville's novel *Redburn*, published in 1849, as well as *Smith's Guide to Liverpool for 1843*.[35]

Clergy Housing

There is no information about where the priests lived in the first two centuries of the chapel's existence, but in the later medieval period, adjoining the church lands was the clergy house. The evidence for this is twofold. Firstly, a house was given in 1470 by Robert Taillour and his daughter to the Mayor and Commonalty for the priests of the chapel;[36] secondly, the King's Commissioners in 1548 note that all the chantry priests – by then four in number – live in a manor house with an adjoining garden worth 20 shillings a year.[37] There is a further, though more imprecise, reference to the clergy housing in 1533 in the King's Rentally, in which there is a mention of the "priests' chambers."[38] We cannot be entirely sure where the property was, and there are a number of references to a 'stone house' in the churchyard, although this more usually refers to the old Chapel of St Mary. There was wasteland on the Chapel Street side of the church, but town-owned houses to the east in what is now 'Old Churchyard', and it seems probable that the house was there.[39]

Although the value of the property is noted in the Report on the Chantries, the fact that the house was owned by the town must have saved it from being confiscated. Even so, the clergy after the Reformation did not have sole use of the property: in December 1565 on of the 'chantry chambers' is assigned to a stonemason, Henry Kaye, and his apprentice as they work on repairing the chapel.[40] By 1574 we can see a slight change in terminology, but presumably the same house, when the town paid for repairs to the "minister's chambers."[41] At some point this arrangement came to an end, because in 1655 the minister of the chapel, John Fogg, petitioned the common council for a new clergy house recently acquired by the town, Cooke's House in Tithebarn Street.[42]

CHAPTER TWO

The Reformation

Prelude: Business as Usual

At the start of the Henrician era there were very few storm clouds to herald the English Reformation. The worshipping life of the town continued as it had for nearly three centuries, but with no religious communities or foundations the running of the town church was relatively straightforward. The only significant connection with a monastic house was with Birkenhead Priory across the river: as well as maintaining the ferry service across the Mersey, the monks came to Liverpool to trade grain. They rented a warehouse on Water Street to store any unsold grain in an upper room until the next market day.[1] It would be wrong to say that the Liverpool Chapel was controlled by the secular authorities, because the constitution of the town was predicated on the centrality of religion. The codification of the by-laws in 1540/1 reveals not just the usual marking of the rhythm of the year by feasts of the church, but also that the liturgical pattern of the day was dictated by the town: *"It is ordered that the priest of Saynct Johns aulter for the tyme beyng dayly shall saye masse between the owre of v and vi of the clocke in the mornyng, to thentent that all labowrers and well disposed people myndyd to have masse maye come to the churche to here masse at the sayd owre."*[2]

In the interweaving of the town and the church, membership of the town's society invariably brought financial responsibilities towards

Herdman's picture of Liverpool Castle. Although a conjectural drawing, the uniformity of design of castles from this era suggests a degree of accuracy. *From W. Herdman,* Pictorial Relics of Ancient Liverpool, *1878*

the church. When a new burgess (land-owning citizen) was admitted to the freedom of the town, a fee was payable to the church. A list of debtors to the church in 1524 reveals a two-tier fee structure, so Henrye Comberbache was charged the lower rate of 3*s*. 4*d*., whereas in the same year John Morehowse was expected to pay the higher rate of 6*s*. 8*d*. Whether or not anyone still remembered the papal bull of the previous century, this system provided the church with a regular income which was not dependent on a donor's hopes of salvation. This income allowed for the maintenance of the building, and the chantries provided the stipends for the clergy.[3]

Administering church property and collecting the income due was cumbersome. Much of this burden was taken by the town authorities. In particular we glimpse the enthusiastic work of William More who appears in a number of documents, including property conveyances and accounts' books. More served as the town mayor on more than one occasion, and he kept his own notes of expenditure. These illustrate how the town authorities directed the affairs of the church. For example, we see More, as mayor in 1511, providing public funds to buy liturgical books for the chapel, and to discharge the fees for some individuals to be entered on the burgess roll.[4] More was a zealous supporter of the chapel, and his will of 1537 indicates that he personally owned books, chalices and vestments. He left most of these to the chapel, and the rest to his family.[5] But the oversight of church property was not just the preserve of enthusiastic individuals: in the by-laws of 1540/1 the mayor *"shall yerelye cause all the churche lands and tenements viewed as often tymes as need shall"* and he should take twelve men with him to ensure that there are no dilapidations.[6]

The majority cause of debt to the church was unpaid rents, although occasional other debts appear, such as Thomas Bolton and Rychard Warmysnam who owed 14*s*. 2*d*. for iron that they sold, presumably on behalf of the church. There were expenses to be paid out as well, such as to William More who took a book to be repaired by a monk at Birkenhead Priory at a cost of 2*s*. 10*d*. The lists of debtors from the 1520s shows that, besides the fee for admission to the burgess roll, the church also charged for the purchase of a 'leystall'. A century later this came to mean a place where cattle (or their waste) were gathered, but in this context it has the older meaning of burial place. Securing a burial place was important, as can be seen from the will of William More. Not only did he allow his executors to pay whatever was necessary to secure burial either in the Parish Church of St Mary, Walton, or in the Chapel of Our Lady and St Nicholas, but he also specified that the officiating clergy should receive 8*d*. each. In addition, he provided for six white gowns to be given to six poor men to bear torches on the day of his burial and to pray for his soul.

The fact that the chapel had a financial life apart from that of the chantries is evident in these glimpses of fees and of transactions relating to the church alone. Alongside chantry lands, it would seem that the chapel accumulated some land of its own. An example of this is in the will of Thomas Gylle of Liverpool who held property in the town itself and in West Derby. In his will of 24 January 1520/1 (probate was granted on 3 February 1525/6) he left land to the Chapel of St Nicholas, to the church at Walton, and also to the chapel at Wavertree, the property for St Nicholas to be held by the churchwardens and the chapel jointly. As the churchwardens were elected by the town, this meant that the control of the chapel's independent wealth remained within the purview of the town at all times.[7]

Unlike some chantries, the priests of Liverpool do not appear to have farmed their own land, but rather they were let to tenants. This also took some management, and there is some trace of the transfer of property or tenancies. The Moore Manuscripts include a property conveyance from 1519 in which William More transfers chantry land to Roger Crosse, and in a further conveyance of 1524 the mayor and 'commonality of Lyverpole' transfer various chantry lands to William More. This includes details of rental and the use to which it was put. For example, one selion (roughly 660 feet by 66 feet) in Wayterthez produced 2*s.* rent for the chaplain at St Katherine's altar.[8]

This altar was the result of the final stage in the growth of the pre-Reformation church in Liverpool. The addition of a fourth chantry – dedicated to St Katherine – was by a will made in 1515, but it was also this chantry which enabled the survival of the old Chapel of St Mary thirty years later. The Crosse family (whose family home was in today's Crosshall Street) were leading citizens in the town – a John Crosse was mayor in 1476 – and landowners. A generation later, another John Crosse, who was a priest at St Nicholas' in the Shambles in London, created by his first will of 10 May 1515 the new chantry of St Katherine. The priest would be appointed by the mayor and by Crosse's brother, Richard Crosse, and his descendants. In addition, the priest was directed to *"kepe gramer scole and to take his avauntage, except all the children whose namez be Crosse and poore children that have no socour."*[9] One of the witnesses to this will was Humphrey Crosse who was also installed as the first chantry priest. This chantry and school seems to have been established immediately before a second will made shortly before John Crosse's death in 1517. This was by no means an unusual arrangement, particularly in the early sixteenth century. For example, just a year earlier in 1514 a chantry to the Blessed Virgin Mary was established by the Earl of Derby in Blackburn with the instruction that the priest should be sufficiently learned in grammar and plainsong to run a free school.[10]

As the deconstruction of the power and wealth of the church began in the 1530s, the theological assault on established practices had yet to reach Liverpool. The will of William More is full of detail about vestments and Mass books, and also the instruction to his son, a priest also with the name William More, to say Mass for his soul. The will is dated in the same year as the closure of Birkenhead Priory across the river, although probate was not granted until 1541. The closure of the Priory without the resistance made by some monastic houses meant that the remaining monks were allowed to work as secular priests. It was possibly the availability of learned and musical clergy which led to a new by-law which appears in the codification of 1541/2 by which the mayor and bailiffs decided to employ a priest who could sing and play the organ, and they instituted a new "leye" (tax) to pay for it.[11]

Chantry Acts

It would appear, therefore, that the gathering pace of the Reformation made no impact on the life of the Liverpool Chapel – at least in the written record – in the 1530s and 1540s. Although the Pilgrimage of Grace of 1536/7 was fomented in Yorkshire and North Lancashire, there is no evidence that there was any active participation as far south as Liverpool. The Abolition of Chantries Acts of 1545 and 1547 were the first jolt to a thriving and accepted system. Edward VI's act of 1547, completing the intention of his father's Act two years' earlier, seized all chantry land as the property of the Crown which, in Lancashire, meant the Duchy of Lancaster. The Duchy had no incentive to hold on to these lands, but there was an immediate wish to realise some cash value. Across the country chantry lands were sold to local landowners,

Liverpool in 1680, although possibly depicting the town at an earlier time.
Courtesy of the Merseyside Maritime Museum, National Museums Liverpool

many of whom were already tenants.[12] This does not seem to be the case in Liverpool, where the chantries of St John, St Katherine, and St Nicholas were swiftly leased in 1548 to Richard Molyneux for 30 years, with their existing tenants.[13] The Molyneux family does not appear amongst the tenants of St Mary's or St Nicholas' chantries in the rental lists recorded in the Town Books in the 1550s, but very likely dating from the 1540s.[14]

The Chantry of St Mary (the High Altar) had a more turbulent period of ownership. The Duchy Rolls show that the lands were let to a Richard Wrightington, but the corporation considered that they had some rights over them. This is perhaps unsurprising, as the corporation now had to make a financial contribution towards a priest at the chapel, but without the chantry lands to provide income. The mayor and corporation took control of the land from St Mary's Chantry, and Wrightington appealed to the Duchy to honour the lease. The judgement was made in Wrightington's favour and an injunction was duly issued to the mayor and corporation.[15] The reverberations from the dissolution of the chantries continued for some centuries. As late as 1779 the Common Council resolved to approach the Chancellor of the Duchy of Lancaster for the purchase of the Chantry Rents payable by the corporation to the Duchy.[16]

Whilst the leases supply the detail of the land held by each chantry in the 1540s, the picture of the activity of each chantry is given in the Reports of the Royal Commissioners appointed first by Henry VIII, and then by Edward and Mary. The Commissioners describe Liverpool as *"one haven towne hauinge a grete nombre of Inhitantes in the same and also grete concurse of strangers bothe by lande and see."*[17] Each of the chantries had one chalice, two vestments, a "sup[er]altare" (the altar stone), and a Mass Book. Elton suggests that there must have been some subterfuge, because the four chantries seem very evenly matched in their equipment, and yet lacking in some of the magnificence which might be expected.[18] However, we have already noted in the will of William More a decade earlier that there were privately owned vestments and plate in use within the chantries, presumably in addition to the property of the chantries themselves. It is not unreasonable to suppose that any private property, including anything owned by the town, was reclaimed before the commissioners arrived. Even so, the official receiver seized and delivered to York two chalices (one of 13oz and the other of 7oz) from the chantries of Liverpool.[19]

A lease of the medieval chantry endowments (St Nicholas' Chantry) to
Richard Molyneux in the time of Edward VI (1548).
Duchy of Lancaster Papers, held in the National Archive

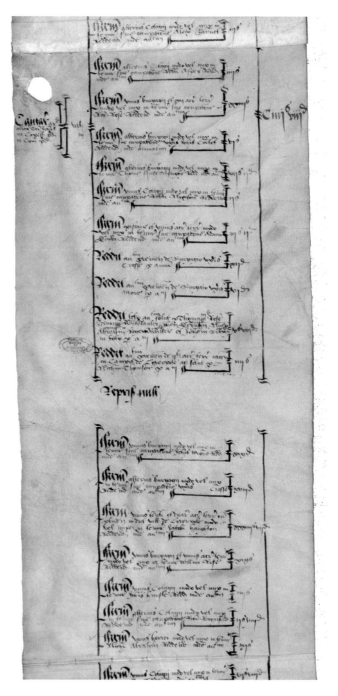

A lease of the medieval chantry endowments (St John's Chantry) to Richard Molyneux in the time of Edward VI (1548).
Duchy of Lancaster Papers, held in the National Archive

The Continuation of the Chapel

The King's Commissioner, Sir Walter Mildmay, was charged with deciding which places of worship should continue and which should go. He issued an order dated 11 August 1548[20] which acknowledged the need for the chapel at Liverpool, "being distaunte foure mylis from the paroche churche, and therfor very necessarie to continewe for divine service and administracion of sacraments to be had and used to the people theare." This refers to the Chapel of St Nicholas which by then was the more significant place of worship. However, the same order breathed new life into the Chapel of St Mary. We can imagine that the relevance of the chapel disappeared as soon as the chantries were abolished and the altar gone, but the Chantry of St Katherine from 1515 had another purpose in the establishment of a school. In 1548 Mildmay reported that the "schole is very mete and necessarie to contynewe." Humphrey Crosse was the priest of the chantry, also the schoolmaster, and clearly of the Crosse family who had founded the chantry, although the exact relation is unclear: he was named in the order as suitable for continuing in this role, and his stipend given as £5 13*s*. 3*d*. We can assume that the school continued in the building of St Mary's. At the end of Edward's reign, following the inventories of church property drawn up in 1548 and 1552 (see below) a new receiver was appointed. When Edward Parker came to Liverpool in October 1553 he found that the town did not own the Chapel of St Mary. When he seized it the Town Corporation immediately bought it from him for the sum of 20*s*., presumably to continue as the school. In addition, he seized a silver pyx which had belonged to St Mary's Chantry, but is absent from the previous inventories drawn up by the Royal Commissioners. He sold this for the greater sum of 33*s*. 4*d*.[21]

Sir Walter Mildmay's order also specified that Humphrey Crosse remain in post as the schoolmaster in the old Chapel of St Mary. He had held the appointment of chantry priest of St Katherine and schoolmaster since 1515, but his impressively long tenure had clearly left him with energy still to spare as schoolmaster. There was, of course, a further advantage that the Duchy was spared the expense of a pension. It seems likely that only one of the chantry priests in 1548 did receive a pension. Richard Frodsham is named as the priest at St Nicholas' Altar in the Report of the King's Commissioners of 1548, in the undated Rental list preserved in the Town Books, and in a further rental preserved in the seventeenth-century Speke MS.[22] In this last source Frodsham's age is given as 80, and so presumably a pension was welcome. The other two chantry priests found other employment. Ralph Hayward (sometimes Howarth) is recorded as the priest at the High Altar (St Mary) in 1533[23] and was still in post when the chantry was dissolved in 1548. However, at an unusual meeting of all the burgesses of the town on 14 December 1565, his name appears again. The mayor summoned the Assembly and had the doors locked. The burgesses remained shut in until sunset whilst all the documents and charters of the town were produced, catalogued, and locked away. Amongst the named documents is one written by Rauffe Hawworth who, in 1565, is listed as "vicar of etc." There was clearly no need to record all the details of a man who was still known in the town, but he had a church appointment elsewhere by this time.[24]

The final chantry priest – John Hurde of the Altar of St John – had a seemingly had a steadier transition within the Liverpool scene. In the Town Books of 1559 he is named as the predecessor of the then incumbent of the town, Evan Nicholson, and it seems likely that he died in about 1555. It seems natural to assume that he moved from chantry priest to incumbent in 1548. However, the Reformation took its toll on some office-holders at the chapel. There is also a note in the Town Books in November 1551 that the "clerk of the church" had fled to Spain, presumably to escape the increasing fervour of the Reformers.[25] The term 'clerk' is uncertain, and is often synonymous with priest. An early historian of the parish, John Elton, made this mistake, suggesting that Hurde died shortly after the report on the chantries of 1548 and was succeeded by a Sir John Ianson who fled to Spain. He was then followed by Nicholson. However, this cannot be the case. Firstly, Elton was mistaken in his assumption of the date of Hurde's death;[26] and secondly it seems natural to assume that John Hurde continued in his post at the chapel after 1548, although as the sole priest rather than in a chantry post. Thirdly, there is a specific reference to Nicholson succeeding Hurde, although it would seem that they did not manage to pay him properly until 1559.[27] Finally, by 1555 there are specific references to the Clerk of the Chapel as a post distinct from the incumbent, and so there is no reason to suppose that the 'clerk' who fled to Spain was the incumbent. The town was concerned with raising money for the wages of Nicholas Smyth, "our clercke of the chapell and teacher of they chyldren." A few months later he is referred to as "clerico et servienti ecclesie."[28] It was not Hurde or Ianson who fled to Spain, but the predecessor of Nicholas Smyth.

Counter Reformation: The Time of Mary

The town records are quiet about the reaction to the change of monarch, although the implications of each change of sovereign were immediately apparent. The transition of Edward VI to Mary is noted only in the usual practice of expressing the date by the year of the monarch's reign. But the change from Edward to Mary brought an abrupt, though temporary, end to the Reformation.

It was not, though, possible to reverse all the changes and revert to the earlier structures. The pace and scale of the changes under Henry and Edward had been so thorough that there was little chance of going back. Locally, we can see that the dissolution of Birkenhead Priory in 1537 had left no opportunity for reconstruction: the buildings and the monks had gone. More significantly for the chapel in Liverpool, which had been funded to a high degree by its four chantries, there was no possibility of their restoration. As we have seen, the Liverpool chantries were immediately transferred to private hands, and this was the case across the country. Both financially and practically, it would have been impossible to gather in so many thousands of parcels of land again. Richard Molyneux, the beneficiary of the availability of many of the former chantry lands in Liverpool, remained a leading citizen in the town, and would have protected his interests vehemently. Furthermore, throughout the country many of those who benefited from chantry lands were themselves Catholic, either through conviction or through the pragmatic diplomacy following the accession of a Catholic queen. Subjects loyal in both faith and allegiance might have their loyalty tested if they had to surrender the lands they had acquired.[29]

The consequence was that the money to pay the clergy had to be found elsewhere, and the town continued to meet this obligation in Liverpool, although not always with ease. There are continual references in the Town Books of the need to raise money to pay the clerk or the priest, or to make their contribution towards the parish church in Walton. For example, on 12 August 1555 "at this assemblie hit is inquired how the priest syr Evan shold be unswaryd of his wayges which is behind this daye."[30] and a similar issue is raised in 1559.

At the same time, there was a modest return to the old ways, and although it was not possible to re-acquire the silver and the vestments which had been seized under Edward, there was some attempt to restore the decoration of the chapel. The production and sale of ale for raising funds for the church was not unknown around the country, and it seems that in Liverpool this provided some funds, to be kept in the custody of the mayor, for the "new aduournyng of the churche" in 1555.[31] This would have been an opportunity to refresh some of the Catholic expression within the chapel which had been lost in the previous few years.

New Furniture and Liturgies

The redecoration of 1555 may well have looked back at some of the inherited forms of religion, but apart from the time of Mary, the move was towards the new Reformed religion. We have already noted the suspiciously sparse inventory of 1548 and noted that there is evidence of other vestments and plate which was not catalogued.

There was a further inventory made on 4 October 1552 when the Privy Council ordered that a comparison was made with the previous lists of 1548. Miraculously, the commissioners discovered a far richer treasure trove than four years earlier. Henry Baylif and Gilbert Rigby Reves, the churchwardens, reported the content of the chapel to the commissioners appointed for the region: the Earl of Derby, Sir Thomas Gerrard, and Thomas Boteler. The inventories of other churches were made the same day: not just Liverpool and her Parish Church of Walton, but also churches from across a broad area including Wigan and Huyton, Sefton and West Derby. It is possible that the paperwork was all drawn up later, but it seems more likely that the commissioners did not personally inspect each church, but relied on churchwardens (all named in the inventories) who were expected to bring an honest account of church possessions. On 6 October the commissioners moved from the West Derby Hundred to the Leyland Hundred (around Chorley), and then on 15 October the commissioners had moved further north to Blackburn.

The extensive list from Liverpool Chapel includes a number of silk or satin vestments and a collection of copes, as well as albs and amices. These were not all reported in the 1548 inventory, but the silence on vestments is matched by the diminishing amount of church plate. Whereas in the earlier inventory the chantries claimed four chalices as their own (although it has been noted that some were taken and sold for the Duchy), now there is just one silver chalice.[32] Although the inventory goes on to declare that the churchwardens had undertaken not to hide from the Duchy any of the declared property, we might still wonder whether there is a small amount of intrigue taking place. Just over a year earlier, on 12 November 1551, the Town Books record that the corporation showed their own interest in the vessels of the church: "We fynde that the churche goodes shall be called fore and put in a place togedder to the townez use, and all the comyns of the towne may be privey to the same."[33] Just as in 1548, it would seem that the town was very conscious of the value of church plate, and of the need to claim some of it for itself.

The liturgical reforms were swift. The Book of Common Prayer of 1549 was incontrovertibly defining of the Reformation, in that the vernacular was used in all parts of the services. In Liverpool the introduction of English passes without comment in the Town Books, but must have made a significant local impact. Many elements, though, did not change, and it would seem that the use of full eucharistic vestments continued. The rubric of the communion service states "the priest that shall execute the holy ministry, shall put upon him the vesture appointed for that ministration, that is to say: a white Albe plain, with a vestment or Cope."[34] The practical application of this is supported by the inventory of vestments and church plate at the Liverpool Chapel in 1552, the same year in which a more protestant Book of Common Prayer was published, which stipulated more restrained vesture and made some theologically significant changes to the liturgies. These cannot have been comfortable changes for the clergy who had been ordained before the Reformation and who had not demonstrated any reforming zeal of their own. Locally, we can see this in Evan Nicholson. There appears to be no complaint about his incumbency (which, within fifty years, will not be the case with his successors), but at his death in 1572 we get a hint of the turbulent and unsettled times through which he had lived: his executor, Thomas Roose, is compelled to reveal that Nicholson had a "decretorie," which is defined as "a big book of service." This was a pre-Reformation liturgical book used in the choir of the church, and seemed to complement the chapel vestments for which Roose gave account as well.[35] Nicholson had become the priest of the chapel half way through the reign of Mary, when the protestant liturgies were suppressed, and although he continued in post at the resumption of the Reformation upon the accession of Elizabeth, it would seem that, until his death, Nicholson found it difficult to conform to the new ways. He was not without encouragement, though. Although votive candles to the saints were not encouraged, in April 1559, less than five months after Elizabeth became queen, the town dignitaries gave instruction for funding the burning of three tapers in the chapel in honour of the Holy Trinity.[36]

Some changes had been forced upon Nicholson, though. The altar stones (superaltars) noted in the 1548 inventories were removed, and in

1559, as the Elizabethan church took hold, the town understood that wooden communion tables were now required. The Town Books record in 1559 that "mayster mayre made the standyng table frame for the comunion in the chapell of Liverpole."[37] Clearly the town was taking its responsibilities seriously to ensure that the chapel reflected the legal expectations of furnishings and worship.

Who Pays?

What is notable throughout the period of the Reformation is that the town took responsibility not just for implementing statute law in its chapel, but also bore the financial responsibility for it. Clergy in the Elizabethan church were generally paid from one of three sources: rectorial income from glebe land or tithes; vicarial income either from

The remaining footprint of medieval Liverpool is difficult to locate, and this solitary dressed stone in the foundations of the tower of Our Lady and St Nicholas is a rare survivor after the Georgian rebuilding of the town. *Author's photograph*

an endowment or allotted from the rector; or the clergy were paid as perpetual curates in their chapels by the minister of the parish. At the Reformation the status of the Liverpool Chapel did not change, but the status of the clergy did. Instead of four fully-funded chantry priests, the 'incumbent' was legally a perpetual curate of the Parish of Walton. We shall examine in the next chapter the strained relations with the church in Walton, and the efforts by the town not to make financial contributions to Walton or to allow the rector any say in the appointment of the priest in Liverpool. This must, in part, have been justified by the fact that no financial support for the clergy came from Walton. The minister was paid in part by the Duchy (£4 17s. 5d., less fees and other charges), and this was complemented by a further £8 from the town.[38]

As well as paying the incumbent, the town also housed him. It seems likely that he continued living in the manor house described in Chapter 1 where all the chantry priests had previously lived.[39] Wherever the minister was housed, the town certainly took responsibility for the upkeep, as we can see from the payment on 1 December 1574 for mending and repairing the minister's chambers.[40]

We have seen that there is evidence of the chapel having its own land, separate from the chantries, but there is little record of the amount or the application of any income. Significant repairs were undertaken by the town, and the cost of the liturgical reforms of the 1550s was borne by the town. Most importantly and rather unusually, the town took immediate responsibility for paying both the priest and the clerk, although the cost of the former was shared with the Duchy of Lancaster. It also seems likely that the town claimed ownership of some of the vestments and plate in use in the chapel. With this financial commitment towards the chapel, by the end of the Reformation period there seems little doubt that the town had effective control and ownership of the chapel and its clergy, setting the course for the centuries to come.

CHAPTER THREE

Liverpool Chapel 1558–1642

A Town Church

As the turbulence of the Reformation subsided, the Elizabethan Settlement brought a degree of stability to national religious life. The chapel at Liverpool had always been subject to a heavy degree of influence from the mayor and commonalty, but now emerged from the period under the complete control of the town. The ministers were appointed, housed and paid by the town, as was the clerk; to complete the picture, the churchwardens were appointed and sworn in alongside other town officials. The town itself was apparently not so settled throughout this period: in Chapter 1 we noted the frequent change of lordship over the town, and by the later sixteenth century there was still a need for royal favour. In February 1566/7 the town's Member of Parliament, Ralph Sekerston, petitioned Queen Elizabeth I, making a strong case that the town belonged to the Queen and asking her to take control of it as her own and to look after it. They were loyal subjects, he said, but the town was, he claimed, the "decayed towne of Liverpole."[1] The petition appears to have been successful, but in fact this was not the first grant of royal favour from Elizabeth, who had already given her approval for the town's right of appointment of the minister of the chapel. Settling this matter gave the town and the chapel the independence required by a proud and growing town, which had already overtaken the population and importance of its parish church in Walton.

The period until the Civil War, therefore, was one of relative steadiness for the Liverpool Chapel. With the town's patronage, the chapel had no financial concerns, and the growing distance between Liverpool and the Parish Church of Walton meant autonomy. The dynamic, though, was very much that the chapel was the servant of the mayor, the bailiffs, and the other leading citizens. The incumbent was afforded a degree of status, but had to conform to the expectations of the town in all matters from liturgical provision to personal appearance. When Thomas Wainwright, appointed as minister in 1598, showed himself to be rather slovenly, he was held to account by the town. And when it was felt that some superior preaching was required, it was the town who recruited and paid a suitable man alongside the minister. This hierarchy of relationship between town and chapel was almost entirely reversed by the eighteenth century, when, although the right to appoint the rector remained with the town, the church had acquired both power and authority.

Most of our picture of this period comes from the Liverpool Town Books which recorded the meetings, portmoots (town court hearings), elections, and other incidents. The books began in 1551 and continued until the second half of the nineteenth century. The chapel was not just a place of religious worship, but also a place where the business of the town could be carried out. For example, in September 1560 Gilbert Moreton, the queen's "feodary" (collector of rents), sent a proclamation to the curates of Walton and Liverpool telling all gentlemen and freeholders to attend the chapel in Liverpool on Thursday 10 October at 9am with their title and rental deeds to prove their right to the land. Similarly, just six months later on 23 April 1561 the mayor ordered all burgesses to appear before him in church after dinner for supplication to Lord Derby for pasturage in Toxteth Park.[2] However, the church was not available for everyone's convenience: although it was the largest public space available for meetings, other uses were not allowed. In 1582 the Assembly agreed that there should be no sail-making in church: presumably this was the largest indoor space available for laying out sail cloth.[3]

Significant occasions were marked in church, both for the purposes of religious devotion, and also as a place where the town could come together, each in their own allotted place. Even in death there was a sense of hierarchy: in 1571/2 Cicill, the daughter of Ralph Sekerston (sometime mayor and by then Member of Parliament) and wife of the

Henry Stanley, 4th Earl of Derby, whose visit to the town in 1577 was
structured around multiple services in the chapel.
Oil on panel, English School, sixteenth centrury, via Wikimedia Commons

current mayor Thomas Bavand, died and was buried in the chancel
before the mayor's stall.[4] Although the burial registers do not survive
from that time, a transcription made in 1800 of the graves in the
chancel show a number of people of status from this period, including
Robert Dobson, a former Bailiff of the Manor of West Derby and Town
Clerk of Liverpool (died 1638), whose name appears frequently in the
Town Books, and who lived in London as well as Liverpool.[5]

The dead make fewer claims on status than the living, because in 1587 the Assembly considered a dispute about where the wives of former mayors and bailiffs should sit in church. The solution, it appears, was that the wives of current and former mayors should sit in the seat closest to the current mayor, in the same order that their husbands were mayor (and the same arrangement was agreed for the wives of bailiffs). If there were more wives of former mayors than space would allow, then the mayor was instructed to nominate another pew for the overflow.[6] Rather amusingly, this was a recurrent issue, and forty years later in 1628 more detailed instructions were given that the mayor and the aldermen should sit together in the chancel, and their wives should sit together in the two upper forms in the middle row in the church. Just to be sure that everything was seemly, the Assembly also prescribed the dress code for the wives.[7]

Although the elite of the town was on show every week in the chapel, there were some more significant civic occasions. Of these the most striking must have been the visit of the Earl of Derby on St George's Day in 1577. The day before Lord Derby came to view the chapel and decide upon the best place to set up the 'cloth of estate', which was a canopy decorated with cloth of gold and representing the queen's throne. This was set on the south side of the chapel. The Earl then came to Evening Prayer at 5pm, accompanied by the mayor, aldermen, and bailiffs. The order of procession is recorded: two bailiffs followed by the rest walking in pairs; the aldermen; the Earl of Derby's men; the serjeant carrying the mace; the mayor; Lord Derby's usher; and finally Lord Derby himself in robes of red and purple, with his train carried by Edward Legh of Baguley. After the service, as they left the chapel, a captain and soldiers were waiting in the churchyard as a guard of honour. The following day, on the feast of St George, there was a solemn procession around the churchyard before entering for a service. A piece of gold was presented to the incumbent (James Seddon), and the Earl's Chaplain, John Caldwell (Rector of Moberley in Cheshire and also of Winwick in Lancashire) preached a sermon on Psalm 81. The Earl attended both Morning and Evening Prayer that day, alongside much feasting and entertainment outside the chapel. On the following day the Earl came to Morning Prayer at which the chaplain to the queen, John Nutter BD, preached on Revelation Chapter 22. Rather sadly for Mr Caldwell, it is noted that the congregation much preferred the second sermon.[8] It may well be this visit to which the novelist Herman Melville refers, though mis-dated to 1588, when he records that "the corporation erected and adorned a sumptuous stall in the church for [the Earl of Derby's] reception."[9]

Religious Practice

Until the Reformation, there had been at least one Mass a day in the chapel, and the presence of four chantries might lead us to presume that there would often have been more than one Mass on many days. The adoption of the new liturgy and the reduction in clergy numbers meant that, along with the rest of the country, the frequency of services was drastically reduced. At the same time, the Act of Uniformity (1558) required all people to attend church once a week. In a town such as Liverpool there would have been obvious practical difficulties: with a population of around 3000, and a small chapel as the only place of worship, it is inconceivable that the law was strictly observed by anyone except those whose absence would be noticed. Peet's estimate that the church's capacity would have been about 550 still leaves a considerable shortfall for the resident population.[10] Furthermore, the Town Books do not contain any reference to disciplining under the Act those who did not attend (the Act prescribed a fine of 12*d.*). However, avoiding any mention of the legal requirements but focusing instead on religious devotion, the mayor did intervene to increase the provision of services during the week. At the October meeting of the Assembly in 1562 it was recorded: "For the further honour of Almyghtie God, and that everie man maye the better knowe his duetie to Hym and love oone another, wee fynd it expedient that mayster maior cause service divine to be sayd in [the] chapell of S(aynct) Nicholas and our Ladie in this towne, everie Wedynsdaye Fryddaye and Saterdaye at evyn, and after as shall se cause."[11] An additional three services every week would certainly have assisted the populace in both godly and legal observance, though universal weekly church attendance remains implausible.

Having said that, the town took steps to ensure that Sunday remained a day for religious devotion. At the October Assembly in 1574 it was decreed that it was permissible to go out fishing from Monday to Saturday, but all work was forbidden on Sundays on pain of a substantial fine. The same rule was extended to butchers.[12] Throughout the town records there are frequent fines, not for failing to attend the chapel, but for indulging in forbidden activities during the time of the service. For example, Peter Jump was brought to the court in 1619 for walking in the streets and standing at the foot of the tower during divine service, as well as "giving evill speeches" to the churchwardens.[13] In 1628 seven men were brought to court for playing 'Carles' at the time of the divine service.[14] The following year nineteen men and women are presented to the portmoot for their non-attendance at divine service, but the emphasis seems mainly to be on the activities they were otherwise doing, rather than any particular contravention of the Act of Uniformity.[15]

We have already seen in Chapter 2 that the town was active in promoting the new Protestant religion, both in ensuring that the new Prayer Book was used, and also in the provision of church furniture and plate to accommodate the new forms of worship. This continued throughout the century, and the town was quick to correct the clergy when it felt them to be in error. In 1587 it was agreed in the Assembly that the lectern should be placed in the middle of the church. Three years later the new incumbent, Hugh Janion, was swiftly fined in the same year as his appointment because he did not read the "latter lesson" at morning and evening prayer in the body of the church. And although imposing fines on Janion was a regular indulgence of the Assembly during his short incumbency, after his successor, Thomas Wainwright, was in post from 1598 there was a further repeat in 1602 of the old order that the lessons be read in the body of the church, "that the people maie heare theim."[16] Some twenty years in 1623 later the matter was settled when it was felt that everyone could see and hear better if the action took place in the middle of the church: not just the lessons, but in fact the entire service should take place there, rather than in the chancel. The town decided to build a new pew of "quare" so that the service and the lessons should be read from the same place.[17]

The instruction on the reading of the lesson in 1610 was given with the added injunction that the epistle and gospel should be read from the pulpit every Sabbath and Holy Day.[18] The inference we might make is that the Holy Communion was celebrated every week, for which the epistle and gospel were the readings. Across the Church of England there was varied practice here, and culturally a weekly communion dropped from common practice: the Canons of 1604 only demanded that the Holy Communion be celebrated often enough that everyone has the opportunity to receive the sacrament three times a year (including Easter), and they also instructed that due notice be given if there was going to be communion the following Sunday.[19] The significance of a weekly Eucharist should not be overstated in Liverpool: the heavily ecclesiastical nature of the Earl of Derby's visit in 1577 was clearly based on Morning and Evening Prayer. However, a weekly communion shows a balance between sacrament and preaching. The same order about the reading of the gospel also says that, if there is no sermon preached, a homily should be given from one of the Books of Homilies (published in 1547, 1562, and 1571) "according to Canons."[20]

As we shall see below, the incumbent was not always qualified to be a preacher, but the town felt that its duty was to enforce the Canons by their own, secular, authority.

It was presumably the active participation of the Town Assembly in enforcing the new liturgies and doctrines which set Liverpool apart from the rest of Lancashire. Whilst the incumbent, Evan Nicholson, may have maintained private Catholic devotions, there is no indication that there was any clerical pressure to lead the townspeople away from Protestantism. A port and market town, frequently thronging with seafarers and visitors, would have been accustomed to a variety of religious practices, but Liverpool's own allegiance was beyond question. As well as the penalties for non-attendance, the 1581 Act of Parliament to retain the "Queen's Majesty's subjects in their Due Obedience" imposed harsh penalties on recusants – those who refused to renounce their Catholicism. The compilation of Recusant Rolls gives a picture of recusancy across the country, and in the sixteenth century by far the largest roll is that for Lancashire. Despite significant numbers of recusants in the towns and villages around Liverpool, the town itself housed remarkably few. This is endorsed by a list drawn up for the King of Spain before the Armada, which said that most of Lancashire was Catholic apart from the Earl of Derby and the town of Liverpool.[21] We can illustrate this from the second Recusancy Roll of 1593/4, in which Liverpool features on only three occasions. The first is unnamed, but a reference to various lands and tenements, including in Liverpool; the second is land belonging to Richard Blundell of Crosby Hall; the third is a spinster, Alice Peper, "lately of Leverpoole."[22]

There is some evidence to the contrary, that Catholicism was flourishing behind closed doors in the town. In 1564 it was reported to the government that there was much papacy in Liverpool, and two priests were named: Sir William More and Sir Robert More. Clergy, presumably ordained before the Reformation, from such a distinguished local family could be sure of protection, and presumably had no need of the stipend of beneficed clergymen. Later in the century the influx of Catholic clergy trained and ordained on the continent began to affect Liverpool. Blackburn-born priest Robert Hawkesworth, was trained in Rheims and Rome, but was arrested in Liverpool in 1595.[23] In the petition of 1629 to the Bishop of Chester, appealing for preachers to deliver lectures, the mayor states that there are "many papistes inhabittinge thereaboutes."[24]

Even if the town's control of religious life meant that there was little appetite for the religious culture which was still more openly prevalent in the rest of Lancashire, there were still traces of the old ways. There are some examples of everyday words and actions which were fast going out of fashion. The Assembly continued for some time to refer to Christian festivals using pre-Reformation terminology, including All Souls' Day, Pentecost, and Candlemas.[25] The doctrinal undergirding of the abolition of the chantries was a prohibition on prayers for the dead, and yet a note in February 1582/3 recording the death of the mayor's mother, Johane Barlowe, ends with the words, "God graunt her a joyfull resurrection. Amen."[26] The visit of Henry, 4th Earl of Derby, in 1577 was recorded with jubilant detail. Lord Derby was an enthusiastic Protestant, but as he entered the chapel in a great procession "he did marke him self unto God," which is to say that he made the sign of the cross.[27] Piping and dancing at church were also seen as Catholic practices: there were specific problems with piping at weddings in Walton parish, and in Liverpool there were problems with piping and dancing during the evening service in 1598.[28]

The town swiftly phased out the pre-Reformation vestments, including those which were initially allowed under the first Prayer Book of Edward VI. In 1572 two copes were made into clothes for the mayor's son so that he could take place in a play. However, this was merely the practical recycling of redundant fabric: in all other respects dignity and order in worship and vesture was expected. At the same time as the copes were remodelled, the town brought together all other vestments, banners, candlesticks, and other ecclesiastical paraphernalia to be audited.[29] Similarly, when Hugh Janion resigned in 1596, it was agreed that the new incumbent should receive "by inventory" all books, surplices and other implements.[30]

The town's concern on vesture was not entirely legalistic in enforcing the new requirements, but the bristling tension in the Town Books suggests that it was also a sense that religion should be done properly and with due reverence. Thomas Wainwright was the focus of this tension, as he was rebuked and fined in 1604 for not wreathing his surplice according to the King's instructions.[31] In 1610 the same rebuke was given, but with the added complaint that he should wear his surplice "at all tymes that he shall meet any corps as wel poore as Riche."[32] The implication might be that he took the trouble to dress appropriately for the funerals of significant people within the town, but did not trouble himself for paupers. Whether or not this was the complaint, the town felt that it had an interest in ensuring that vesture and funerals were beyond disagreement.

Walton Parish: Friend and Foe

The regular despatch of money to the Parish Church of Walton must have been a continual source of irritation. Very often the payments attract no particular comment in the Town Books, but as well as a church rate, there was surprisingly frequent need of capital sums for repairs. For example, on 12 August 1555 the town contemplates how they would make the required contribution towards the "reparacions of Walton churche."[33] A decade later the same matter arose again, and they decided to impose a tax of one fifteenth upon personal property to fund the Liverpool contribution towards the repair of Walton Church. A list of the taxes levied for this is preserved, with typical sums ranging from 1*d.* to 12*d.*[34] And then again in 1573 and 1574 there is a significant contribution made to the repair of Walton Church, "our parishe churche."[35] This pattern of extra taxes and payments to Walton Church continue, with a significant payment made every ten years or so, in addition to regular contributions.

It is surprising that there is no record of discontent at this stage, as Liverpool appears to have received little benefit from being situated within the parish. Queen Elizabeth's grant that the Assembly could appoint the clergy of Liverpool (see below) was a formal severing from the principle legal rights held by the incumbent of Walton. A more peculiar incident occurred in 1614 when Lawrence Bridge, Clerk of Walton Parish Church, appeared in Liverpool and asked the Assembly for his wages. The Assembly judged him to be honest and agreed to pay him.[36] There is a faint trace of cordial relations with Walton Church: as a response to a plea in 1629 to the Bishop of Chester for clergy to be allowed to come and lecture (preach) once a month, the bishop named Neville Kay (or Keye), the Vicar of Walton, as one of those empowered to make a suitable appointment. He undertook to find a suitable preacher for two months of the year.[37]

Church Land and Property

For many decades after the abolition of the chantries the lands associated with them were still known by their former owners. For example, a property conveyance from John Crosse to Thomas Roose in 1564 described the parcel of land by the adjacent plots, including "lands late of the Chantry of St. John" which were already in Thomas Roose's possession.[38] Roose was one of those in the town who adapted to the new religious situation pragmatically and profitably: as well as benefiting from chantry lands, we have already noted him as the executor of the will of the incumbent, Evan Nicholson, in 1572 when pre-Reformation books and vestments were acknowledged.[39] The dissolved Chantry of St Nicholas caused more problems for the town: the land was leased to Ralph Sekerston (the Member of Parliament) on 13 January 1558/9,[40] but he was persistent in not paying what was due to the town. At the portmoot on 21 October 1566 he and Thomas Secum were fined for non-payment; the following year at the October portmoot the outgoing mayor, Robert Corbet, was fined for not enforcing the penalty from the previous year, and in October 1568 there is a note that the rents from St Nicholas Chantry had still not been paid.[41]

The Duchy of Lancaster still kept the designations of the land they seized in 1547. The accounts of the Duchy Lands (Compotus Rolls) made by the Receiver of the Duchy in 1619 list the separate chantries of Middleton, Newton-in-Makerfield, Liverpool, Halsall, Rufford, Becconsall, Clitheroe, Tunstall, Thurland, Salford and Ormskirk.[42] A century after the Reformation, there is still the occasional reference to chantries, such as in a lease from the town to John Lurting, a blacksmith in 1653. There is a passing reference to a plot of land which, although its current owner is named as Thomas Tarleton, is noted as being former chantry lands.[43]

As well as land and property, the chapel received a fee income, although this was not always forthcoming. In 1578 the Assembly had to rule that the churchwardens should receive burial fees before any earth was broken for the grave. Likewise, the stewards should receive the wedding fees before the service.[44]

The Clergy

As a chapel in the parish of Walton, the appointment of clergy for Liverpool would naturally fall to the Vicar of Walton. However, as successive clergy arrive after the Reformation, Walton is never mentioned. The town considered the appointment to be theirs, and in the Town Books the incumbent was often listed amongst those 'elected' on an annual basis, along with the churchwardens and other officers of the town. It is difficult to ascertain whether or not they were actually elected, but there is evidence to show that the town considered both the appointment and the despatch of clergy to be entirely within its gift.

There is no record to suggest that the parish of Walton resisted this arrangement, and yet the procurement by the town of specific authority to make the appointment might suggest that there was some complaint about their ability to do so. Either way, and presumably as a result of some petition, Queen Elizabeth granted the mayor and burgesses of Liverpool the right to "nominate, elect, pace and appointe suche a mete sober and able personne to be Mynister". Such appointment was, of course, dependent on the consent of the Bishop of Chester, in whose Diocese the town continued to reside. The grant was probably made around February 1564/5, but the loss of the original, and the enthusiasm of the town to procure a copy the following year, suggests that the document and the rights it conferred were dear to the town.[45] The possession of the document did indeed prove useful a century later, when the Revd Thomas Marsden, Vicar of Walton from 1660 until 1720, attempted to claim his right of appointment. Following a complaint to the Privy Council, reported to the Assembly on 30 November 1669, the town met again on 21 December 1669 and cited in its defence the "ancient grant in the 7th year of Queen Elizabeth and our constant usage ever since."[46] The town had no intention of relinquishing its control over the chapel.

The arrangement at the Reformation that the incumbent should be paid by the Duchy of Lancaster and the town jointly remained in place, but with increments on occasion. By 1559 the town was paying Evan Nicholson £19 4s. "for the mayntenaunce and continuaunce in servying of cures and administracion of sacraments."[47] The incumbent, along with the schoolmaster serving in the former Chapel of St Mary, were expected to go to Halton Castle to collect the Duchy's portion of the stipend. In 1568 this caused a particular problem because the Duchy accused the town of not paying their share of the schoolmaster's stipend and so refused to contribute their share. The incumbent, John Mylner, collected his stipend, but it must have been an awkward journey together back to Liverpool.[48]

The inability to pay the clergy persisted throughout the Elizabethan age. For example, in 1581/2 the town found itself in debt to the incumbent, James Seddon, and had to levy a ley to raise £5 to settle up. Just a few years later, in 1588, alongside a shortfall in the schoolmaster's wages, it is noted that the incumbent received only part payment of his wages of 20s., and that he was still owed 54s. 5d.[49] By the 1620s the incumbent, Edward Lappage, was receiving £20 a year, but this was supplemented by a milk cow, which presumably provided him with both sustenance and income.[50]

At the time of the grant, Evan Nicholson had been the incumbent for nearly ten years, and he survived until 1572. He was obviously missed, as within months there is reference to the need to keep the churchyard as "cleane and honest" as it was in Nicholson's time. A more turbulent period then followed with the appointment of John Milner (or Mylner) in 1572 on wages of £1 6s. 8d.[51] Milner did not last long, but the willingness of the town not only to pay Milner's funeral expenses when he died in 1574, but also to pay off his debts, illustrates that the Assembly continued to be protective towards the incumbency as an asset of the town.[52] By this time James Seddon had been appointed as the new incumbent: his time appears to have been reasonably harmonious, although there are complaints about the state of the churchyard. The first instruction from the Assembly on this came in 1575, but the complaint later became that he was not opening the gate to the churchyard on Sundays and Holy Days at the time of the service: this is mentioned in 1587, but becomes a theme for the rest of Seddon's time, as well as that of his successor.[53] The explanation for the closing of the churchyard gate becomes clearer under Hugh Janion, who followed Seddon in 1590. In 1594 he was fined for keeping horses in the churchyard and for not taking away their dung, which presumably explains why he needed to keep the gate closed, and also why in the previous year he was fined for cutting down the great thorn in the churchyard without a licence.[54]

There seems to have been frequent discontent with the clergy. In 1585 the Earl of Derby wrote to the mayor to try and force the appointment of James Martyndall in place of James Seddon, "whoe for some impediment is thought a man insufficient for that function." Whether or not the inspiration was Lord Derby's reputation for advocacy of the new religion is unclear, but the mayor threw open the matter to the Assembly. Despite advocacy of Seddon by those who felt that only the loss of the bishop's support should hasten his departure, Martyndall overwhelmingly won the vote, perhaps because the burgesses thought it politically expedient to support Lord Derby.[55] We do not learn the end of this rather awkward situation, and Seddon appears to have stayed in post for five more years.

Janion's incumbency following Seddon was hardly a success. At the time that he was listed as the new incumbent, a note was included that he should not go off to Chester has much as he had been doing.[56] Within days of his appointment, he was fined for not reading the second lesson at Morning and Evening Prayer in the body of the church. Together with the issues in the churchyard, it was obviously felt necessary to keep

Janion on a short leash, and in October 1594 it was made clear that he could be removed from his appointment by the mayor, and in 1595 it was clarified that either Janion or the town could give six months' notice to terminate the contract.[57] Within a year he had gone. The new incumbent, Ranulph Bentley, was elected in December 1596, and at the next portmoot he was also fined for not keeping the churchyard gate open during the time of divine service. Bentley was not a success: on 31 March 1598 he was summoned before the Assembly and asked if he was minded to continue as the Minister. He replied that because the previous mayor, William More, had spoken to him in such a way that he thought that he had been dismissed, he had found for himself another position and would leave before St Luke's Day (i.e. the required six months' notice).[58]

A plan of Liverpool in about 1600.
Courtesy of the Athenaeum, Liverpool

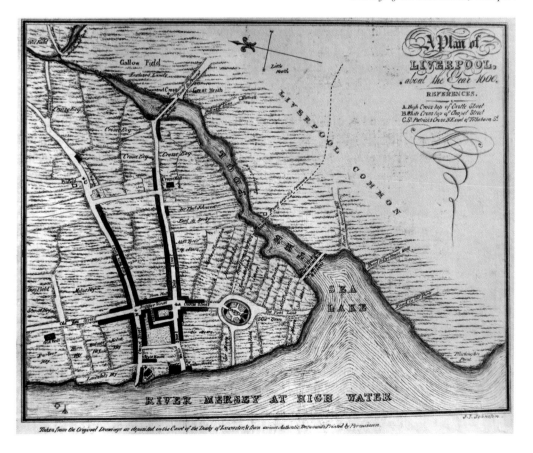

The appointment of Thomas Wainwright in 1598 brought a period of stability, as he remained for twenty-eight years. There were disagreements, of course, such as his dilatory attitude to wearing the surplice and, rather more amusingly, the Assembly's command in 1613 that he should get his hair cut "a comly and seemely length in such decent maner as best befitteth a man in his place."[59] They were lucky to keep Wainwright for so long, because the unusual tradition of the annual appointment by election did not afford him the level of job security enjoyed by beneficed clergymen, such as the Vicar of Walton Parish.

There was, though, no expectation that all clergy could preach. The Canons of 1604 suggest that there should be a sermon (rather than the reading of one of the homilies) at least once a month, and that the beneficed clergy should arrange this.[60] Without beneficed clergy, the town clearly had a mind to plug the gap, and in 1616 the Assembly considered whether to employ a preacher for the town. There is no reason to consider this a criticism of Wainwright, who clearly did not have the requisite learning. He had other uses, though, as in March 1622/3 he especially asked for a clock on the chapel for the benefit of the inhabitants of Liverpool: he agreed to set the clock himself, or personally to pay himself for someone else to do it.[61] It was five years, though, before a suitable man was found to be preacher, and in January 1621/2 it was proposed to appoint a Mr Swift on a generous salary of £25 a year. This was a short-lived appointment, and in the following year James Hyatt, a Batchelor of Divinity, was employed, though on the slightly lower salary of £20 a year, but with his accommodation costs paid.[62]

It would seem that, at least in some years of this period, the town felt that the appointment of the clergy was on an annual basis. Given that it was not always easy to find clergy for the chapel and that the income was not always paid reliably and steadily, it seems bold to maintain a degree of insecurity of tenure. However, on 25 October 1568 there is a note that the appointment of the incumbent, John Mylner, was agreed for the following year.[63]

Maintaining the Chapel

Throughout this period, there was an assumption by the town that they would maintain the chapel. This was always both practical and financial. The Assembly of October 1563 decided that both now and in the future the mayor should see, view and overlook the church walls and windows. At least every three of four years the Town Books record the details of the repairs needed to the chapel, often alongside other public buildings. For example, in December 1564 the Assembly enquires about the repairs needed at the chapel, as well as at the Common Hall and the stone bridge. In the following March there were more repairs required to the chapel walls and the wooden roof of the steeple.[64]

Financially, the maintenance of the chapel was a shared responsibility. The oath administered to those admitted as a Free Burgess of the Town in 1621 included the injunction: "You shall further be lyable and contributorie at all tymes necessary to all reasonable and convenient taxacions and payments which shall be assessed upon you… as alsoe for the uphouldinge and reparacion of the Chapell within the same [Liverpoole] called the Chappell of Our Ladie and St Nicholas accordinge to the auncient orders, uses and customes of this Towne."[65] However, throughout this period there were often additional taxes levied for repairs to the chapel, just as we have seen the burgesses discharge their financial responsibilities towards Walton Church. For example, in October 1578 it was agreed that the church walls should be repaired with some haste, but by the following May there had been no progress, presumably because of lack of money. As a result, they levied a special ley (tax) to raise £20 to repair the chapel walls.[66]

One of the most dramatic moments in the history of the chapel building occurred in December 1565. A fleet of ships, together with their owners, gathered in Liverpool to give safe conduct across the Irish Sea to Sir Henry Sidney, newly appointed Lord Deputy of Ireland (listed in the Town Books as the 'Lord High Deputy'). Shortly after setting sail a storm of wind, snow and frost occurred, and on the morning of Sunday 23 December "*all Christen people calld and cryed, praiyng and making theyr moost humble prayers unto all myghtie to amend the weyther… and to save the forsaydes shypps.*" The storm, though, grew worse and by 24 December considerable damage had been done to the chapel. Stone pinnacles fell from the tower, smashing on the ground below, the chapel windows were broken, and the sea breached the walls where the chapel abutted the shore. Some of the larger stones were left six or seven yards out of their places.[67] Although Sidney reached his destination, a number of ships were lost.

Instantly the town set about repairing the chapel. On 24 December the mayor summoned a meeting, and an immediate double tax was imposed (i.e. two fifteenths) to pay for repairs. In the following days the hunt for builders and masons took place. The local mason, John

Knollis, seems to have dithered over costs, but in the end agreed to do the work for £7, so long as he also had help from the town. Meanwhile, a second quotation was obtained from three masons from Aughton. Leading citizen Thomas More then reported that he had been to Warrington and met a mason called Henry Kaye (possibly from Dunham-on-the-Hill) who felt that he could do the work. Kaye was also asked to come and give a quotation. In the end, the work was split between Knollis and Kaye, with Knollis providing the ashlar stones, and Kaye working on the west wall of the church, above the high water mark. The total cost of the works came to £6 15s. 4d.[68] It must have been a relief to the townspeople, as well as to the incumbent, that just a few months later there was a heatwave in May 1566, followed by hot weather in June and July which was tempered with sufficient rain for crops.[69]

Not all building contracts were for urgent remedial work such as this: on 1 August 1589 the town signed an agreement with William Browne of Ormskirk, a glazier in the pay of the Earl of Derby, for the ongoing repair and maintenance of the windows of the chapel. For an annual sum of 5s. Browne was to supply the materials and the labour to keep the windows in good repair. It was also made clear (unlike the arrangements with some other contractors) that although the town would supply the ladders and fire whilst he was working, they would not supply him with food and drink.[70] There were occasional other references to developments in the building: there is an annual instruction from the Assembly that the clerk of the chapel ring the curfew bell throughout the winter months, but only in 1574 was there a reference to a new chapel bell. It seems likely that until that point the bell from the old Chapel of St Mary was still being used.[71]

CHAPTER FOUR

Civil War and Restoration

The Civil War

Liverpool was always a royal town. From the early associations with King John, Henry III and the Dukes of Lancaster, through to successive charters from reigning monarchs, Liverpool was swift to pay allegiance to the sovereign. However, despite evidence of some desperate petitioning for royal favour, such as Ralph Sekerston's requests to Queen Elizabeth in 1566/7, there are surprisingly few references to the monarch in the Town Books, beyond referencing the date to the year of the reign. Rare exceptions include the day of rejoicing on the start of the 19th year of the reign of Queen Elizabeth on 17 November 1576.[1] The accession of Charles I was no different, in that the town continued its royal patronage with a new Charter in 1626, confirming the town in its inherited powers, and conferring new ones upon them.[2] Some time after the Civil War, in November 1667, the town was pleased to receive back this and its previous charters.[3] But at the start of Charles' reign the oath of the mayor retained repeated clauses of loyalty to the monarch and his successors.[4]

The people of Liverpool, however, were divided in their loyalties, although in reality perhaps most of them had no particular allegiance. The Town Books record some of the vicissitudes of war, but remain surprisingly silent on some of the major events, including Prince Rupert's bloody invasion of the town in June 1644. Despite a seeming lack of

A copy made in 1861 of an original map of the fortifications of Liverpool in the Civil War. Although the original manuscript no longer survives, this is one of the oldest depictions of the chapel.
Courtesy of the Athenaeum, Liverpool

Detail of the above, showing the chapel.

engagement with the politics of the Civil War, civilians were drawn in by conscription if by nothing else. Lord Derby was the recruiting officer for the Cavaliers, and his officers

> *had taken up a custom of summoning... many older person, upon paine of death, to appeare at generall musters, and thence to force them away with such weapons as they had, if they were but pitchforks, to Bolton; the reare being brought up with troopers, that had commission to shoot such as lagged behind, so as the poor countrey-man seemed to be in a dilemma of death, either by the troopers if they went not on, or by the great and small shot out of the towne if they did.*[5]

But at the same time, at the outbreak of war, the bailiffs and Members of Parliament for Liverpool seemed generally parliamentarian in their disposition, even if others of the leading families were royalist, as of course was the governor of Liverpool Castle, Colonel Norres.

Liverpool therefore began the Civil War as a royalist town, and as the parliamentarian forces swept across Manchester in 1642/3, just Liverpool, Wigan and Warrington held out. In consequence, Colonel Norres was governor of a royalist town from June 1642 to April 1643. In summer 1643 the parliamentarian forces, under Colonel Assheton, took Liverpool after a siege which is not even mentioned in the Town Books. The new governor, Colonel Venables, established his garrison in Liverpool, but early in 1644, partly at the request of the town, Colonel Moore became the garrison commander.

The history of the Civil War in Lancashire and Liverpool is covered in detail elsewhere,[6] and we shall examine the place of religion below, but our focus on the ecclesiastical life of the town highlights the possibility that at times the church building itself may have been drawn into the battle. There is a passing reference in a tract dated 1643 which appears to describe the parliamentarian occupation of Liverpool in May of that year:

> *About which time one of the ships, under the command of the Earl of Warwicke, stroole into the Harbour called Leverpoole, into the River of Merse, which commeth to the said towne, and put the enemy into a great feare; and although the ship came in, rather by accident than with any intent to aide the Earl of Derbyie's forces; yet within two days after, the Manchester men having gotten the great street, and planted their Ordnance on the Church which commanded the towne, the Popish forces sent to desire a parley with Colonell Aston."*[7]

The Manchester garrison took Warrington after an uneventful siege, and it seems that Liverpool had fallen before then to the same garrison (the "Manchester men"). This is a vague reference to fortifications in the Church, and without corroboration. Churches, though, were a good position for armaments: in the same month a royalist garrison had taken up residence in Winwick Church, but were dislodged by parliamentary forces. We certainly know that the Liverpool Chapel was drawn into civil defence from the 'Certificate of the Musters' in 1639. This snapshot of the militia for the county on the eve of the Civil War lists guns held in reserve, and also that match, powder, and ball were stored in the steeple of St Nicholas' Chapel in Liverpool.[8] We know that the stockpiling of arms was an ongoing issue, and just a fortnight before Prince Rupert's storming of Liverpool there was a delivery of 100 muskets, 100 bandalliers, and 100 rests to the mayor and aldermen for the defence and safety of the town.[9]

It was Prince Rupert's arrival in Lancashire in 1644 which changed the temperature of the war in the county, and the brutality of his capture of Bolton is well documented, along with other major towns such as Manchester. Liverpool was still a small town with a population of under two thousand, but with the strength of being a port with easy access to Ireland. The capture of Liverpool by Prince Rupert in 1644 was, though, undoubtedly violent. Adam Martindale, after describing in detail the butchery in Bolton and other towns, gives a shorter narrative of the fall of Liverpool. This occurred overnight on 12/13 June 1644, and Martindale describes the slaughter of all those with whom the invading army met, totalling 360 people.[10] Another tale of the church's involvement, though thoroughly without corroboration, is two centuries later in Melville's *Redburn*. He states that Prince Rupert "converted the old church into a military prison and stable."[11] It is an interesting piece of invective, which is not just unsubstantiated and unattested, but perhaps also less likely given the political association between the royalist cause and the church. It was only a few months before Liverpool changed hands again, but this did not mean that the town was fervently parliamentarian, although from this point it was not to return to royalist hands. In September 1644 the parliamentarians, under Sir John Meldrum, took the town, largely because the royalist garrison itself capitulated: 60 English soldiers of the garrison escaped (along with some of the cattle), and the remaining Irish soldiers realised that there was little point in resisting and opened the gates of the town to the enemy.

Liverpool Puritanism

It has been suggested that the majority of the townspeople of Liverpool were Puritan,[12] but it is difficult to see any evidence for this. Some events are open to interpretation, though. We have already seen that there was provision in the Canons for a reading from the book of homilies if the incumbent was not up to preaching, but the town was keen to appoint and pay for a preacher. In 1621/2 Mr Swift became the first, and there is no particular reason to judge his preaching to be puritan. A document reported in the Town Books in 1654/5 but purporting to date from June 1628 gives an indication of the source of finance: an indenture provides that two closes called Two Far Heys containing five acres were given to William Fox, Robert Williamson, Ralph Sandifort, and Thomas Tarleton and their heirs on condition that they pay £4 a year to an able and preaching minister "who shall every sabbath preach the word of God in the chapel of Liverpool, and shall be approved of by the Mayor of Liverpool and five of the frequent communicants living in Liverpool."[13] At the same time, we know that puritanism was present in the region: the Ancient Chapel of Toxteth has its origins in a dissenting school built in 1611, and although its first minister, Richard Mather, was later ordained in the Church of England (from which he was subsequently suspended), the chapel remained in the hands of dissenters throughout the Civil War and Restoration periods.

However, the town's enthusiastic petition to the Bishop of Chester in 1629 for regular preachers could well indicate a wish for more puritanical teaching, especially as the request includes the observation that there were many papists in the region: the preacher was clearly meant to be injecting a different flavour into the town's religion. The consequence of the petition was to establish a pattern of monthly 'lectures' for which different people took responsibility for organisation. The Vicar of Walton supplied preachers in November and February, Mr Broxopp looked after March and July, and the mayor was responsible for the rest, although some individuals volunteered to take on the task. Whether or not they were puritan, they were expected to conform to the doctrine and discipline of the Church of England.[14]

In itself, conformity with the Established Church was an unremarkable agreement to make with the Bishop of Chester, but perhaps it was also a reaction to some puritan teaching in the town which took Christian faith and teaching outside the realms of the church: in 1630 the Archbishop of York's metropolitan visitation detected a James Chambers who was charged with 'repeating sermons in his house and entertaining people to hear him, the same being held to be conventicles' (that is to say, unauthorised religious gatherings led by lay people).[15] Conventicles were a mainstay of puritanism, both because it fostered the puritan emphasis on household religion, and it also took religion out of the control of the Church of England. In addition, of course, they were a place where dissatisfaction with the establishment could be voiced. In the Restoration period conventicles were banned by Act of Parliament in 1664.

Although the fervour of hearing sermons or lectures may have persisted, the enthusiasm of the town to pay for it wore off, and in 1642 the Assembly decided that the mayor should henceforth 'on his own cost' find two preachers to preach every exercise day, to work alongside the town's preacher. The Assembly also decided that they would no longer pay to 'keep' all the ministers in the town. Since the Reformation the town had provided accommodation as well as stipend, and it is possible that the growth in the number of preachers was making this impractical.[16] We have an account of typical puritan preaching in the region. In about 1643 we hear of a Mr Smith preaching at St Helen's, described as pious and serious. In his sermon he spoke of the 'desperateness and damnableness of a natural state without conversion.' Adam Martindale, who recorded the occasion, named this as the principal influence on his own conversion.[17] Whilst there are traces of puritanism in individuals at this time, there is little evidence of religious feeling within the population of Liverpool itself. On the eve of the Civil War we can also see a reaction against puritanism, the most amusing being John Mannwarring in August 1642, who was charged with abusing a general fast and saying that "if the king had comanded a Fast he wold then have kept it but because a companie of Puritanicall Fellowes had appoyned it hee wold keepe none nor cared not a fart for it." Mannwarring's invective against puritans is more significant than his disregard for their instructions, as only a few months earlier in January 1641/2 he was charged for abusing the mayor and bailiffs 'going upon the King's service' and also for 'abusing and infringing the liberties and privileges of this town.'[18] Mannwarring was clearly a troublemaker, whoever was in charge!

After the fall of Liverpool to parliamentary forces in May 1643 and it was established as a garrison town under Colonel John Moore, there was a notable change in religious direction. In September of that year Joseph Tompson was appointed by the Assembly as the minister (there is no mention of the fate of the previous minister). As in every previous regime, financing the incumbent's stipend was a continual problem, especially now that the Crown (through the Duchy of Lancaster) could no longer be relied upon to produce income from the former chantries. In August 1643 there was a petition drawn up about the payment of Liverpool clergy and signed by the mayor, Thomas Bicksteth and twenty members of the corporation. This was referred in September firstly to the Committee for Plundered Ministers, and then to the Deputy Lieutenants of the County.[19] By November the perspective of the Town Books reflects not so much the Assembly but rather the governing officers of the garrison, and their surprise is noted that there was no endowment for the ministry of the chapel. In January, on the authority of Colonel Moore, the tithes relating to Liverpool, but belonging properly to the parish church in Walton, were requisitioned for the purpose of appointing 'two able and orthodox ministers' for the town. Those appointed were Joseph Tompson, the minister already in post, and David Ellison. This new financial arrangement was aided by the desertion of Dr Andrew Clare, the Rector of Walton. All tithes from Liverpool, Formby and Kirby were sequestered for their local area. In addition, all "Papists and Malignates" were ordered, along with their wives and children, to leave Liverpool (unless they were prisoners) on pain of being plundered and deprived of their personal goods.[20] In fact the recusants paying the poll tax in Liverpool in 1641 numbered only five, so the expulsion of the Catholic population created no great upheaval. At the same time, following the protestant massacre in Ireland, non-Catholic Irish refugees were pouring into Liverpool at such a rate that Parliament granted £200 to be distributed to relieve their needs.[21] The influx of Irish protestants did more to change the religious tone of the town than the removal of the remaining Catholics.

Policy was clearly driven by a puritan agenda, but this was not always matched by domestic religious practice. Colonel Moore himself took into his household a young man called Adam Martindale, a puritan who later became a Presbyterian minister. His description of Moore's household (his 'family') indicates no great religious enthusiasm:

> *His family was such an hell upon earth, as was utterly intolerable. There was such a packe of arrant thieves, and they so artificiall at their trade, that it was scarce possible to save anything out of their hands, except what I could carrie about with me, or lodge in some other house. Those that were not thieves (if there were any such) were generally (if not universally) desperately profane and bitter scoffers at pietie, and these headed by one that had a mighty influence over the colonell, and was (I never knew why) become mine implacable enemy.*

This was not universal, though, and others with religious fervour such as Martindale's were drawn into the service of the parliamentary side. Martindale reports gathering every night with some of the more religious officers to read scriptures, engage in holy conversation, and to pray together.[22]

There was, though, an enthusiasm for enforcing puritan fervour through regular attendance at church. As we have seen, the enforcement of the Elizabethan laws on conformity and attendance was patchy, and the size of the chapel in Liverpool meant that it was impossible for the entire town population to attend every Sunday, but Liverpool under the Roundheads was one where prolonged absence was noticed. An example of this is the public admonition in June 1647 of Jane Gerrard and six other women for not attending church for the previous month.[23] There was no chance of avoiding weekly church attendance for the leading citizens of the town: either through religious zeal or political expediency they decided in 1648 that they should be listening more intently to the content of the services. Complaining that they could not hear properly from their seats in the chancel, the mayor and aldermen relocated to new seats elsewhere in the church, leaving their former places in the chancel to merchants and strangers. After noting in Chapter 3 the implication that there was a regular (weekly) celebration of Holy Communion in the Liverpool Chapel, the complaint that the mayor could not hear in the chancel suggests that the focus was no longer words from the communion table, but rather from the pulpit. Puritan religion had taken hold.[24]

Clergy and Church Before the Restoration

The frequent changing of hands of the town presented difficulties for the clergy. The church was generally loyal to the King, but political expectations were sometimes stronger. There was also the matter of preserving the dignity of town life. In January 1644/5, six months after Prince Rupert stormed the town and less than four months after the town fell again to parliamentary forces, the continuing bloodshed was such that the Assembly ordered that those who were 'murdered' and buried out of the town should be covered over properly, and townspeople should be sent out with spades to accomplish this.[25] We do not know how long the bodies had been there, but this appears to be an aspiration towards religious and human dignity, rather than an immediate reaction to bloodshed. Within the formal structure of the town the clergy continued to be honoured: in an era when any garrisoned officers appear to have been made burgesses 'gratis', the clergy were granted the same rights. In September 1646 William Warde, the Rector of Walton, and William Dunne, the Vicar of Ormskirk, were both made burgesses.[26] Similarly in October 1655 Robert Eaton, the 'parson of Walton' was made a freeman 'gratis'.[27] The town also elected a new minister, John Fogg, in 1645. Although, at the time of election, Liverpool was in parliamentary hands, Fogg appears to have been a royalist: by October 1650 he had been suspended, and his reappointment in January 1651/2 was only on the condition that he "declare his submission to the present government."[28]

The tussle over Fogg was both political and religious. Bishops and Archbishops were abolished in September 1646, and the county was rearranged for Presbyterian government. There were nine 'classes' across Lancashire, and Liverpool lay within the fifth 'classis' of Walton, Huyton, Sefton, Ormskirk, and Aughton. A carefully prescribed system allowed a minister and lay representatives from each parish to attend an area meeting.[29] We do not know if Liverpool attained separate representation at a provincial synod, but the historically analogous situation of the town chapel appears to have allowed life to continue as normal: the town appointed the minister, and he remained accountable to no one else. The church 'Inquisition' surveys of 1650 do, though, acknowledge the independence and pseudo-parochial status of Liverpool. They list John Fogg (before his suspension) as the minister, and state the right of appointment as resting with the mayor and council. His salary is from the tithes within the town, and an augmentation from Walton and also from the "late king's revenues" (in total over £90), although he also has to pay for the upkeep of the widow of Dr Clare, who deserted his post at Walton. The Inquisition makes no recommendation of its own, but notes that the parochial chapel is remote from any other church, and therefore "doe conceive itt fit to bee made a parish of it selfe."[30] The generosity towards Dr Clare's widow is despite the town's order that a report be drawn up "showing the violence he used against this town and how he preached here."[31]

Fogg, though, was dismissed in some circumstances which were not recorded. There was an ongoing dispute about the allocation of tithes from Walton, and it would seem that Joseph Tompson, who had been appointed under a previous parliamentary regime, still had possession of some of the tithes, despite remaining for under two years in Liverpool before moving to the rectory at Sefton. Fogg's departure presumably had both the political implications of a minister who was, at heart, a royalist, and also someone who did not suit the puritan expectations of the garrison. There is a telling statement in June 1651 when the mayor proposed the election of a new minister. It was decided to elect "two orthodox ministers" as there was hope of "better maintenance than before, as it is the chief port and only garrison in the area." In other words, ministers who were acceptable to the local garrison could be paid for. The ministers appointed were Peter Stanynough and Michael Broscowe, but in less than three month Stanynough resigned. James Rigbie was appointed in his place, but then Briscowe went on grounds of ill health. There cannot have been a superfluity of clergy in the vicinity, and so the town turned back to Mr Fogg "if he, by subscribing the judgement, agrees to officiate in the garrison which the town is very desirous of."[32] As we have noted, Fogg was also expected to submit to the government, which he swiftly did. Town and church life then continued, and there is also no further mention in the records of James Rigbie, the other minister.

However, the ongoing financial tussle with paying the clergy continued. In January 1653/4 Mr Fogg appeared before the Assembly and, in a manner acknowledged as apologetic, made a number of requests before withdrawing whilst the Assembly considered them. Firstly, he asked whether he could have the surplus of a year's profit from the tithes which were collected in his absence from the post, and whether he could have the £50 paid back by Joseph Tompson. To this the Assembly replied that he could not, as any surplus money was used to pay ministers in his absence (presumably Stanynough, Broscowe, and Rigbie). Secondly, could he be free of all leys (taxes) which concession he claimed had been promised to him when he took up the post. The Assembly refused this as well, compelling him to pay his taxes. Thirdly, he asked for all church dues (i.e. fees), to which the Assembly replied that he could. And fourthly he asked for a six-month notice period should he be removed from office. To this the Assembly replied that he could, but only as a courtesy, and not as a right.[33]

Meanwhile, the town's responsibility for maintaining the church continued. In March 1645/6 the town ordered that the lead on the south side of the chapel be removed, melted down, and replaced on the roof. Two years later the town ordered that the church wall by the water be repaired quickly because it might damage the foundations of the church. And again in 1648 it was decided that two new bells should be cast for the church.[34] The pattern that every decade or so some significant repairs were required continued, and in October 1656 the Assembly ordered that the church, "being in decay", should undergo repairs to the roof and to the walls. They later decided that the costs should be offset by a ley to which all foreign burgesses should contribute. Repairs were obviously piecemeal, because in March 1658 it was necessary for more repairs to the church walls and roof: they were evidently fairly urgent as it was decided to raise the money at a later date.[35]

The Restoration

The first consequence of the Restoration in May 1660 appears to have been a vacancy at the chapel. In October of that year the Assembly ordered that there would be 20 shillings for every sabbath day for any minister taking services during the vacancy. There was obviously a scarcity of suitable candidates for the permanent post, and in that month the appointment of a minister was deferred. It was not until the following October that the new minister was named as John Leigh.[36] In other ways the business of the chapel continued as before: there was still a frequent need for repairs because of the weather and the effects of the water, and in 1663 it was ordered that all freemen should be assessed for a contribution towards the £100 required. Six years later the situation was severe again, and in the pursuit of just £50 it was decided that any freeman who refused to pay would be disenfranchised and made incapable of any benefit of the Freedom of the Town which they possessed. Just a year later the Assembly ordered the raising of a further £60 towards repairs.[37] The continuing willingness of the Assembly to take responsibility for the repair of the church did not deter individuals from pious donation, just as they had in pre-Reformation times.

The 1660s saw many repairs executed by the town, but there also remains a draft receipt from 1667 stating that Edward Moore had repaired the chancel in the chapel.[38] Moore was the son of Colonel Moore, who had been governor of the town during the Civil War and Commonwealth. Colonel Moore's property is referred to in the Indemnity and Oblivion Act of 1660, which granted a pardon to most of those involved in the Civil War. Edward Moore appears to be a loyal subject of the Crown, and an enthusiastic citizen of the town. Despite the repeated leys on the burgesses, Moore's understanding of his obligations towards the repair of the chapel are nuanced:

> *I find that you are not obliged, in the common laws, to repair the chapel, without it were either the parish church, or you was an inhabitant in the town; but if they lay you in the general amongst*

> *the foreign freemen, provided it be in reason, equally as others,*
> *then if you be a freeman of the town, you are bound by your oath*
> *to contribute proportionably.*

In fact Moore's responsibility towards maintenance was more than just his oath as a freeman, but also his ownership of pew:

> *both where I sit myself, and servants, to hear divine service in*
> *Liverpool church, know that you must maintain it with glass,*
> *flags, doors, seats, and all other materials whatsoever; otherwise*
> *the bishop and the ordinary may remove you, or order others to sit*
> *with you, it being not sufficient for you to prescribe it.*[39]

At some point, some of the responsibility for the incidental fabric and fittings of the church shifted from the town to the pewholders.

The life of the chapel was more than a struggle for financial existence. There are glimpses of genuine and faithful worship, and an outward looking congregation. An example of this is in the 'briefs' which survive from the chapel. These were orders, signed by the Sovereign, which provided for the collection of money for specific causes from churches across the country. There is provision in the Book of Common Prayer for "Briefs, Citations, and Excommunications" to be read, and this practice continued into the nineteenth century, although there was also the opportunity for much corruption. A selection were listed in the registers of the 1660s, including ecclesiastical causes both local and afar. There are nine 'briefs' listed for 1663 alone in the chapel, from a collection in March of £1 1s. for the rebuilding of the church of Wytheham in Sussex, through to 5s. raised on 18 September for the relief of Gilbert Greene and his son in Wigan. Although the burial registers present no evidence that the Great Plague of 1665 made any great impact in Liverpool, a total of £4 11s. 2d. was raised at the chapel for the relief of the poor of London and elsewhere affected by the plague.[40]

The religious life of England had always been intertwined with politics, and the Corporation Act of 1661 restricted public office to members of the Church of England. Although this was later associated with a campaign to remove Catholics from public life (and this was particularly the issue in the campaign before the repeal of the Act in 1828), the initial impetus was for the removal of Presbyterians and Puritans. The Act was applied to Liverpool in November 1662 and resulted in the removal from office of six aldermen, seven councillors, and the town clerk. In particular, we can note that all six aldermen had held office as mayor in the 1650s under the Commonwealth: the Act was not a defence of the Reformation so much as a purging of political opposition.[41]

Puritanism had been put aside, but biblical learning and religious devotion had not. One of the more intriguing documents of the time is the *Moore Rental*: a candid account by Edward Moore of his land and tenants written in the 1660s for the benefit of his son, William, when he came to inherit, and possibly also an embittered complaint against those tenants who failed to support Moore in his bid for Parliament. Sadly, William did not live to read the book as landlord, but it remains for us as a glimpse behind the doors of Restoration Liverpool. Here we learn of John Monely, a tailor described as "a base fellow, and a knave, and his wife worse." Or perhaps John Lorting, "A sour dog fellow, yet one who loves me and my family."[42] This practical manual of people and property management is, though, cased in the language of prayer:

> *And whoever thou art, that opens this Book, know that it is by Christ Jesus' permission; or else thou couldst have no power here: therefore as thou art a Christian, and wilt answer me in another world, do this my endeavour no hard; neither wrong me nor my children by the knowledge of it; for the time will come (and that very shortly) that I shall see thee face to face, to give an account of it.*[43]

The book reveals the author not just to be literate, but also learned in Latin and well-read in church history and doctrine. Most significantly, Moore's defence of the faith which he holds is explicitly that of the Church of England, but he demonstrates familiarity with both the books and the authors from a wide spectrum of traditions. He quotes not just Anglican divines, but also his friendship with Catholic priests. In a statement of Anglican identity which would be anathema to the puritan, he promotes the identity of the "Reformed Catholic," amongst whom he numbers early reformers such as John Wycliffe, and Anglican divines such as Jewell, Laud and Hooker.[44] Given Adam Martindale's account of life in Colonel Moore household in the 1640s (probably after Edward Moore had left his father's house), which he found to be like hell on earth or full of thieves, Edward Moore's interest in Roman Catholicism and Anglican piety is surprising, but the Moore family – whose ancestors were the subject of the thirteenth century property conveyance in which the Chapel of St Mary receives its first mention – were always adaptable.

Moore's religious disposition seems genuine, but also reflected the acceptability of a more Catholic flavour to religious practice. We can see from the extensive provision of bread and wine in the church-wardens' accounts in the 1680s that there were frequent communion services, but a more Laudian approach to worship was also promoted. Thomas Cartwright, the Bishop of Chester, recorded in his diary for 21 September 1687: "*I went at 11 of the clock from my Lord Molineux to Liverpool, where the mayor and aldermen met me in the church, and I commanded the churchwarden to set the communion table altar wise against the wall. They gave me and Mr Molineux and Mr Massey a fish dinner.*"[45] This removal of the communion table from a likely 'free-standing' position, around which people could stand, to an altar position, of the sort with which we are more familiar today, showed a significant shift in religious and doctrinal practice: only forty years earlier the mayor's seat had been moved away from the chancel so that he was closer to the place of preaching, and now the prominence of sacramental worship was being restored.

Status and Display

Apart from the Common Hall of the town, where the Assembly met, the chapel was the only place where the leading citizens could be seen by the populace. Both alive and dead, the position one occupied in the chapel was of significance. In the Tudor period there was a set order of precedence in the chapel for officials, their wives, and their widows. During the Stuart era there was no diminution of attention from the mayor and corporation to this detail. In December 1629 the Bishop of Chester granted confirmation of the allotment of seats within St Nicholas' Chapel made by the mayor.[46] A list from about 1660 of the land and property of Edward Moore, who had personally paid for repairs to the chancel, included pews or seats in both Walton Church and the Liverpool Chapel.[47] A few years later Moore wrote of the responsibility of being a pew holder in the chapel:

> *For your chapel, (the seat you sit in is so called,) and for the servants' seat, you must repair the glass windows, forms, and flags, with all things else belonging to them, of your own charges. And remember, all the compass within them is your ancient burial place, and so hath been for many hundred years, there never being any but your kindred of blood and name there interred.*[48]

Although the position of the church in the Commonwealth was much diminished, and puritanism frowned upon excessive display, the town church in Liverpool continued as a place to parade civic status. Even without the mayor's stall, there was still a place for mayoral status to be displayed after death. The extant registers begin in 1661, but a plan of the burial places in the chancel was made in 1800, including the grave of John Walker who died in 1651 after having held the office of mayor on four occasions. Another occupant of the chancel was Thomas Hodgson, recorded in the inscription as having been Mayor of Liverpool in 1649, before his death in 1653. Other prominent people from this period managed to secure a place in the chancel, with either civic or ecclesiastical connections: Alderman Thomas Williamson was buried in 1691, followed by his son, the Revd Thomas Williamson who died in 1696. The younger Williamson obviously chose not to be buried in the parish of West Kirby, where he had been rector since 1670.[49] The plan of burials in the chancel are corroborated by the record of fees received: Alderman Thomas Williamson's grave cost 6*s*. 8*d*. in the chapelwardens' accounts of April 1692, though the chapelwardens' accounts for the year of his son's death are not recorded.[50]

The Church Ascendant

Throughout the seventeenth century the chapel had gradually been acquiring the independence and confidence of a parish church, although it had to wait until the end of the century to acquire the legal independence. The physical appearance of the chapel remained largely unchanged since medieval times. It had a nave aisle and a north aisle, and the architecturally precise drawing in Enfield's *History of Leverpool* of 1773 reveals a buttressed nave with a low roof, which Peet estimated as 100 feet in length, divided into six bays (he made this measurement partly, one imagines, on the basis of the current building, which occupies almost exactly the same footprint). The nave had a low roof with no clerestory, and there was a square tower at the west end of the building.[51] The earliest drawings of the church are small and short on detail, but date from the Civil War itself, though only survive now in nineteenth-century copies. The first is a plan of the fortifications of Liverpool in 1643–4 based on a plan by Sir Bernard de Gomme, a royalist who travelled with Prince Rupert. The second also shows the various batteries erected in Liverpool, and was a map amongst the Leland Papers.[52] Both drawing show rudimentary drawings of a church with a nave and a square tower. A more detailed depiction of the church appears in a painting dating from 1680, though supposedly representing an earlier period, which is known as the "Ralph Peters" painting, as it was once in the possession of a man of that name (it now hangs in the Mersey Maritime Museum). The building is clearly identifiable as the one in Enfield's book a century later, with buttresses, porch and tower in the same arrangement.

A curious and unexplained circumstance reveals the only piece of furniture from the seventeenth-century chapel still in existence. In the now disused church at Ladykirk near Berwick-upon-Tweed is a carved oak chest with an incised inscription stating that it was the gift of Edward Williamson in 1651 to the Church of St. Nicholas, Liverpool. Williamson served as mayor in 1653–4, and this ornate gift is decorated with both armorial badges and religious scenes (although it is possible that some were added later). The parish chest was the place where

The 'Ladykirk Chest', made for St Nicholas' Chapel in 1651, and mysteriously now held by a church on the Scottish borders.
Photograph by Tommy Newlands

registers were stored, but the additional inscriptions, if at all original, suggest that the chest may have been related to poor relief. At the top it says, "Edward Williamsons Gift to ye Trulye Poore and Aged of this Parish." And then below, "My Trust is in God alone." At the very bottom on the plinth is says, "I was hungrie and ye gave me meat, I was thirstie and ye gave me Drinke, a stranger and ye tooke me in, naked and ye clothed me, I was sicke and ye visited me" (biblical quotations from Matthew Ch. 25). It seems likely that this is the oak chest listed in the inventory of 1702.[53] Quite why the chest came to be released from the Liverpool Chapel, and how it found its way across first to an estate in Sheffield, and then to auction in Edinburgh before settling in Ladykirk, remain a mystery.[54]

It is at the end of the seventeenth century that the vestry records begin. From 1681 until 1834 extremely detailed minutes were kept of vestry meetings which detail not just the life of the church, but also the administration of the Poor Law (see Chapter 6). There is no reason given for the sudden commencement of this written record, although it is possible that it was a continuation of records which are now lost. But in many respects the business and financial details are those which previously appeared in the Town Books. The accounts given on the first page, at the Easter Vestry Meeting in April 1682, include not just the details of fees received, but also every detail of building upkeep and repair, along with the cost of bread and wine "for the Sacrament." There is also an inventory of "all the plate, bookes and other ornaments and necessaries belonginge to the Parochiall Chappell of Liverpoole. This inventory lists not just silverware, but also details such as the cushion in the mayor's stall. Sadly it does not mention the chest now in Ladykirk.[55]

The town was growing at a rapid rate, and there are plenty of indications that there was not enough space. In 1673 the Bishop of Chester granted a faculty for the erection of a gallery on the north side, in which pews were then place subsequently by individuals, rather than by the church or corporation. There was a similar grant made in 1680 as more seats were added, and the right to allocate (in return for a fee!) the space was given to the mayor and corporation. Then in February 1681/2 a faculty was granted authorising the mayor and corporation to build three galleries: one on the south side of the nave, one over the north chancel and one at the west end of the nave.[56] The churchwardens' accounts for 1682 in the Vestry Books record much of the financial activity connected with these new galleries and seating, and also considerable expenditure on the building of a new vestry: with the levelling of the churchyard and the provision of new flagstones, this would appear to be a new structure added to the old building.[57]

Some seats were allocated directly by the Bishop of Chester, as Bishop Thomas Cartwright records in his diary for 1687: "*A seat in the church of Liverpool, upon Mary Hesketh's resignation, granted to David Poole, merchant, and his heirs*"[58] However, the Vestry Books also record some of the allocations from the mayor and aldermen of spaces in the galleries for the installation of private pews in September 1683.[59] Each allocation would have been accompanied by an elaborate document, of which a considerable number survive in the church archives. The earliest of these is from 1696, assigning a seat (to be installed at his own expense) to Joseph Briggs in return for £2 5s. The maintenance of the seat rests with Briggs, but the allocation of the space remains his, to be handed down to his heirs as property.[60] At the same time, a pew for a 'choir' to lead the singing of psalms was also put up by a faculty dated January 1695/6, authorising a singing gallery to be built over the chancel.[61]

The expansion of the population of Liverpool now continued unabated: by 1700 there were approximately 5000 people[62] but still with just one place of worship. Although this was to change in the next few decades with the building of a number of new churches, the immediate response was to extend not just the existing seating plan, but also the building. In March 1696/7 a Faculty was granted to William Preeson, Thomas Johnson, and Ellen Willis to build an 'Out Aisle' on the north side of the church. This appears to have involved removing a portion of wall and extending the building out to the north, before reinstating the wall and installing new windows. The new space was, of course, to be filled with pews.[63]

Separation from Walton

The attack on the parish structure by the commonwealth government at last gave Liverpool some financial freedom from Walton. It was made explicitly clear that Parliament allowed Liverpool and its minister to benefit from all the tithes in the town.[64] We have already seen that Mr Fogg was paid from some of the revenue from Walton, but in this period the frustration of Walton's demands for support from Liverpool built to a head. The Assembly seized the opportunity of a change of authority to ask for independence. Without citing Queen Elizabeth's grant that they could appoint their own clergy, the Assembly noted in 1654 that "time out of mind" they held the right to nominate the minister, clerk

and churchwardens. They therefore decided to send a petition to the
governor to make the town a separate parish, distinct from Walton,
"especially in view of demands for an allowance toward the repair of
their church which this town is not willing to pay unless compelled by
law." The response was some time coming, but in February 1655/6 a
letter from the late governor, Colonel Birch, was read to the Assembly,
asking for a list of the town's wishes. Almost at the head of this list was
that the town become a separate parish, citing the status as the only
port in the county as justification.[65] There is no record of a response, but
the campaign continued, and in May 1657 it was ordered that the Town
Clerk, John Winstanley, should go to London to try to have the town
made into a parish distinct from Walton. The town later gave him an
allowance of £5 a quarter towards this mission, and they also allowed
Mr Fogg, the incumbent, to go with him.[66]

Throughout these years there was an ongoing tussle over whether
there was a legal obligation for Liverpool to contribute towards Walton
Church. Mr Moore, the Vicar of Walton, along with a churchwarden
produced a warrant in May 1654 to say that £12 was needed for the
repair of Walton Church, and that Liverpool should pay £2 13s. 4d.
towards this sum. The Assembly decided that the warrant was not

Indenture from 1696 recording the sale of a pew in the newly-built 'out-aisle'.
OLSN Archives

well-grounded or legally issues, and referred the matter to the Recorder for legal opinion. Walton tried again in 1657 when the vicar, Edward Moore, produced another warrant for Liverpool's share of the £12 needed. Again, the town refused to pay and decided to defend any law case. In addition, it would seem that James Standish, one of the officials in Walton, seized the plate and goods of Gilbert Formby, who occupied church land, which were "distrained" (seized in order to obtain payment of the debt). The bailiffs of Liverpool immediately took legal action against Standish, with the town paying the legal costs.[67] The case began in August 1658 with a suit in chancery: the case was brought by Edward Moore against Gilbert Formby and others; in response there was another case against Mr Standish of West Derby for the taking of Gilbert Formby's silver in place of the leys for Walton Church. The case dragged on, and in October 1658 it was agreed that if the justices of the peace signed the warrant against Liverpool then the town would pay up. The case, though, had still not been heard, and new papers were drawn up, alongside discussions about which land should constitute the tithes of the town. Arguments about the conduct of the case were still going on in in January 1658/9.[68]

After all of this, it seems rather surprising that, shortly after the Restoration, the new incumbent of Walton, John Heywood, should be admitted as a freeman of Liverpool 'gratis'.[69] This was, perhaps, a brief rapprochement, because in December 1669 the next Vicar of Walton, Thomas Marsden, made a claim to the right of appointing a minister for the Liverpool Chapel and demanded the keys as his own right. Given the preceding history, this seems to be a rash foray into an old battle, and the Town Assembly – now in a position to cite royal favour again – quoted the grant of patronage given by Queen Elizabeth before declaring that for them to surrender the right of appointment would be a "loss and dishonour to this ancient corporation." Moreover, they decided that if Marsden took any action against the minister in Liverpool or anyone else then they would indemnify the defence.[70]

The result of the court case is not recorded, but the town continued to appoint the incumbent. We have already seen that, with the addition of preachers, there were often several clergy in the vicinity. In October 1670 Robert Hunter was elected as minister of the chapel, but the list of Free Burgesses in April 1671 contained his predecessor, John Leigh, who was obviously still resident.[71] This was perhaps a precursor to the unusual arrangement made when Liverpool finally won its own parish. In the meantime, Hunter was followed by Samuel Smalhorne in 1674, and then in 1688 both William Atherton and Robert Stythe

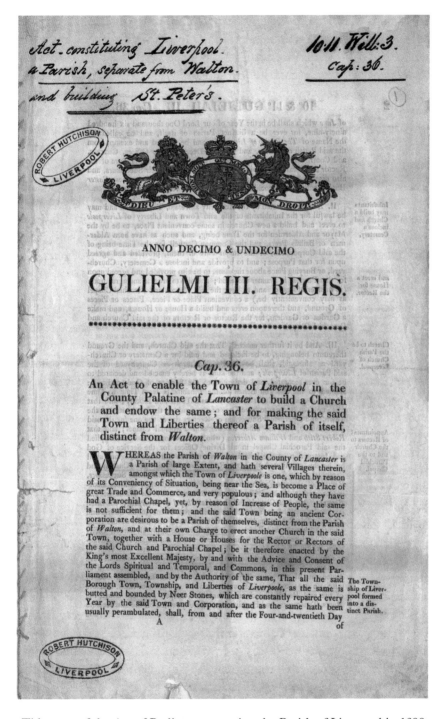

Act. constituting Liverpool.
a Parish, separate from Walton.
and building St. Peter's.

10.11. Will: 3.
Cap: 36.

ANNO DECIMO & UNDECIMO

GULIELMI III. REGIS.

****

Cap. 36.

An Act to enable the Town of *Liverpool* in the County Palatine of *Lancaster* to build a Church and endow the same; and for making the said Town and Liberties thereof a Parish of itself, distinct from *Walton*.

WHEREAS the Parish of *Walton* in the County of *Lancaster* is a Parish of large Extent, and hath several Villages therein, amongst which the Town of *Liverpoole* is one, which by reason of its Conveniency of Situation, being near the Sea, is become a Place of great Trade and Commerce, and very populous; and although they have had a Parochial Chapel, yet, by reason of Increase of People, the same is not sufficient for them; and the said Town being an ancient Corporation are desirous to be a Parish of themselves, distinct from the Parish of *Walton*, and at their own Charge to erect another Church in the said Town, together with a House or Houses for the Rector or Rectors of the said Church and Parochial Chapel; be it therefore enacted by the King's most Excellent Majesty, by and with the Advice and Consent of the Lords Spiritual and Temporal, and Commons, in this present Parliament assembled, and by the Authority of the same, That all the said Borough Town, Township, and Liberties of *Liverpoole*, as the same is butted and bounded by Neer Stones, which are constantly repaired every Year by the said Town and Corporation, and as the same hath been usually perambulated, shall, from and after the Four-and-twentieth Day

The Township of Liverpool formed into a distinct Parish.

A   of

Title page of the Act of Parliament creating the Parish of Liverpool in 1699.

arrived. Eleven years later they were to become the first rectors. In the meantime, the campaign for independence continued: the Town Books record that the matter came again before the council in 1697 and the mayor undertook discussions with the Rector of Walton, and the Liverpool Members of Parliament, Sir William Norris and William Clayton, were asked to take the issue forward in Westminster. The resistance from Walton over the preceding one hundred and fifty years had largely been financial, and so the mayor, after consulting with the Patron of the Living of Walton, Lord Molyneux, made an offer to the Rector of Walton to compensate him for the loss of tithes within the town of Liverpool. The final arrangement was that the Rector of Walton would be given £55p.a. during his lifetime, and the vicar should receive £6. 10s.[72] The Rectors of Liverpool would also give one sixth of "all First Fruits, Tenths, Procurations, Synodals, and all other Ecclesiastical Charges" to Walton. At the same time, the Town Corporation would made financial compensation to Viscount Molyneux (spelled 'Mulleneux' in the Act) for the loss of his rights as patron over the Liverpool portion of the Parish of Walton.

And so in 1699 Liverpool finally gained her Act of Parliament, providing for two rectors and a new parish church alongside the parochial chapel.[73]

CHAPTER FIVE

The Georgian Parish

A Parish Church

The Act of Parliament of 1699 contained a significant eccentricity: a parish needs an incumbent, but Liverpool was granted two of them. The Act read: *"…and that there be Two Rectors to have Care of the Souls of the Inhabitants of the Town, and a perpetual Succession of Rectors there… And be it further enacted, That the said Rectory shall be called and esteemed a Mediety, that is to say, equal betwixt the said Two Rectors that shall preach at the new Church and Parochial Chapel."*[1] This was not an entirely unknown situation (for example, St Helen's Church in Trowell, Nottingham), but remained unusual. Quite quickly the rectors were often designated as 'junior' or 'senior', depending on the date of their appointment. Initially they were given a housing allowance until suitable rectories could be built for them, although in 1715 a number of individuals subscribed £300 towards the building of rectories.[2] Before the new church was built, the rectors presumably co-existed in the same building, but by the end of the eighteenth century a pattern had developed whereby each rector officiated in one church only for a year, and on the third Sunday of July each year they exchanged their churches.[3]

The new parish came into existence on 24 June 1699, the feast of the Nativity of John the Baptist. The first task was the building of the new Parish Church of St Peter: the vestry continued to levy higher rates for the poor than for church maintenance, but largely absent from the record is the cost of the new church. This was, though, financed by an annual 'ley', possibly around £600.[4]

Although the corporation had initially explored building on the site of the castle, this was not immediately available. The rate lists of 1708 show 34 streets, with the most densely populated area being around the original 'seven streets' of Liverpool, and the place chosen for the new parish church just a few years before was in a relatively sparsely inhabited area, but one which would soon be built up by extensive Georgian townhouses. The building itself was unattractive on the outside, with an octagonal tower and a selection of neo-classical features to create a Georgian contrast to the medieval parochial chapel, but it was never considered architecturally successful. The inside was much more ornate, particularly in its carved wood decoration, and although photographs from the beginning of the twentieth century do not show an interior of great beauty, it was practical.[5] Underneath a great barrel

An eighteenth-century print of the parochial chapel. The adjacent building may originally have been part of the Chapel of St Mary del Quay. *Author's collection.*

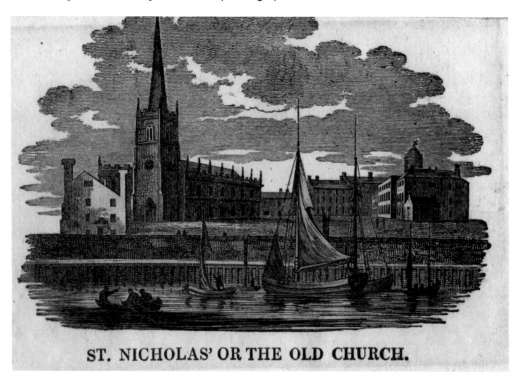

ST. NICHOLAS' OR THE OLD CHURCH.

roof there was substantial seating at ground level, and even more capacity in galleries arranged around three sides of the church. In 1717 it was even resolved to build a second west gallery above the first, to seat charity children.[6] The central place of the pulpit raised up above the nave captures the dominant ecclesiastical tone of the age, but the elegant altar at the east end reflected the High Church inclination of the clergy, evidenced not just in the restoration of the altar in St Nicholas to the east wall in 1687, but also in the Tory ideals of the rector which we glimpse in Chapter 6. A feature of the church which persisted until its demolition in the 1920s was a library in the vestry: the first reference to this is a complaint from the churchwardens in 1735 that Edward Green, the former clerk at St Peter's, allowed people to borrow books without checking them out properly. At that stage there were 54 books, although a further catalogue (not surviving) was made in 1752. The catalogue made of a much augmented collection in 1893 reveals a significant number of sixteenth- and seventeenth-century printed books ranging from patristic scholarship through to the Anglican divines.[7] It was a significant room for some, at least: in 1765 Henry Wolstenholme (Rector 1753–71) claimed his right of burial in the Library of St Peter's. There was to be no marker, but the floorboards should just be put back as before.[8]

The consecration service itself on the feast of St Peter (29 June) 1704 was rather grand. Henry Prescott, Deputy Registrar of Chester Diocese, recorded in his diary:

> *The Clergy 42 in number, two halberteers makeing way go first, myself next alone, next the Dean and the preacher Mr Styth, next the Mayor and the Bishop preceeded by the sword and their Several Maces next, the Chancellor, then Gentry and others... The Bishop enters the Church alone takes possession and in a few minuits returns. That door and the rest are open'd and people like a torrent flow in with irresistible force at every door; many complain, cry out, and loose parts of their habits, but a good and great providence prevents mischeif... The office begins by the Bishop with a prayer of Consecracion, hee sits in a Throne near the pulpit, next the 1st chaplain Mr Taylor begins the service of the day, the Bishop intermixes proper prayers, an anthem, 89 psalm is sung by Holcomb, after the Nicene Creed the sentence of Consecracion read by the Bishop. Mr Styth has a very sound discourse on 3 verses of those of Solomon at the Consecracion of his Temple, justifies our Consecracion and service takes occasion to rebuke the*

papist and dissenter; Commends in generall the piety of the Town in raising a structure so magnificent among Warrs losses, taxes in 4 years, and enumerates particular Benefactors. After Benedicion by the Bishop, the people flock out, the Bishop follows in the Churchyard… and reads the sentence of Consecracion of it.[9]

As soon as the new church was consecrated it became part of the fabric of the town, although equipping the building continued for some years. For example, payments relating to new bells appear in the church-wardens' accounts in 1714, and in 1715 there was permission given for the building of new pews. The vestry meetings alternated between the parish church and the parochial chapel, and although other churches were later built within the parish, St Peter's and St Nicholas' remained the seat of the rectors, and the places where the business of the vestry – and therefore the town – took place.[10]

More People, More Churches

Liverpool Castle had ceased to dominate the town, but still had the ability to produce an income. In 1704/5 the corporation leased the castle from the Crown with the explicit purpose of raising the £200 required by the 1699 Act towards the rectors' stipends.[11] The site, though, was soon put to a different use. Despite the recent arrival of St Peter's, the rapid growth of population meant that capacity for worshippers was always stretched. Population estimates are difficult to make, but it is possible that the town grew from about 1300 people in 1664 to around 20,000 in the mid-eighteenth century.[12] Numbers were always significant, but the building of churches was also about need and location. Although the mayor had always had a pew in St Nicholas', the development of the civic seat in Exchange Building – later rebuilt as the Town Hall – and the final demolition of that other locus of authority, the castle, meant that civic Liverpool wished to move its ecclesiastical gaze.

Following an Act of Parliament in 1714 to build a new church within the parish of Liverpool, in 1715 the mayor and Common Council resolved to give the land they had in the castle to the building of a new church.[13] The delay in pursuing this plan was probably connected with the Jacobite Rebellion in the same year, which led not only to the fortification of the town, but also to the imprisonment and trial in Liverpool Castle of the rebels captured after the Battle of

The new Parish Church of Liverpool dedicated to St Peter, consecrated in 1704. *OLSN Archive.*

Preston. When the town attempted to reclaim the costs of fortification from the government in 1718, they resolved to use any funds obtained for the building of the church. We do not know if they were successful, but by 1725 plans were being drawn up for the new church.[14] When St George's was opened in 1734 it was possibly built on the foundations of the (much smaller) garrison chapel in the castle grounds,[15] and it was designed and built by Thomas Steers, who built the world's first wet dock in Liverpool (1710–16). Although we can see from the pew plans of the eighteenth century that the mayor continued to maintain a seat in St Nicholas', and indeed an earlier inventory in 1702 shows that it was furnished with a velvet cushion, he began to attend St George's as the principal civic church.[16] Unlike St Peter's, the layout of the new church was not conducive to Eucharistic worship. Filled with pews and galleries, the dominant feature was a vast triple-decker pulpit in the very centre of the nave aisle, effectively blocking any view of the altar behind. This church was designed for preaching and little else.[17] According to an anonymous writer in the nineteenth century, this was "*the* church of churches." He wrote that "we used to rush down to

The interior of St George's
Church, opened in 1734.
*By Courtesy of the University
of Liverpool Library, Peet
Collection 2/4/1*

Castle Street, about a quarter of an hour before the service began, to
see the mayor and his train march to church! We were never tired of
watching that procession. It was super-royal in our estimation."[18]

St George's was the first of many churches built within the parish.
Acts of Parliament followed to build a considerable number of new
churches (dates of opening shown in brackets): St Thomas (1750),
St Paul (1769), St John (1784), St Anne (1772), St James (1775), St
Mary (1813), St Catherine (1776), Trinity (1792), St Stephen (1792),
St Matthew (1795), Christ Church (1797), St Michael (1826), St Mark
(1803), St Andrew (1815), St Philip (1816), St David (1827), St Catherine
(1829), St Martin-in-the-Fields (1828), St Bridgett (1831 – from the
beginning known as St Bride's), St Luke (1831), St Matthias (1834).
In the Victorian period further churches were established, so that by

1870 the parish contained thirty-four Anglican churches. Many of these churches were built at the expense of the corporation, although a number were private ventures. For example, St Andrew's Church in Renshaw Street (opened in 1815) was built at the sole expense of John Gladstone, who lived around the corner in Rodney Street. Gladstone was a merchant and father of the future Prime Minister, William Ewart Gladstone, who later bought the patronage of the Parish Church. William Gladstone was baptized at St Peter's on 7 February 1810. The exception to private or corporation funding was the Church of St Martin-in-the-Fields in Great Oxford Street North (now Silvester Street), which was funded entirely by the government following the Church Building Acts of 1818 and 1824. St Martin's was the only "Commissioners' Church" in Liverpool, and was often referred to as the "National Church". As a sign of the times, there were delays in its construction because of finalizing the route of the new railway. Although funded by the government, the new church became the property and responsibility of the parish, who were swift to shake off this financial incumbrance and secured an Act of Parliament in 1829 to transfer ownership to the corporation.[19] There was another category of chapel within the parish recorded by the librarian of the Liverpool Athenaeum, John Jones, in his commonplace book in the 1860s as "not regularly belonging to the Established Church thought the National Liturgy is said to be constantly used in them." Jones begins his list with "St Mary's or Mr Bragg's Chapel built in 1775 and licensed about that time by W. Markham DD then Bishop of Chester (Rector T Maddock strenue sed frustra obstante) which licence being revoked by a succeeding Bishop in 1788 it was afterwards licensed under the Toleration Act by the Magistrates."[20]

All of these churches were inferior to the Parish Church of St Peter, and the Parochial Chapel of St Nicholas, but they acted independently. For many years the town repelled the right of the incumbent of Walton to appoint the clergy of any chapels within the parish, and so with the arrival of new churches within the parish of Liverpool, the town often retained the same principle and appointed the clergy themselves, rather than deferring to the rectors. The principal clergyman of each church was usually referred to as the 'Chaplain' of the church, or sometimes the 'Minister', and each church also retained a number of curates. Each church had its own ministry, and although the churches in the eastern part of the parish were often not endowed and largely catering for a poor population, some of those in the heart of the town were every bit as grand as the two principal churches. Foremost amongst these remained the Church of St George, whose chaplain and lecturer often succeeded to the rectory of Liverpool. For example, in 1829, the chaplain was listed as Jonathan Brooks and the lecturer as Augustus Campbell.[21] In the same year both moved to be the last rectors who held the incumbency in mediety. Brooks' death in 1855 enacted the provisions of the *Act for uniting the Medieties of the Rectory of Liverpool* (1838). They were not the only clergy to move from St George's to the parish churches: so did Thomas Maddock, Henry Wolstenholme, George Hodson, Samuel Renshaw and Roughsedge. In fact between the foundation of St George's, and the appointment of Brooks and Campbell, only two Rectors of Liverpool had not first served at St George's. There were other family links as well: George Hodson's son, Frodsham Hodson, was licensed as lecturer in the parish (1794–6) and then as lecturer at St George's (1796–1812) and was perpetual curate at St George's (1812–22). He simultaneously held other appointments, including as Principal of Brasenose College, Oxford, from 1809.

One of the more unusual daughter churches within the parish was the Mariner's Church in George's Dock, Centre. This was formerly the Royal Navy ship HMS *Tees* which was given by the government for use as a floating chapel in 1827. It was fitted out like a conventional church, including the provision of galleries to create a seating capacity of a thousand, and regular Church of England services took place in it. The first chaplain was the Revd Dr William Scoresby, who was an Arctic explorer and scientist. Scoresby was noted for using nautical language and illustrations to engage his congregation, such as the mariner's compass as an analogy for the Spirit of Christ, or Christ as the life boat of the soul.[22] It was not the only waterborne place of worship, as there was also a non-conformist floating chapel, but the Mariner's Church reached the end of its life in 1872 when it sank on its moorings.

The relationship between the two principal churches and their offspring varied. Some of the churches were very much left to be self-governing, but both the corporation and the vestry felt a need to be involved in the affairs of the more significant churches. Foremost amongst these was St George's and as early as 1735, just a year after it opened, the rectors complained that they and the churchwardens were being denied their right to use the money given at the offertory at communion at St George's for whatever charitable purpose they saw fit. They reminded the vestry that the chaplain of St George's was technically only a curate of the parish.[23] This was an awkward relationship, because the appointment of many of the clergy rested with the corporation, and the maintenance of the buildings fell to the corporation. Whereas the parish church and parochial chapel levied a Church Rate to maintain their buildings, the corporation took direct financial responsibility for other churches. For example, in March 1757 the large and splendid spire of St Thomas' fell down in a storm: "About 42ft of the lofty Spire of St Thomas's Church (which was esteemed one

The exterior of St George's from Enfield's *History of Liverpool, 1773*.

of the most beautiful in Europe) fell upon the Body of the Church, broke through the Roof and has torn down the West galleries." On 19 April the Common Council passed a resolution to repair and rebuild the spire entirely at the expense of the corporation.[24]

Provision of additional churches for the living also extended to the dead. The parish church and the parochial chapel both had churchyards, but these were insufficient for the population and efforts were made to equip at least some of the new churches with burial grounds. The first of these was the purchase in June 1750 of an additional piece of land for a churchyard around St Thomas'. Fifteen years later the Bishop of Chester granted a faculty for another new burial ground "by reason of the vast increase of people in [the] Maritime Town the present burial places therein are become very insufficient to contain the great number of inhabitants daily dying."[25] By 1792 there were discussions about the need for an additional two burial grounds.[26] The growth of population and commerce since the opening of the first docks meant not just an increase in graveyard provision, but also an increase in fatalities connected with the river: in 1775 the corporation funded the establishment of the 'Institution for Recovering Persons Apparently Drowned.' At some point a 'Dead House' was also opened in the basement of St Nicholas' where bodies recovered from the Mersey were on public display until they were claimed, or until burial at public expense became a necessity.[27] The old churchyard at the parochial chapel continued to be used until the mid-nineteenth century: alongside the graves of the known influential people of the town sits the first written record of a black resident of Liverpool. Abel, a slave belonging to a Mr Rock, was buried in October 1717. By the end of the eighteenth century, the baptism registers record a number of people of African origin, showing not just the presence of enslaved Africans, but also their connection to the life of the town.[28]

Status and Income

The status of seats in the churches of Liverpool cannot be overstated, but nor can the revenue derived from their sale. When St George's was built, it was established that the corporation had the right to sell all the pews, and they reserved for themselves only the seats for the mayor, aldermen, bailiffs and common council (and all wives). The annual income from pew rents slightly exceeded the figure established for the income of the clergy (the Revd Henry Wolstenholme was appointed the first chaplain/curate). The town did not wish to profit from the church and, although undoubtedly relieved that all ongoing costs were covered, turned over any surplus to the income of the clergy.[29] St George's was the place to be seen, and despite seating for 817 people being listed by 1829, from the outset there were disputes about pew ownership.[30]

Disputes about pews were not confined to St George's. The parochial chapel had almost continuous arguments about pews, especially those which belonged to the rectors. The pew plans show that a substantial proportion of the ground floor seating belonged to the incumbents, not for their families, but as a source of income. When the chapel walls were rebuilt in 1775 this meant an actual pecuniary loss of £60 13s. 2d., for which they were compensated.[31] With seating always in short supply, some management was needed: in 1708 it was ordered that locks be put on the seats of the bailiffs and that the sexton, as the keyholder, should only allow authorised people to sit in them.[32] Free seats were provided,

Ground floor pew plan of Our Lady and St Nicholas.
OLSN Archives

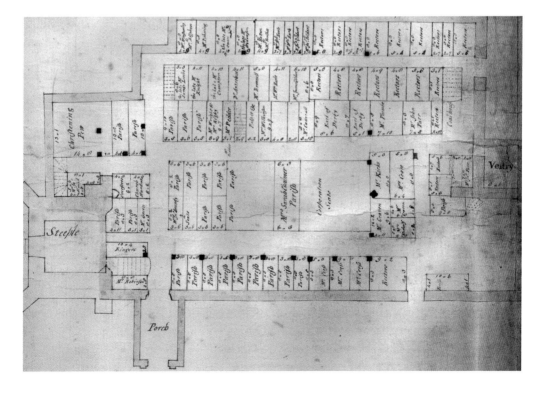

though they were often limited in supply. St Nicholas' maintained some "Sailors' Seats" under the north west gallery, and in 1753 the font was moved from the north west corner in order to create more space for public seat, but on the whole the other churches catered for the poorer classes. At the same time, it was decided to build a new church at the north side of the town (possibly St Paul's) where the "whole body or nave of the said church be laid open and appropriated to publick use." It was later decided to sell the seats in the gallery of St Paul's for as much as possible on 900 year leases in order to repay the loan for the building of the church. In 1792 The vestry debated whether they should take as many seats as possible in Trinity Church on an annual rent for the use of the poor. In fact they decided against this motion.[33] The problem only increased, and in 1808 it was noted that there were inadequate churches with accommodation for the poor. It was recognized that despite an increase in population since 1792 of some 30,000 people, there had not been additional provision for the poor since that date. Although it was decided to build a new church, a particularly egalitarian vestry felt that it was desirable that "the rich and the poor should ever meet together" to worship. Despite the solution that fifty galleries of the church be endowed for the poor, and only ground floor pews put up for sale,[34] it seems unlikely that this genuinely brought rich and poor together in worship. But unlike in the parish church and chapel, at least they were worshipping under the same roof.

Pews, once bought, became a tradeable commodity, sold with the language of a modern estate agent. For example, in Gore's General Advertiser from June 1795 the following small advertisement appears: "TO BE SOLD. A large, commodious PEW, in the North Aisle of the OLD CHURCH. A note will be found on the door of said Pew to be entered on in August. Apply to James Gildart Esq. Duke Street, or Mr George Clutton, No. 20, Islington."[35] The large collection of pew 'indentures' which survive show not just the initial grant of the pew from the mayor, but also transfers between owners.[36]

Non-Anglican Churches

The comfortable ascendency of the English church at last allowed for some relaxation of the laws of conformity. The glimpses of puritanism through conventicles in the seventeenth century persisted in expressions of non-conformity in the following century. In 1707 the Assembly noted the dissenting chapel built in Key Street as being in accordance with the liberalizing laws of William and Mary.[37] This was the first recognition of small but undoubtedly widespread non-Anglican practice across the town. By 1737 some problems were arising, as several Quakers were refusing to pay the church rate. This situation was worse by 1754 when it was reported that in addition to Quakers refusing the taxes, the churchwardens needed defending "against any insults, abuses or suits… brought against them by the people called Quakers."[38] The Quaker Meeting House had first opened in 1706 and was at the start of a steady growth of places of worship outside the Established Church. By 1766 there were a number of non-conformist clergy in Liverpool, named as attached to Key Street Presbyterian Chapel, Benn's Garden Presbyterian Chapel, the Octagon Chapel, and the Baptist Chapel in Frog Lane.[39] There was some fluidity, though, such as the Octagon Chapel which was built as a non-conformist chapel in 1763, but in 1776 was converted into the Anglican Church of St Catherine.[40]

Non-conformity showed the Church of England to be a remarkably cohesive and harmonious denomination, at least in the eighteenth century. The proliferation of non-conformist chapels catered not just for growing numbers, but also different doctrinal positions. The most notable in Liverpool was probably the Revd John Johnson (1706–91), who was appointed pastor of the Byrom Street Baptist Chapel in about 1741. Johnson's high Calvinism became a little extreme for some of his congregation, although doctrinally appears surprisingly palatable to twenty-first century Anglicanism, and he was forced to leave in the late 1740s. The Johnsonian Baptists were soon found in Wisbech in Cambridgeshire and also in Norwich.[41] The Byrom Chapel had been built in 1722, although later relocated to Byrom Hall when the original chapel was sold to the Church of England and opened as St Stephen's Church in 1792.

Catholic worship had taken place in private chapels since the Reformation, either open to or hidden from the gaze of others, but the first public Roman Catholic chapel was St Mary's Catholic Chapel, founded by the Jesuits in 1727. Following the Jacobite Rebellion, the chapel was attacked by an anti-Catholic mob and its contents burned. The priest, Fr William Carpenter SJ, forced his way through the crowd of rioters to the High Altar, where he removed the Ciborium containing the Blessed Sacrament from the tabernacle, and carried it with dignity out through the mayhem until he reached the house of a (protestant) friend who gave him safety. Clearly frightened by this outbreak of violence, and perhaps inspired by the ecclesiastical conformity which prevented Catholics from holding public office, the mayor and corporation refused permission to rebuild the chapel. The building which went up on the site of the chapel was still in the hands of the Jesuits, but was made to look like a warehouse, complete with large folding doors which were closed in the evening. This in turn was also destroyed, but the chapel remained in existence – albeit in different locations and buildings – until St Mary's, Highfield Street closed in 2001.[42]

Worship

Bells were a frequent sound in the town. A new peal of six bells was introduced at the parochial chapel in 1724–5,[43] but every service was signalled by the ringing of at least one bell. As the number of churches increased, so did the number of bells. In 1734 the sextons of both St Peter's and St Nicholas' were admonished for not ringing the bells before the service. However, it would seem that they were a little more enthusiastic about ringing the 'passing bell' (the ringing of a bell to signify a death), for which they received a shilling for an hour's ringing. The vestry decreed that not only should the passing bell not be rung between 9pm and 5am, but it should also not be rung for more than an hour unless the family of the deceased were to pay the extra fee.[44]

The introduction of a choir pew to St Nicholas' at the end of the seventeenth century is evidence of the use of singing to enliven worship. The audience was not always appreciative: in October 1711 Henry Prescott recorded in his diary, "I come to Leverpool before 12. I step up to the old Chapel and hear an Anthem, 89 psalm rudely attempted, yet it pleases that audience."[45] Clearly the use of singing was to the taste of some, but not others. In October 1751 the town council ordered "that chaunting divine service, or such parts thereof as are usually thus performed, be introduced and performed in the said service in St George's Church. And that the management thereof be left to the direction of Mr Shaw, who is to agree with some proper persons to instruct some persons in the knowledge and exercise thereof." Clearly the experiment did not go well. In July 1752 there was a new order "that chaunting the publick service in St. George's Church be for the future discontinued."[46] Even so, singing remained part of the diet in Liverpool. Emulating the choir pew in St Nicholas', a 'singing pew' was also built in St Peter's, and another one was installed in St Thomas'.[47] Similarly, the churches all gradually acquired organs, which were occasionally upgraded. St Nicholas' had had an organ since medieval times but in this period was replaced in 1764, the old one being given to the Charity School (i.e. Blue Coat Hospital); at St Peter's the west gallery was altered in 1765 for the installation of an organ.[48] St Thomas' had to wait until 1770 for its organ, which was inaugurated with a performance of Samuel Arnold's oratorio *The Resurrection*, which had received its first performance at Covent Garden a few months earlier. By 1775, the vestry was again contemplating renewing the organ at St Nicholas',[49] and in 1800 the vestry debated using the surplus of the church and rectors' tax to fund an organ at St John's.[50]

Thomas Maddock,
Rector of Liverpool 1772–83.
OLSN Archives

The injunction in the *Book of Common Prayer* that one should receive Holy Communion at least three times a year might lead one to assume that infrequent communion was normal. This was not the case, and the equality between communion and preaching is often evident. For example, Henry Prescott, the Deputy Chancellor of the Diocese, recorded in his diary that in 1711 he received the Sacrament on All Saints' Day, and then again three days later on Sunday 4 November, along with "a very considerable number."[51] Although the frequency of Holy Communion in the worship of Liverpool is attested by the regular sums of money given for the provision of bread and wine, and for the occasional disputes over the use of the 'Sacrament money' given at the offertory, there is no doubt that the majority of Christian worship centred on the spoken word. In addition to Mattins and Evensong, the provision of a weekly or fortnightly 'lecture' became part of the regular provision. In effect, this was just a long sermon divorced from liturgy. As the principal civic church, the corporation felt that there should be a lecturer at St George's. In 1734 they recorded,

> *Mr Mayor now also recommends that an assistant to Mr Wolstenholme be now appointed, and nominates the Reverend Cuthbert Sewell to be assistant to the said chaplain, which this Council agree to and recommend him accordingly, and that the chaplain or his assistant do preach a lecture sermon on every other or second Thursday in the afternoon throughout the year, and that the prayers in the weekdays be at tenn aforenoon, and six a'clock in the evening dureing sumer season and at three in the afternoon in the winter season.*[52]

It seems likely that the town had the heart only for one significant lecture provision, which led to the demise of the 'Lecture Service' at St Nicholas' and its eventual discontinuation in 1753.[53]

Old Church, New Walls

Despite the expansion of church provision in the town, there was little to diminish the status of St Nicholas' as the historic church of Liverpool. A *History of Liverpool* written in 1796 described the parochial chapel as "the real mother church of the parish."[54] Four hundred years of constant repairs and rebuilding made it a difficult building not just to maintain, but also to adapt to the needs of the eighteenth century. The addition of the galleries in the previous century will have had an impact on the acoustic, and in 1700 it was decided to use the £35 not required for the building of St Peter's to replace the stone pillars in the parochial chapel with slimmer wooden ones which would "obstruct the voice" less.[55] The extensions to the building had not finished, though, and in 1716 it was agreed that the out-aisle of 1697 be extended because of the demand for extra seating.[56] Shortly afterwards, in 1723, the pulpit was moved back against a pillar to create an extra pew for women who had come to be 'churched'. Further alterations took place to the pulpit in 1757, and the pew for bailiffs' wives was converted into space for women to be 'churched'.[57]

The next enhancement to the building was the addition of a spire. In April 1736 it was decided that a spire would not only be ornamental, but also useful for guiding ships in and out of port. It was another decade before, in 1745, it was agreed that Henry Sephton (who was also the architect of St Thomas' Church) and William Smith should build the spire following plans drawn up by Thomas Gee. It was at the same meeting that the final demolition was ordered of the old school building

St Paul's Church (opened 1769) from Enfield's *History of Liverpool, 1773.*

adjoining the chapel which had once been the Chapel of St Mary del Quay.[58] It was still a crowded site, and the remains of older buildings still visible in the basement of the church are difficult to identify. These may relate to warehouse buildings to the north west of the eighteenth-century chapel, or possibly to the late seventeenth-century extensions to the building (the out-aisle).[59]

The church and vestry appeared autonomous, but the obligations of the church towards the town were always evident. Although the Seven Years' War against France did not particularly affect the town, the diversion to Ireland in 1758 of the French privateer François Thurot must have alarmed Liverpool. In 1759, a year before Thurot was killed in battle off the Isle of Man, the vestry agreed to allow a new extension to the churchyard to be used for the fortification of the town. A contemporary print shows battlements facing the water, and fourteen guns were installed. The guns remained in place until 1772.[60] Defence continued to be the responsibility of the vestry who were responsible under various Acts of Parliament for raising the militia. In 1803, in the midst of the Napoleonic Wars, there was a meeting at the request of the town residents to discuss the installation of military defences. The vestry resolved to raise £28,000 immediately for floating batteries, gun boats, and other defences.[61]

Herdman's print of the gun fort at St Nicholas' in 1749.
From W. Herdman, Pictorial Relics of Ancient Liverpool, *1878*

By the eighteenth century there was little precise knowledge about the origins of the old church, as the chapel was often known. Written in 1774, William Enfield's description is unappealing:

> *This church affords little matter of curiosity either to the antiquary or architect. In its structure there is no appearance of magnificence or elegance. The body of the church within is dark and low: it is irregularly though decently pewed: it has lately been ornamented with an organ. The walls have been repaired and supported by large buttresses of different colours and forms; and a spire has been added to the tower.*[62]

In the same year, the need for repairs to the east wall necessitated investigation, with the hope that at the same time it might be possible to reboard the ceiling and commission a painting. Neither turned out to be possible, as within a fortnight it was reported that the church was in such a bad state of repair that much of it should be taken down and rebuilt. This began with the north wall the following March. In a slightly eccentric move, though financially necessary given the private ownership of the pews which would attract significant compensation claims, it was decided to leave the interior intact, including the pews, and merely replace the outside walls, with the exception of the steeple and spire which could remain.[63] This remodelled church was largely that which survived until the bombing of the church in 1940. The steeple and spire, though, had a different fate. Despite a report from stonemasons in June 1788 that the steeple was unsafe and in danger of falling, and the immediate instruction to the churchwardens to arrange repairs,[64] any work was insufficient to prevent the tragedy which followed.

On Sunday 11 February 1810 the congregation was preparing to worship. There were about ten minutes to go, and the bells were ringing as the people were assembling, some of whom were in the chapel and others were outside. The Revd Mr Pugh, the curate who was to officiate, was not yet in the building but was approaching the south door; the Revd Robert Roughsedge (the rector) had decided not to walk through the building, but was approaching the vestry by an outside door at the west end., but there were fifteen or twenty adults inside, and the procession of children was arriving from the Moorfields Charity School. The boys were in the rear of the line, but the girls were inside or just entering the chapel when a stone fell inside the tower and struck one of the bells, causing the bellringers to run from the ground floor ringing chamber of the tower. As the interior of the tower began to fall, the keystone gave way and the whole spire fell through the roof along the central aisle, pulling down as well the west gallery and the organ. Twenty-five people – mainly girls aged nine or ten – were killed, and twenty four were badly injured. The nineteen schoolgirls who were killed were buried at St John's Church on Tuesday 13 February, mourned by their contemporaries who walked together dressed in white.[65]

Work started immediately on clearing the site, and it was reported at the Annual Vestry Meeting in April 1810 that Thomas Harrison of Chester had been engaged to make the site safe and to examine the cause of the collapse. By September Harrison had drawn up plans for a new gothic steeple, but also suggested the entire rebuilding of the chapel. This was rejected, although the walls were to be examined in

St Nicholas' Chapel after the collapse of the tower in 1810. *OLSN Archives*

St Nicholas Church, Liverpool. after the fall of the Spire.

case further demolition was necessary. In December the vestry received three reports on the foundations: the first two gave an alarming report that the walls rested on a shallow foundation which was being undermined by graves dug to a greater depth around them; the third gave a cheerful endorsement that the walls were sound and well-built with an excellent roof. This final report was more acceptable to the vestry, and they voted to proceed with the building of a tower alone. The faculty from the Bishop of Chester permitting the building was dated November 1811, although the new tower was not completed until August 1815.[66]

It was, perhaps, this experience which led to a different course of action in 1829 when the belfry at St Peter's was found to be in a dangerous state because of the decay of the principal roof timbers. Without much deliberation, the churchwardens closed the church entirely until repairs had been carried out, and they took the opportunity to paint and clean the interior.[67]

The Civic Role of the Clergy

Throughout the eighteenth century we also see the clergy involved in the establishment of charitable institutions for the benefit of the sick and the poor. The involvement of the clergy in these institutions was in addition to the responsibilities for social care described in Chapter 6: it complemented the administration of the Poor Law, increased the social outreach of the church, and drew on the Georgian tendency towards philanthropy. The first of these acts of charity was the establishment by one of the rectors, the Revd Robert Styth, of the Blue Coat Hospital in 1708 (now the Blue Coat School in Wavertree). This charity school for boys and girls was funded by subscription, and also by a grant of £20 from the church's 'sacrament money' and authorized by the Bishop of Chester.[68] The school was very much a church foundation, although the finances were handled by Bryan Blundell, a ship owner and merchant who, amongst other interests, was involved in the transportation of enslaved Africans. Blundell later served as Liverpool's mayor. The church made frequent financial contributions to the school: for example, the list of collections "for pious uses" in 1716 includes the payment to Blundell and the school-master "for the use of the Charity Schoole" of £30 2s. from St Peter's, and £32 15s. 7d. collected at St Nicholas'.[69] In fact, the founders of the hospital established a more historic link with the church: from 1722 until 1806 the trustees received the grant from the Duchy of Lancaster towards a school in Liverpool which had its origins in the payment of a priest-schoolmaster through the Chantry of St Katherine established in the medieval chapel by the will of John Crosse in 1515.[70] Today the Rector of Liverpool remains *ex officio* one of the Guardians of the Blue Coat Foundation.

The continuing interest which the church took in the Blue Coat Hospital perhaps detracted from their involvement elsewhere. The Free School of the town – the immediate successor of the school which used to meet in the old Chapel of St Mary – found itself entirely ignored by the middle of the century by the church which had previously provided governance and instruction. The corporation seized the opportunity to assert itself against the church and in 1748 delivered a withering criticism against the rector, Thomas Baldwin, accusing him of neglect, and also against the schoolmaster, the Revd Mr Martin. Taking the school under the control of the corporation, the common council decreed that "no clergyman shall be admitted Schoolmaster or Usher of the said school in any capacity whatsoever."[71]

The other great charitable institution of this century was the Liverpool Infirmary, first founded in 1749. Unlike the Blue Coat Hospital, this was not the initiative of the church, but rather some other (now unknown) group who established a subscription fund in 1744 towards an infirmary. The opening ceremony was performed by the Earl of Derby, but the trustees listed on the lease of the land show a majority were merchants, validated by the addition of two lawyers, a surgeon, and the Revd Thomas Baldwin, Rector of Liverpool.[72]

Power, Authority, and Money

With the diocesan bishop at a distance in Chester, the rectors appropriated a quasi-episcopal role over the churches in the parish. There were occasional episcopal visits which left a written record, such as the bishop's appearance in Liverpool in June 1709 for a Confirmation service.[73] In 1754 the Bishop of Chester came to Liverpool for his visitation, and the vestry agreed that the rectors and churchwardens entertain him at parish expense, "but we recommend it to them not to make the entertainment too publick and general and expensive." In the same year, the power of the rectors was curtailed by the division of the parish into six districts. Although much of the power of patronage was already in the hands of the corporation rather than the rectors, the opportunities for income from the different churches was considerable. Many of the 'surplice fees' (the income from performing baptisms, weddings and funerals) belonged by right to the incumbents

Bill of Mortality for the Parish of Liverpool, 1833.
By Courtesy of the University of Liverpool Library, Peet Collection 17/1/2.

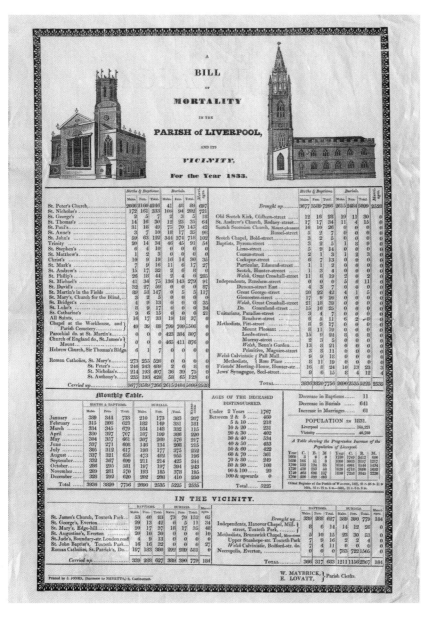

rather than the officiating clergy. By separating the parish into districts
and making, in effect if not in law, separate parishes, the rectors lost
considerable income for which, in the short term at least, the vestry
decided to offer compensation.[74] Although inflation rates were low
in the eighteenth century, often interspersed with periods of negative
inflation, the value of the fees reduced considerably throughout the
century. Although there was compensation in the large increase in the
services which attracted fees – though with a commensurate increase in
the work required to earn them – in 1802 it was noted that the fee table
had not been revised since 1733. The vestry was keen to amend this,
but the simmering power of the corporation, as patrons of the parish,
became apparent in their objection.[75] Despite an Act of Parliament in
1786 to increase the stipends of the Rectors of Liverpool, the value
of the income of the rectors continued to decrease, and in 1811 the
vestry decided to pay each rector £150 in addition to their salaries.
This payment continued to be made without comment until 1827 when
there was clearly an objection. It was proposed that the vestry and
corporation petition Parliament to legalize this additional payment: a
three-day poll on the proposal ensued which was eventually lost. And
yet in the accounts of 1828 the payment by the vestry to supplement
clergy income continues without further reference to the dispute.[76]

Glimpses of individual characters emerge occasionally, such as pen
portraits of the clergy from the opening years of the nineteenth century.
We learn of the Revd Mr Kidd, who remained as a poorly-paid curate
in Liverpool for many years, but who despite benefiting from the kind
hospitality of many, was shy and awkward in company. And of the Revd
Mr Moss, whose horror of innovation and, in particular the Manchester
to Liverpool railway, may have been motivated by the large number of
shares he held in a canal which would lose its freight to the railways.[77]
The two rectors were clearly regarded fondly. Robert Roughsedge, who
was inducted as rector in 1796, was mild, amiable and good-hearted,
"with much more of the innocence of the dove than of the wisdom
of the serpent… He was utterly ignorant of the world and the world's
ways."[78]

Although the clergy usually chaired meetings, the real power
lay with the churchwardens, but held in check by the other elected
members of the vestry and, annually, by the meeting of all the parish.
It seems to have been possible for the churchwardens to have made
financial decisions and alterations to the buildings in full view of all,
only to be called to account at the end of the year with accusations of
acting without authority. For example, the Annual Vestry Meeting of

1727 heard a complaint that the churchwardens had laid flagstones in the churchyard at St Peter's without the consent of the vestry.[79] This was, though, nothing compared to the actions of John Dennison in 1817–18. There was clearly some suspicion that there might be an issue with financial management, because in the same meeting that Dennison was appointed churchwarden in April 1817, it was also resolved that a Committee of Finance be appointed to act with the churchwardens in making contracts and financial transactions.[80] A year later, the first suspicions were brought to the Annual Meeting that Dennison had spent a lot of parish money without authority. The meeting refused to approve the Churchwardens' Accounts, and a full investigation was launched.[81] The report took two months to assemble and identified a total of £2,149 11s. 10d. of unauthorized expenditure. The list is impressive in a number of ways, and yet it seems difficult to imagine the expenditure of £441 on the building of a Gothic Arch in St Nicholas' Churchyard as an act of profligacy which was carried out in secret. Preston Parish Church was supposedly the first religious building in the UK to be lit by gas in 1816,[82] and so it might be thought progressive that just a year later Dennison spent nearly £391 on tubes and columns for gas, but the outlay of nearly £33 on "hatbands at the funeral of Doctor Barrow" does seem implausibly expensive. A more vague complaint was made about him providing "an excess of wine to the Clergy." This was a financial scandal which stopped the vestry in its tracks: the dispute continued for many years as they tried to reclaim as much money from Dennison as possible.[83] Dennison, for his part, continued to deny any wrongdoing. Although the official minutes of the vestry record only condemnation, Dennison had his supporters. In 1851 the Revd David Thom, a non-conformist minister in the town, wrote of the parochial chapel: "A handsome Gothic Gateway leads out of the Church-yard into Chapel Street. Very unpleasant and protracted discussions, arising out of a refusal on the part of the Vestry to pay for it, were the result of its erection by one of the Churchwardens, about thirty years ago."[84]

CHAPTER SIX

Vestry and Politics 1681–1834

The Elizabethan Poor Law

Whilst the poor have always been with us, the changing society of Tudor England, with its increasing departure from a wholly agrarian economy, made the presence and growth of the poor more evident. Charitable giving (including through legacies) remained the expectation for dealing with the poor under the 1531 Poor Law, but in 1563 a further Act allowed for an organised collection for the relief of the poor, and in 1572 Parliament distinguished between the deserving poor and vagrants.[1] Despite the distance from London, the inhabitants of Liverpool always remained well-informed about legislative events. Throughout the immediate post-Reformation period, we have seen that the Town Assembly was keen to enforce the changing religious requirements as enacted by law. Members of Parliament were expected to report back regularly, and so on 27 August 1572 Ralph Sekerston, the Member for Liverpool, gave his account of events in Parliament to the Assembly, including the latest phase of development of the Elizabethan Poor Law.[2] The Town Books reveal that the poor were a constant source of concern. The Assembly turned their attention to the matter in 1598, clearly concerned about the amount of begging and taking place, and the inconvenience being caused to householders and gentlemen. However, this was tempered by a concern that proper provision was

The exterior of St Nicholas', the Parochial Chapel of Liverpool, before the rebuilding of the walls in 1775. *From Enfield's* History of Liverpool, *1773.*

being made: there was a register of the poor, and a house was taken (in fact the corporation rented it from the mayor for the year, William Dixon) to house them, though it was unfortunately termed a 'house of correction' – a phrase used two centuries later in a specifically punitive context, but at this time merely referring to a place where vagrants and beggars could be housed on a relatively short-term basis. In addition, a poor box was set up, presumably in the chapel, for the relief of those in need.[3]

Although the detailed records of the administration of the Poor Law in Liverpool only began in 1681, the separation of the role of churchwarden and overseer of the poor ('guardiani') occurred much earlier. The first reference is in 1636 when John Boulton and

William Dwarrihouse were appointed.[4] The election of these minor town officials was not noted every year – either because there was no change, or because chroniclers did not always consider it significant. Occasionally, more detail is given, such as in 1654 when it was noted that a Mrs Derby and Robert Williamson had given £17 10*s*. for the use of the poor, and the Assembly agreed that 20*s*. should be give yearly to the overseers to be distributed where most need was. In the same year, it was recorded that a bastard child was being kept at the town's expense, and that there were attempts to trace the father in London.[5] The inclusion in the town records of an individual instance of bastardy illustrates the small size of the community. However, the growing port town continued to attract visitors who thought that there was more chance of survival in Liverpool: in December 1656 the Assembly decided that the town should keep its own poor, but that the poor from elsewhere should be prevented from begging in the town, and the beadle should keep out the "country poor". It was agreed that the churchwardens should be the overseers of the poor (rather than separately elected officials) and that they should keep a register of the names of the poorest people. At that time, the number of the poor was calculated to be about sixty, and a monthly ley (tax) of £3 was to be levied by the merchant appraisers and distributed by the overseers. New and ingenious ways were found to raise funds: it was felt that there was a problem with swine wandering the streets, and so the Assembly decided that the owners should be fined 12*d*. in each case; 6*d*. to go to the official who caught the swine, and 6*d*. would go to the poor.[6] At the same time legacies frequently produced income for the poor. For example, in 1698 Captain Edward Tarleton left £45 which by 1717 was producing an income of £2 5*s*. which the rectors were able to distribute. When Ann Molineux died in 1729 she left £300 for the relief of sailors and their widows, and £200 for the relief of poor prisoners[7] (this bequest survives today in the Molyneux and Warbrick Charity).

Despite a temporary reversion to the fusion of the roles of church-warden and overseer, it was soon realised that the demands of both roles were too much. In July 1666 it was decided that the church-wardens of the *preceding* year should henceforth be appointed as overseers of the poor, and for those unwilling to assume the post then there would be a fine of £5. The first men to be appointed under the new rule were Henry Crane and Richard Williamson, and they were commissioned to undertake a monthly survey of the town to find what poor there were.[8]

Housing the Poor: from Almshouse to Workhouse

Grants of cash were not the only way for the town or vestry to provide for the poor. In 1568 there is a record of the town leasing a house to Henry Wirrall (described as a 'very poor man') at an extremely low rent.[9] Housing provision by the authorities complemented that by charity: the will of Richard Warbrick enabled the building of almshouses on Lord Street, which were then left in trust to the overseers of Liverpool, but there were other almshouses in the town as well.[10] These were not sufficient for all those in need of housing, and in 1723 the overseers attempted to take control of provision and rented from Bryan Blundell (who had also founded the Blue Coat School with the rector some years earlier) thirty six new houses. The idea was to move poor families into these and out of private rented accommodation: those who refused to move to the new houses would be struck from the roll of the poor.[11] In fact this was not always the case, and there was much more discretion exercised than was planned. For example, in 1736 Lawrence and Sarah Robinson petitioned the parish for relief. They found themselves in arrears and although they felt able to meet the rent, they could not clear the debt. The vestry readily agreed to pay the arrears on their behalf, presumably because the alternative was more expensive if they became dependent on the parish for Poor Relief.[12]

The Elizabethan distinction between deserving and undeserving poor, and the subsequent development of a dual system of indoor and outdoor relief, all increased the stigmatisation of the poor. The Town Books and the vestry minutes do not suggest any particular lack of compassion, but the growth in numbers meant that the processing of the poor became industrialised. The gradual slipping away from the official record of the names of the individual poor, giving way to categories and numbers, was also reflected in practice. The Poor Act of 1697 required that all those receiving poor relief should wear a badge on their right shoulders indicating the parish on which they were dependent. The requirement was not enforced in all parishes (despite the risk of a fine), and the first indication of this Act being enforced in Liverpool was in 1713 when the vestry ordered that those poor who did not wear a badge would lose their weekly allowance. This order was repeated in 1718, and then in 1758 the vestry ordered that the poor of the parish who were in the workhouse should wear the letters L.P. [Liverpool Pauper] in a badge cut out in red cloth, to distinguish them from the other poor. The idea that the poor should be labelled persisted, and was occasionally repeated in primary legislation: in 1823 the vestry decided to petition against the clauses of a Bill in Parliament making the poor wear badges, but in the same discussion it was also felt that magistrates should be able to send the poor to join the militia.[13] In fact, this arrangement suited the parish well, as the vestry remained responsible for providing recruits to the military, which in a period of frequent British intervention across the world, was both necessary and burdensome: for example, in 1796 the vestry was compelled by Act of Parliament to recruit 95 men for the Army and the Navy, and there is a faint hint in the vestry minutes that the committee formed for the purpose began to look at what inducements they could offer to volunteers. In 1803 the issue arose again as a result of further Acts of Parliament, with the parish retaining responsibility for raising the militia.[14]

The move to 'indoor relief' from a system of grants and housing was a response to rising costs and complexity. However, it was always going to be a less desirable option, so from the moment of the joint decision in 1732 by the vestry and the common council that a workhouse be built, it was also decided that no rent or relief should be given to the poor outside the workhouse. In fact, 'outdoor relief' continued throughout the eighteenth century, although not without criticism. In addition, there were emergency scenarios, such as when several poor families were made homeless by severe weather in 1790, and the parish committee was asked to provide assistance.[15] Responsibility for the building of the workhouse was given to the trustees of the charity school, and an overseer of the workhouse, John Brookes, was appointed. Given the resources being poured into this project, the vestry decided to keep a tight hold on it, and the instruction was given that the proceedings of the trustees of the workhouse be read and approved by the vestry.[16] The first workhouse was built on the corner of College Lane and Hanover Street, and the governance and oversight of the institution became a significant pre-occupation of the vestry. Initially the appointment of the superintendent and governess were renewed annually (during the 1730s these positions were filled by Thomas Cockshutte and Mrs Devias), but the staffing increased rapidly: in 1736 the vestry agreed that the governess needed an assistant, and when Cockshutte died in 1742 he was replaced by two men, Thomas Halls and Charles Gore.[17] By 1757 the workhouse was too small, and plans were made to extend it. However, by 1769 it was clear that a new, larger workhouse was required, and building work commenced on a new site on Brownlow Hill.[18] This was a significant venture made jointly between the vestry and the corporation: the latter providing £2,250 towards the new poor house.[19] The workhouse became an industry in itself, providing not just a solution to the problem of provision for the poor, but also providing employment both directly and in ancillary services. Whilst the Liverpool Infirmary was a charitable institution, admission of patients was still often as a result of recommendation by subscribers or benefactors, or the largest contributors to the infirmary.[20] The parish therefore provided an annual salary to an apothecary who could treat the poor. This continued until 1778 when it was felt that a public dispensary, built as part of the workhouse development, would be more economic. The building of the dispensary was overseen by the parish in 1780 and provided a more efficient service which was a less attractive financial opportunity for those who had been employed as apothecaries.[21] The next element of health and social care provision made by the parish was the building of a House of Recovery, which in 1805 William Roscoe, shortly before his election to Parliament, proposed should be completed at the expense of the Poor Rates.[22]

It was not the case that the vestry delegated responsibility for the poor and took no further interest. In 1762 leading people in the town were appointed to do a monthly inspection: four people were appointed for each month, and the list was published for the entire year. Other details are preserved, such as the decision to exempt the poor from burial fees.[23] Even so, there remained a romanticised view of the work and atmosphere of the workhouse. An observer in 1843 wrote:

> "*The Workhouse was opened in 1772, and is situated on the space of ground between Brownlow Hill and Mount Pleasant; the front of the principal part of the building, before which is a large lawn, facing the former street. The interior accommodation is good; aged persons inhabiting apartments on the ground floor. Each individual is employed in some trade; the male adults as joiners, tailors, shoemakers, bricklayers, slaters, blacksmiths, spinners, etc., and the females as sempstresses, bonnet-makers, etc. Boys are instructed in various trades to fit them for becoming apprentices. The establishment is supported by the poor-rates, and is under the control of the parish authorities.*"[24]

Similarly, in Sir Frederick Eden's 1797 survey of *The State of the Poor*, a very positive picture is painted, although he does acknowledge that too many children are crowded together at work.[25] Although it was not long before the vestry paid its officers to administer the Poor Law, there was genuine commitment from the leading figures in the town to find out the poor and assess them for assistance. Papers survive in the parish archives of the division of districts in July 1805 and the nomination of eighteen men to visit and assess those receiving outdoor relief. They had clearly not been consulted first, as they were asked to accept or decline the appointment by the end of the month. Letters were sent by the vestry clerk saying, "I request to be informed… whether it will be agreeable to you, to be appointed to the Office to which you have been nominated by the Parish Committee."[26] The size of Liverpool parish – far bigger than most other areas – meant that working within the Poor Law system was attractive: when the governor of the workhouse died in May 1833, thirty seven applications to replace him were received within a week. The man appointed (with his wife as matron) was the governor of a smaller workhouse in Holborn, London, and so coming to the Liverpool workhouse was a promotion.[27]

The sheer cost of the workhouse also meant that the vestry was unlikely to take its eye off the administration for long. In fact, there had been occasional lapses of attention which proved costly. In 1800 the churchwardens augmented the allowances of the outdoor poor, in some cases even doubling the grants, and in 1801 it was reported that the level of expenditure had increased considerably. Outdoor relief was always more costly, but the rise was exponential in the second decade of the nineteenth century: in 1815 it was £5,588, but by 1818 it was over £18,000.[28] The dual purpose of creating income and finding employment for the poor became an incentive for a new approach. In 1809 the vestry resolved to look into what sort of work was done in the house, and it was discussed whether the inhabitants should start making their own clothing. The following year the vestry decided to purchase eight looms for the workhouse which could employ 150–200 women, providing them with a level of support and, more importantly one imagines, making a profit for the workhouse. The initial outlay for the looms was £234 11*s.* 7*d.*, but it was a profitable business: in 1825 it was reported that the weaving manufactory had made a profit for the parish in the previous year of £450; in 1827 it was reported that in the previous year the looms had produced 251,490 yards of fabric. The economic advantages were plentiful: the sheets and shirts of the workhouse were produced 'in house'; they were able to sell the produce; children were taught a skill which made them more attractive as apprentices (and therefore no longer the responsibility of the parish).[29] There were other areas of job creation which, despite explicit denial, benefited the town: in 1821 it was decided that relief could be given to the poor "by the medium of labour", and 38 men

Printed minutes from the vestry of the division of the parish into districts for the better administration of the Poor Law, 1805.
OLSN Archives

PARISH OF LIVERPOOL.

At a meeting of the Committee, the 9th July, 1805,

"It was RESOLVED,

"THAT the Town be divided into nine Districts, and two of this Committee "be appointed to each District, for the purpose of occasionally visiting "the Poor receiving out-relief; and that the undermentioned Gentlemen "be nominated; but, before appointed to the duty, that application be "made to them by the Vestry Clerk, to know whether it will be con- "venient to take upon themselves the trouble, which such an appoint- "ment will unavoidably occasion.

Viz.

"Mr. HARDY,	"Mr. COPELAND,
MILBURN,	GRIFFIN,
ALLEN,	BAINBRIDGE,
ABRAM,	GREGSON,
FARRER,	JOHN TAYLOR,
HOLMES,	S. RATHBONE,
J. TAYLOR,	JOSEPH
WILCKENS,	THOMAS WILSON,
CROOKE,	R. SUTTON."

"It was ALSO RESOLVED,

"THAT it be requested of the Gentlemen nominated to favour the Vestry "Clerk with their determination, to accept or decline the appointment, ", by a note to be left at his Office on or before Monday the 29th Instant."

---

were put to work on making a road from Kirkdale, and a further 61 were working on the new infirmary. Not all projects proved beneficial, and in 1823 the vestry decided to discontinue employment such as the breaking of stones and making a pin factory, and turn the workers over to the looms instead.[30] Children were ready for apprenticeships sooner when they were trained in skilled work, but job creation also took place outside the walls of the workhouse: the poor were even sent out to whitewash the cellars of the town, so that in the end everyone in receipt of relief was put to work, unless they were prevented by age or infirmity. The financial benefit for the vestry was obvious as the income generated subsidised the costs, but a more significant effect was to discourage people from seeking assistance from the parish in the first place: this may, of course, have been the intention in the first place, following the observation in 1817 that the numbers claiming relief had increased considerably.[31] The figures of those in receipt of relief before and after the change of policy in 1821 are striking: in 1819 there were 6,410 receiving indoor relief, and 14,800 receiving outdoor relief, at a total cost of £21,210. In 1822 this had halved to 3,901 receiving indoor relief, 6694 receiving outdoor relief, and a total expenditure of only £10,395.[32]

Throughout the period, curates from the parish churches provided the spiritual provision in the workhouses. Services may not have been all that regular, and Sir Frederick Eden's description in 1797 was that the inmates "all dine together in a large room, which serves occasionally for a chapel."[33] By 1822 the increase in poor and therefore of clerical duties led to the proposal that the workhouse should have its own stipendiary curate, rather than rely on the parish. The corollary was that the following year the four parish curates each had their stipends reduced to enable £50 to be available for the new workhouse curate.[34] The arrival of a permanent curate in the workhouse meant that more appropriate provision was needed, and in 1825 it was suggested that a purpose-built hall be erected for worship.[35] Different provision was made for Catholics: in 1829 it was decided that children of Catholic parents in the workhouse should be allowed to go to a Catholic place of worship on Sundays and at other times when their Anglican counterparts would also be expected to attend worship.[36]

Essential Services

The power and financial resource of the vestry was considerable, but there were fine lines of demarcation with the common council, which often led to dispute. The churchwardens often had responsibility for particular areas of infrastructure. One of the first of these was fire engines. Two engines were presented to Liverpool by Thomas Bootle, but in 1731 they were given into the care of the churchwardens to pay for maintenance and keeping them permanently available for action. Within three years there were problems, and the churchwardens were rebuked by the vestry for allowing them to be moved and used to spray salt water into new ships, meaning that they were not ready for emergencies.[37] As the town grew, the need for provision for firefighters increased. In 1745 sixty leather buckets were bought to be kept with the fire engines. At the same time, the growth of the insurance industry provided new possibilities for cover. The Sun Fire Office opened in London in 1710 as the first fire insurance company in the world, and in 1762 it was ordered that the town clerk, who also served as vestry clerk, should write to the Sun Fire Office and ask for a hundred fire buckets, which would be matched by the parish increasing their own stock from sixty to a hundred. A few years later, in 1773, the churchwardens were instructed by the vestry to provide another fire engine and fifty more buckets: this provoked another application to the Sun Fire Office for match funding.[38] The insurance industry grew quickly, and in 1782 there was no need to refer to a London firm: the insurance with the Sun Fire Office was cancelled, and a new policy taken out with the Liverpool Fire Office.[39] By 1826 the need for a regular and professional fire service was clear to both the vestry and the common council, who established together a "Fire Police" in the town, based in two buildings – one to the north and one to the south – and equipped with horses and fire engines. Although the funding remained from the parish (at a half penny in the pound of rates), the control moved further from the vestry itself and became a separate civil enterprise.[40]

Just as the vestry took responsibility for a fire service, so they were often the enforcers of regulations and criminal justice. Legislation needed implementation, and so, for example, we see Joshua Tunstall appointed in May 1750 as an inspector to ensure that no meat was brought to market without certificates to show that the cattle free from disease. Criminal justice was a more complicated matter: with no police force, all prosecutions brought before the courts were essentially privately funded. There are occasional indications that the vestry felt that some prosecutions were in the public interest: in August 1750 a Mr Young was prosecuted at parish expense for an attempt to commit sodomy on a poor boy of the parish who was not able to launch a prosecution himself. Six years later it was decided that the vestry should continue to prosecute at their own expense all felons, and the crimes were extended to include receiving or buying stolen goods.[41] Depending on the crime, detaining the guilty fell to either the corporation or the parish: the castle and the tower had traditionally provided the place for incarceration, and the corporation continued to maintain a gaol in the town, but it had often been easier just to send criminals for imprisonment in Chester or Lancaster. In 1806 the corporation proposed giving the parish a wing of their new gaol for their use. More local provision was required for minor offences, and in 1776 the parish and the corporation acted together. The vestry decided to build a 'House of Correction' on Brownlow Hill, next to the new poor house. The capital outlay for this came from the corporation in the form of a loan: although the corporation chose not to take on joint responsibility through funding, they did readily agree to let the parish off £500 of their debt, which was a contribution by stealth.[42] In fact by 1814 the vestry decided that they were not obliged to maintain a House of Correction, and so they rescinded their previous motion and informed the mayor and magistrates that they would no longer be responsible.[43]

Darkness is a familiar friend to lawlessness, and the vestry employed watchmen to patrol the streets at night. The number employed increased steadily, from an unspecified additional number in 1738, through to the realisation in 1787 that sixty watchmen were not enough, and a Bill should be prepared for Parliament to increase the number.[44] By this time, the management of the watchmen had been delegated by Act of Parliament in 1748 (which also established the Church of St Thomas) to commissioners, comprising the mayor, recorder, borough justices (who were also aldermen) and eighteen inhabitants chosen by the vestry. The minutes of the meetings of the commissioners give an overview of the areas of oversight exercised by the watchmen: apart from consid-erable emphasis on the disposal of excreta and the sweeping of the streets, the main task was to patrol the streets between 10pm and 6am, challenging those they encountered, confronting disorderly behaviour, and escorting strangers through the streets. The parish paid for both lamps and lamplighters throughout the town, and the streets were also dotted with watch-boxes, where the watchmen could take shelter and rest within each of their districts.[45] Like the fire police, the need for law enforcement separate from the parish became evident. Although the Lancashire Constabulary was not established until 1839, the decision to employ police officers in Liverpool was made in 1829 by the Grand Jury of the Common Council.[46]

Surprising additional responsibilities fell on the vestry. In 1799 the committee decided to oppose a petition to the House of Commons from the mayor and Common Council asking for an Act to pave the town. Despite the request from the mayor for a meeting, the obvious problem was who should pay for it. The dispute continued for some years, during which the condition of the streets continued to deteriorate. By April 1803 it became clear that the parish had lost, and not only would the streets be paved, but the vestry would have to pay for it.[47] Even so, not every road was a public thoroughfare: the surviving deed and plan of the laying out of what is today known as the Georgian Quarter shows that building the streets and the sewers were done at the expense of the landowners. This arrangement, made in 1800, and the construction of sewers and streets in 1803, included the "Rector's Fields" which lay at the eastern end of the space between Faulkner Street and Myrtle Street. Creating this scheme in the Georgian Quarter required a bold and co-operative approach which treated the development as one plot of land, before it was divided up again after construction.[48]

Some twenty years later in 1822, the parish opposed the Liverpool Waterworks Bill, which proposed the funding of new infrastructure from parish rates.[49] In fact both of these issues remained within the remit of the parish for some time. In 1829 notice was given of an intended new Sewerage Bill, and the resulting Liverpool Paving and Sewerage Act of 1830 provided for the election of twenty-four commissioners to be drawn from both the Common Council and also the ratepayers.[50] A series of Acts in the 1840s took paving and sewerage even further from the oversight of the vestry.

Rates, Taxes, Debt and Imprisonment

The explosion in size from a small town to a thriving port across the course of a century or so relied on the provision of money for the public purse. Even in the seventeenth century, a 'ley' was imposed for a specific purpose, and in a town with only a few thousand residents the collection must have been relatively easy. Even so, costs were increasing: for example, in 1683 there was a ley to raise £40 for the poor, and £30 for the repair of the chapel; by 1687 they needed £70 for the poor, and £40 for the chapel. By 1691 the annual bill for weekly payments to several poor inhabitants came to £56 9s. Around this time there was a significant change, in that the poor ceased to be named individually in the vestry minutes, although local detail, such as the need to keep a sick soldier's child still appears.[51]

By the eighteenth century, rates could no longer be imposed for short-term aims, but needed to finance increasingly large and complex projects, alongside the salaries of large numbers of employees. Remarkably, despite the employment of people to run the workhouse, the church, civil defence, and even sixty night-watchmen, the office-holders who administered this large and complex organisation remained volunteers until the nineteenth century. In 1816 it was felt that the roles of overseer, treasurer and collector of the parish had become so onerous that they should become paid posts, and it was decided to petition Parliament for an Act to enable public officers of the parish to be remunerated.[52] The result of this growing financial machine meant that flat rates of taxation had to be levied. Income tax was not imposed by central government until 1799, but the local taxes were based on property. At the Annual Vestry Meeting of 1727 the ley for the poor was given as 15*d.* in the pound on houses, and 18*d.* in the pound on land value.[53] However, landowners found themselves caught by a triple layer of tax. On top of both the contribution towards the vestry and also the corporation, they were obliged to pay a 'County Tax' as well. The unfairness of this was not just the objection (made in 1829) that Liverpool paid one sixth of the entire county rate, but also that other circumstantial expenses fell to Liverpool which were not experienced elsewhere in the county. For example, a significant cost was the repatriation of Irish vagrants to Ireland, and in 1823 the vestry attempted to pass this cost to the county (the success of the endeavour is not recorded).[54]

The tension of responsibilities between the vestry and the corporation was matched by the complexity of their interchanging finances. The workhouse and the House of Correction were both parish building projects, financed by loans from the corporation. In addition, the parish claimed rates from corporation property, including tolls and other dues. This was balanced by the rent and interest claimed by the corporation from the land on which the workhouse was built on Brownlow Hill.[55] A delicate financial balance was never properly achieved, and disputes arose readily: the most significant was over the docks. By 1800 the vestry tried to charge the corporation for rates on the docks, which the corporation refused to pay. The matter went to court, and the magistrates decided against the parish, stating that "as there is no one in the beneficial enjoyment of the duties, they are not objects of taxation." This was a statement of judicial principle, that you can only tax something owned by an individual, and not a corporate entity.[56] It is difficult to see how this principle can be aligned with another court judgement over a different dispute between the parish and merchants over a shipping rate which continued for four years from 1800. This was not a dispute confined to Liverpool, and the court judgement from Hull in 1804 ruled that non-resident merchants should not have to pay rates.[57]

The vestry minutes illustrate the constant friction not just with the corporation, but also with individual ratepayers. The final decades of the Georgian era were a constant struggle to reduce the burden which had been borne by relatively few. In 1821 there was a vestry motion to increase the number of rateable dwellings by including properties which were let for between £6 and £20 *per annum*, but with the obligation on the owner/landlord to ensure payment is made. This was put to a poll over three days, in which 825 people voted, eventually carrying the motion.[58] This was not the end of the matter, and the subsequent Cottage

Assessment Act obtained from Parliament only infuriated even more of those drawn into the rank of ratepayer when they saw that shipping and stock remained outside the category of rateable property. This came to a head at the Annual Vestry Meeting of April 1832 which lasted four hours at the parochial chapel, with participants entirely filling the pews on the ground floor, and the front few rows in the galleries as well. With the Revd Jonathan Brooks, Senior Rector of Liverpool, in the chair, the meeting was conducted with thorough bad humour throughout, and reported with relish by the *Liverpool Mercury*: 'Mr Samuel Holmes said, he was well acquainted with cottage property, and begged leave to say a few words on the subject. He knew that a good cottage might be built

The exterior of St Peter's, the new Parish Church of Liverpool.
From Enfield's History of Liverpool, *1773*.

Lancaster Castle, June 3rd 1826

Mr. Blackstock

Sir

I received a Letter this Morning from my Daughter, in which it mentions if I would send you my own note of hand for 33£ Law expenses &c. and consent for my Daughter to remain in the workhouse, I should have my discharge sent on receipt of my Answer to You. I have only to say that I do agree to your Proposal, and also have herewith enclosed to you my promisory note for the money but I hope you will shew me as much lenity as you can in the payment thereof after you send my release. — I return you my most sincere thanks, and I hope you will send my discharge Forthwith according to Promise —

I am Sir,

Your most obt & hble St.

Dan.l Christian

£ 33.0.0   *Lancaster June 3rd 1826*

On Demand, I promise to pay to the Church Wardens and Overseers of the Parish of Liverpool, or order, the sum of Thirty three Pounds, for Law expences incurred against me. —

Witness. Thomas Blaisdale   Dan.l Christian

Letter to the vestry clerk from Daniel Christian in 1826, imprisoned in Lancaster gaol for a £33 debt to the churchwardens. He generously allows his daughter to remain in the workhouse if he can be released, and his IOU provides surety.

OLSN Archives

for £65 or £70. – ("*Hear him.*" "*False! false!*" and great uproar.) He knew that there were a great number of cottages in this town which were not fit for any human being to live in; and many of those persons who talked so much about the poor, and pretended to be friends to the poor, were the worst enemies the poor ever had. – (*Hisses.*) – Twenty yards of land might be procured at an average of about £1 per yard, and a good cottage might be built for something short of £70. – ("*Hear him,*" and "*No, no.*").[59]

In such a climate, collecting taxes was onerous and a strategic approach was needed to make it achievable. The first plans to divide the parish into districts were made in November 1753 and agreed a year later in December 1754: officers for the poor would be appointed for each district, but taxation would not be broken down in this way. However difficult it was, the 'Tax Gatherer' was a significant position. In 1780 there was an election for the post: Rowland Hunter received 272 votes; Thomas Deare came second with 270, but he alleged that some of those with no right to vote took part and he requested a scrutiny. Although we do not know the result of this, in subsequent years Mr Hunter is named as the Tax Gatherer.[60] Unexpected benefits for the town came from taxation. In 1773 it was decided that unnumbered houses should be numbered at Parish expense in order to make it easier to collect taxes.[61] However, collection remained fraught as we can see from two instances in the 1820s. Firstly, in 1825 one of the assistant collectors in the treasurer's office absconded with over £125 of parish funds. Some of the money was swiftly recovered, but there is no record of the apprehension of the miscreant. The ensuing conversation, though, highlighted the lack of control which the vestry had over the appointment of collectors, and also their work.[62] The second instance is a correspondence which survives – albeit only from one side – of an individual who was in debt to the parish. The churchwardens began a legal case against Daniel Christian in 1826 and he was committed to the debtors' prison in Lancaster Castle. In a series of letters in June 1826 he wrote to the vestry clerk, Edward Blackstock, pleading for his release, and generously offering that his daughter (who also acted as an intermediary in this correspondence) would stay in the workhouse until his debt of £33 was discharged. The only record of the conclusion of the case is a scribbled note from Blackstock that he had sent a note of discharge.[63] The burden for the vestry was that the clerk and other officials were constantly dealing with the minutiae of tax collection.

National Politics, Local Campaigns

As a town of seafarers and merchants, Liverpool generally knew what was going on: throughout the Civil War the factions became increasingly obvious, and in the late seventeenth century, as party factions emerged, Liverpool reflected this as well. An election fraud of 1694 exposed the political leanings of the town: Alexander Norres, the mayor for the year, returned the Tory candidate, Thomas Brotherton, as Member of Parliament. Brotherton had polled only 15 votes, against the 400 votes of the Whig, Jasper Maudit. Norres was summoned to Parliament where he confessed to the fraud and was imprisoned.[64] The result of this was a new charter for the town from William III in 1695. This charter effectively did away with a generation of local politicians, and a selection of new men appeared in the list of councillors. They were able to co-opt new members, and the mayor and bailiffs were to be chosen by them rather than by all the freemen.[65] This effectively created a Whig hegemony which, although reflecting the majority view according to the election result of 1694, possibly encourage political dissent.

Reflecting an age when churchmanship and politics were often aligned, it is no surprise that in a church arranged along High Church lines the clergy were Tory in disposition. The Junior Rector in April 1711, Henry Richmond, instigated a Tory revolt in the town. He questioned the validity of the 1695 charter, causing the leading Whigs to take legal advice on defending the challenge. Most significantly, the Town Books record that the council was "greatly divided into parties of High Church and Low." This was not a doctrinal dispute, but a political one, and the Whig council retaliated in October 1711 by presenting Richmond to the portmoot, charged with absence from his ministry resulting in the increase of "vice and debauchery". The political motivation was hardly disguised, because after the complaint that he was absent between January and June 1711 the charges continued to include that he had published libellous statements against the common council. Richmond managed to get the charges dropped in 1712 on the technicality that they were presented in English rather than in Latin.[66] There was further conflict in 1714, but nothing further was heard from Richmond beyond that, perhaps partly owing to a decline in health. By 1720 he was no longer taking services, and the vestry books discreetly refer to his "indisposition" whilst limiting his stipend and increasing that of the curate, Thomas Baldwin, who succeeded Richmond as rector upon his death in 1721.[67] At some point following this, the corporation decided that the clergy should enter into a personal

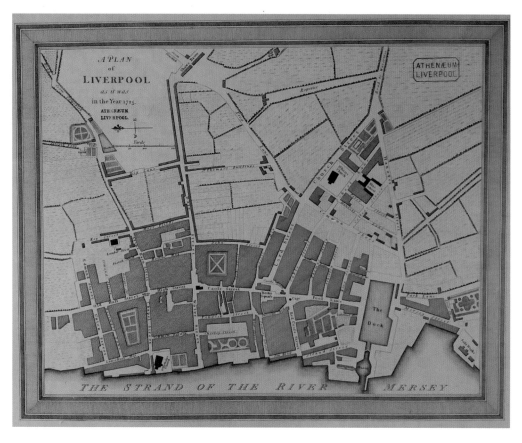

Liverpool in 1725.
Courtesy of the Athenaeum, Liverpool

bond to guarantee the performance of their duties, with a penalty of £2,000, which would ensure that the corporation maintained greater control over the clergy. In 1812 this was then rescinded, but it was felt that the immediate result was a relaxation of standards. In 1820 the personal bond was reintroduced, but won the immediate disapproval of the Bishop of Chester, who understood this to be an affront to his authority to institute and discipline the clergy. Moreover, in the subsequent correspondence he reminded the corporation that if they sought to interfere with the licence of the clergy, even if they were performing their duties inadequately, then they would be restricting the legal rights which licensed clergy held. The corporation swiftly capitulated and suspended their resolutions, thus kicking the issue into the long grass. However, the allocation of stipends still lay with the corporation, who henceforth added the line "so long only as he shall personally perform the duties of the said Church, unless prevented by sickness or infirmity."[68]

Political partisanship rarely shows itself in the ecclesiastical history of Liverpool, but engagement with national politics becomes increasingly apparent. It was not uncommon for men of the town to go to Parliament to request an Act to achieve a local aim – from forming the parish itself, to the lobbying in 1807 for the right to levy rates against property in the

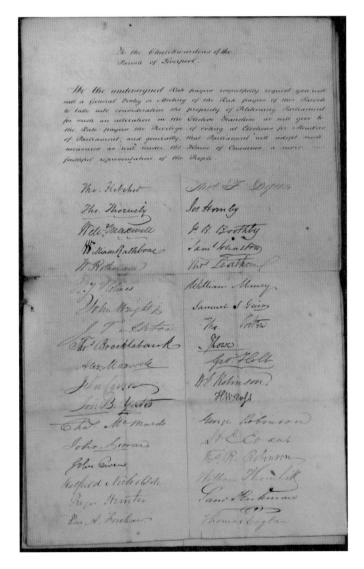

First page of a petition of 1830 from the ratepayers of Liverpool to the church-wardens to lobby for electoral reform.
OLSN Archives

town owned by non-residents (although this particular request was then withdrawn).[69] The ratepayers increasingly looked for ways to exercise influence. Locally, this is evident in the increase of three-day polls, sometimes on seemingly minor matters. For much of the history both of the common council and the vestry, decisions taken by vote were immediate and dependent on those who were present. By the 1820s, the vestry began to have increasing numbers of polls, so that there was much greater participation in decision-making. For example, in 1830 there was a three day election for a new vestry clerk: it was not an unimportant position, but having such a painstaking selection process would have been unimaginable a generation earlier. Was this really because there was such burning enthusiasm to be involved in local affairs? It seems more likely that the polls became an outlet for the frustration at being denied participation in national politics.

With such limited suffrage which favoured the freeholder above the wealthy merchant, there must have been considerable tension in a system which could tax the merchant far more harshly, both in the relatively new income tax, and also in local rates. Voting at the Annual

First registration of a ratepayer, John Eaton, as an elector under the Reform Act of 1832. This is possibly the same person listed as a churchwarden of St Paul's in 1808. *OLSN Archives*

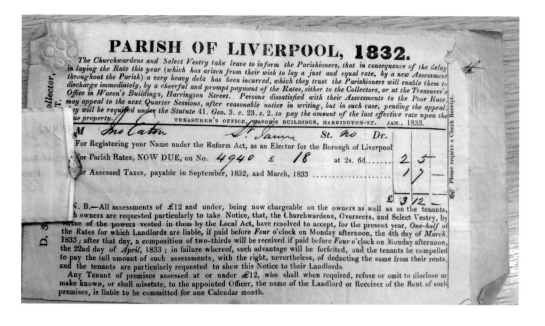

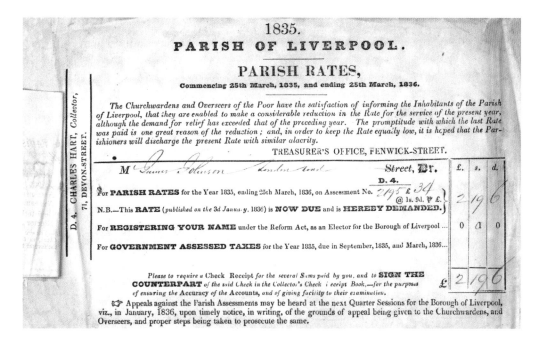

Rate assessment for James Johnson in 1835, by which time a fee was listed but not charged for registration as an elector.

OLSN Archives

Vestry Meeting, and increasingly in local polls, was the closest most ratepayers came to democracy, and the ratepayers of Liverpool echoed the demands across the country for wider voting rights. One way of exercising collective influence was through petitions.

In 1830 the ratepayers presented a petition to the churchwardens, requesting them "to call a General Vestry or Meeting of the Rate-payers of this Parish to take into consideration the propriety of Petitioning Parliament for such an alteration in the Elective Franchise as will give to the Rate-payers the Privilege of voting at Elections for Members of Parliament, and generally, that Parliament will adopt such measures as will render the House of Commons a more faithful representation of the People." A number of pages of signatures then follow, which illustrate that even leading citizens (names such as Rathbone persist in the city today) were denied the franchise. At the end of the petition is a note written by the churchwardens, setting the date of a meeting in December 1830, the minutes of which are sadly not preserved. In 1832 Parliament passed the Great Reform Act, under which many

Liverpool ratepayers were given the vote. The parish archives preserve a number of assessments of rates, including one dated 1832 for a John Eaton of St James' Street, which prints notice of his first registration as an elector under the Reform Act.[70] This was not the last petition, though. In February 1832 a very similar petition was presented to the churchwardens requesting a meeting to discuss making funds available to protect against the spread of cholera, which three weeks earlier the Board of Health had warned was approaching Liverpool. And yet another petition is recorded in 1841, asking for a special Act of Parliament (passed later in 1842) to regulate the implementation of the New Poor Law in Liverpool.[71]

The Victorian Church

By the 1830s the structure which held together both ecclesiastical life and social welfare was beginning to feel strained. Maintaining a single parish unit for the increasingly large number of churches in a thriving port town had ceased to be viable, and the following century saw the continued splintering of the town into districts, and then into separate legal parishes. More significantly, the common council, who had exercised considerable control over the church in Liverpool since the Reformation, decided that they no longer wished to maintain this interest. In addition, the administrative functions of the parish were also changing: the passing of the Poor Law Amendment Act in 1834 were less significant in the town than the Liverpool Select Vestry Act of 1842 which created a board of guardians who were mostly directly elected, rather than under the authority of the vestry. The involvement of the parish was not entirely over, as the rectors, churchwardens, and the overseers of the poor were *ex officio* members of the board, but the administration of the Poor Law became a secular function.

Secularising the Parish Function

The unpicking of the responsibilities of the parish happened relatively swiftly. Although the fiftieth anniversary of the Select Vestry Act was marked by the presentation in 1893 to the Board of the Select Vestry of a portrait of their chairman, Canon Alexander Stewart,[1] this was a mere vestige of the genuine intertwining of the church and responsibility for the infrastructure of Liverpool, and the following year the Local Government Act of 1894 severed all connection.[2] The Act of 1842 was detailed in its prescription of duties and rights within the administration of poor relief, and the role of the chaplain which was described illustrates the central place which religion was given in the disciplined regime of the workhouse, but there was no longer to be the elasticity of boundaries between the church rate and the poor rate which had been evident for the previous three centuries. There were many advantages in the new arrangement, including greater continuity of governance. Given the level of spending, this was a necessary step: the total expenditure of the poor rate rose from £103,458 in 1856 to £140,799 in 1882.[3]

In the same year as the Select Vestry Act, an "Act for the Improvement, good Government and Police Regulation of the Borough of Liverpool" was passed (1842), superseding previous Acts which had combined these civic responsibilities with granting permission for the building of new churches. Half a century before, it had been expedient to combine Liverpool churches, pavements, and watchmen in one Act of Parliament: by the 1840s the matters appeared only distantly related. Perhaps out of courtesy, copies of the new Acts were delivered to the parish church by the town clerk, and signed with his compliments[4] but in reality the parish now had little use for copies of the legislation. There had already been disquiet in Parliament about the financial intertwining of clergy, parish, and the provision of essential services. It was argued in a debate on the Liverpool Police Bill of 1835 that the corporation was using clauses in secular legislation to secure the right to fund the clergy out of the rates. William Ewart, the MP for Liverpool, spoke vehemently: "Though this was called a Police Bill, the real object of it was to provide payment for the clergy of the parish of Liverpool out of the funds of the Corporation. It bore the name of a Police Bill, it was true, but it contained a clause which enabled the Corporation to make provision for the clergy of Liverpool out of their funds... The real object of the Bill was to render the clergy of this parish completely free from anything like popular control, in fixing their provision by Act of Parliament."[5] The vestry was indignant at the opposition to the Bill, claiming that the provision of day police was a necessity for the safety of the people of the town, and that moving the payment of the clergy to the corporation was, in fact, a matter of justice, because it would help Dissenters not to be paying the church rate for Anglican clergy.[6]

Under the Select Vestry Act of 1842, the Brownlow Hill workhouse remained the primary place for providing relief for the poor, as outdoor relief virtually disappeared. With the parish 'ownership' of the workhouse diminished through legislation, its main influence was religious. After its enlargement in 1842/3 to a capacity of over 3000 (though often, in effect, much more), there was need for provision for worship. A new chapel was licensed for worship in December 1855[7] within the parish of Liverpool, but of course for the workhouse chaplain to minister. There was a Roman Catholic chaplain later in the century as well, and one of the concerns of the select vestry was whether he should be paid. It is doubtful whether there was much concern about the spread of Catholicism amongst the paupers of the workhouse, but the institutionalisation of Anglicanism was considered a right of the Church of England.[8]

Religious provision did not mean that the moral state of the workhouse was beyond reproach. Just a year after the Act came into

The licence of 1855 from the Bishop of Chester for services to take place in the new workhouse chapel.
OLSN Archives

force, an article in the *Satirist* magazine claimed that the Liverpool workhouse was the largest brothel in England. There was an immediate investigation, chaired by one of the churchwardens, looking into both sexual immorality within the workhouse and also some other allegations, such as that an inmate had been refused a Bible, and that other inmates had not been permitted to attend church. The birth of three illegitimate children to long-standing residents within the previous year clearly indicated that the regime was not as rigid as the rules required. The chaplain was called to give evidence and, perhaps mindful of the need to demonstrate the effectiveness of his moral teaching, said that all the statements were faulty, and praised the running of the workhouse.[9] The workhouse chapel survived until a fire in September 1862 which entirely destroyed it, as well as killing twenty two children and two women who were suffocated in their beds.[10]

The secularisation of the parish cut the business of the church off from the population of the town. The wealth of the town experienced rapid growth, and much of this was centred around the docks. From 2946 ships visiting the port in 1816, the figure rose to 9338 in 1850, and by 1857 there were twenty-eight wet docks to accommodate them,[11] as well as a huge labouring population to service this growth. Unsurprisingly, this working class population was confined to a relatively small area: in 1844 the population density of the town was 140,000 people per square mile, which was more populous than Manchester, London or Leeds. The two worst areas were around Tithebarn Street and Crosshall Street, and also in Vauxhall around Scotland Road. Of the seven largest towns in England, Liverpool had the highest mortality rate.[12] Although some of the churches in the parish undoubtedly found a ministry with the poor, there is nothing to indicate that, for example, St Nicholas' genuinely reached out into the deprivation which was literally just up the road. The engagement with both indoor and outdoor relief which was evident through the vestry disappeared with the Acts of 1834 and 1842, and the vestry confined itself to elections and appointments only, hearing nothing of the conditions of the town.

That is not to say, of course, that individual church members were not involved in private charity, of which there were a number of charitable organisations in Liverpool to assist individuals in discharging their philanthropic urges. However, whilst statutory relief was far from compassionate or equitable, it had a degree of consistency; on the other hand, charitable organisations could exercise their discretion in whichever partisan way they wished. An example of this was the Central Relief Society of Liverpool, which operated under the presumption that poverty was avoidable by the individual, and those seeking relief were subjected to intrusive examination to assess their worthiness to receive relief. This in particular drew criticism from the Revd Henry Postance, who said in a speech to the Liverpool Clerical Society in 1884 that the CRS visitors "often times excel the Relieving Officers in their unnecessary painful enquiries."[13] Postance himself was one of the parish clergy who was demonstrably dedicated to ministry to the poor. He was the incumbent of Holy Trinity Church, built in 1858, and he saw education as the most practical way of combatting poverty. Under his supervision a school was opened in Ashwell Street in 1860, and the Beaufort Street Ragged School in 1868. He was enthusiastic in collecting private donations, inspiring even pennies from children in the city, for which he meticulously placed newspaper notices of gratitude.[14] Postance used the schools to reach out to poor children in large numbers: for example, on Sundays he was able to feed breakfast (of bread and milk) to 160 children in Beaufort Street as a result of private subscription.[15]

One Parish, Many Churches

As well as necessitating the secularisation of the health, employment and social care provision in the town, the continued growth of Liverpool and its changing population distribution meant that the church's response had to be more nuanced as the century progressed. In the eighteenth century and the first half of the nineteenth century the response to population increase had been merely to build more churches. In the 1850s, there were a remarkable thirty-two churches within the parish of Liverpool alone, as well as growing numbers of churches in the increasingly urbanised outskirts of the town.[16] There was, of course, a commensurate number of clergy: an illuminated address by the clergy of the parish to the Senior Rector, the Revd Jonathan Brooks, in 1848, to celebrate his fiftieth anniversary of ordination was signed by sixty-five clerics.[17]

By the time of the Religious Census of 1851 the honest evaluation revealed that capacity did not meet the population, but that attendance did not fill capacity. The population of the entire municipal borough of Liverpool was reckoned to be 375,955, where a total of 165 places of worship provided seating capacity of 122,386. The majority of churches of all denominations provided three services on Sundays, with a total attendance of 169,859 people (including Sunday School children and, presumably, some repeat attendance). However, at any one of the Sunday services, only the Roman Catholic churches could claim to be full (with a seating capacity calculated at 14,218, they had a morning attendance of 38,182, and a further 16,108 in the afternoon and evening), though it should be remembered that it was usual for there to be more than one Mass in the morning, and so attendance was split across a number of services. The Church of England seems to have been most successful in the morning (which was not the same for all denominations) when 63 per cent of their 60,545 seats were filled.[18] Caution has to be exercised in the provision of the figures, as some churches refused to submit any data, and some (including St Nicholas') provided only partial, or completely implausible figures. Both of these scenarios suggest that there was an under-recording of attendance, but with a margin of error of just a few thousand, the basic narrative remains the same.[19] The imprecise nature of the statistics is echoed in the Register of Services books at St Nicholas' which began in 1856, where notes record only that it is a good congregation or a full church; when numbers begin to be used in the 1870s (a decade after the collection began to be recorded), it was confined to those receiving communion.[20]

The statistics caused some stir nationally, and locally they were studied in detail by the Revd Abraham Hume (1814–84) who published his analysis, but also gave evidence in May 1858 to the Select Committee of the House of Lords on "Spiritual Destitution in Populous Places." Hume was vicar of the new parish of Vauxhall, and he sent summaries of his annual parish work to *The Times*. As well as being a prolific author of books and pamphlets, he was an enthusiastic participant of the establishment of the Diocese of Liverpool, and he even designed the seal for the first Bishop of Liverpool. Hume calculated that by 1851, despite the addition of numerous churches over the years, the Church of England could only accommodate 15 per cent of the population, and the provision of free seats in churches only catered for 6 per cent of the poor of the town.[21] In fact, the highest the figure which was ever reached for accommodation of the population within Anglican churches was 21 per cent in 1785.[22] All of this must be measured against the well-argued opinion that Anglican clergy (and perhaps those of all denominations) tended to be generous in their estimates of attendance.[23] Although the Church of England accounted for the majority of residents of Liverpool, there were significant minorities. By 1871, 15.5 per cent of inhabitants had been born in Ireland and were predominantly Roman Catholic.[24] Although the parish is primarily conceived as an Anglican structure, the social care provision was for all.

Despite the under-provision of seating for the population, within Anglican churches there was clearly over-provision for the usual congregations, and also disparity between the resident populations within each district. In 1879 the incumbents of Holy Trinity, St Michael's, St Thomas' and St Philip's claimed not to know exactly where their boundaries lay, and the clergy of some of the other churches claimed not to be aware that they had assigned districts at all. It is plausible that this was to avoid the obligation to visit the resident population, although by the end of the nineteenth century it seemed prudent to claim large areas, not only to justify a church's existence, but also to obtain funding from the Ecclesiastical Commissioners.[25]

The vast capacities of many of the churches were not always matched by their population. One report from 1877 suggested that St Martin's Church in the parish only had 107 Sunday worshippers, of whom 53 were children.[26] If this is true, then this shows a rapid decline from the figure of 500 given in the *Liverpool Mercury* in 1853. The same table of statistics records the percentage of working class attendees which illustrates great variation between churches which were geographically neighbouring. 53 per cent of the congregation of St Thomas', Park Lane, were working class, the historic Chapel of St Nicholas' had 21 per cent, whereas St Saviour's (Huskisson Street/Falkner Square) had just 6 per cent.[27] Whatever the nature of the population around a church, the clergy were not necessarily to be found there at night. A surprising number of the clergy lived in the (then gentrified) area of Everton, or the Georgian splendour of Upper Parliament Street. None of the Anglican slum priests in Liverpool appears to have lived with their people, which created a striking difference from the Catholic clergy, whose presbyteries were usually attached to their churches.[28] Doubtless there were many examples of good clerical practice within the city, but sometimes the disparity between the educated clergy, often financially independent, and their people must have grated. The Revd J. Howard of St Bartholomew's, one of the poorest district churches at the turn of the twentieth century, once wrote in the parish magazine upbraiding his working-class congregation for not attending his magic lantern slide lecture on a 'holiday tour of the Lake District'.[29] Howard lived in Chatham Street in what is now termed the City's Georgian Quarter, nearly two miles from his church in Naylor Street.

These various census statistics were striking, but Thomas Snape, elected as MP for Heywood (Lancashire S.E.) in 1892, commissioned friends to go into the churches in 1893 and discover the reality of their congregations. St. Luke's had a large congregation; St. Thomas' had only 139, most of them children; St. Michael's had 200 (including children); St. John's had 101; St. George's, with a capacity of 2,000, had a congregation of only 76; St. Paul's, who could seat 1,800, had only 16 in the congregation, most of whom were children; St. Martin's, in the midst of a large working class district and with a capacity of 1,900, had a congregation of only 32; St. Ann's had 16 adults and 15 children; Trinity Church had 14 adults and 47 children. St. David's was reported as having a unique position as a church in England as it had a Welsh service, but had a congregation of just 39.[30] Snape's friend who visited St George's obviously found them on a good Sunday: in 1889 a visitor had found the four worshippers outnumbered by the incumbent, clerk, verger, organist, organ blower, bell ringer and "one lady singer". The visitor also complained that the church, belonging to the corporation, was brilliantly lit with gas even for such a small congregation.[31] It was also said that the incumbent, James Kelly, who had presided over and undoubtedly initiated decline since his arrival in 1863, linked the church up to the vicarage gas supply and rigged up one pew as his bedroom, another as a kitchen and a third as his servant's bedroom. Two decks of the three-decker pulpit were converted into a wine store and whisky supply.[32] Kelly was eccentric or mad or both, and frequently found himself the subject of both attention and ridicule, but events such as his appearance in the divorce court in May 1869 when his wife sued for judicial separation on the grounds of cruelty did not help. Nor did his authorship of a substantial pamphlet about the case in the following year. It is unlikely that the people of Liverpool had also forgotten that five years' earlier he had been in court on the charge of assaulting the organist, for which he was fined five shillings plus costs, and four years' earlier he had sued the proprietor of the *Liverpool Mail* for libel.[33]

The inevitability that some churches would find themselves superfluous meant that legislative intervention would follow. First came the Liverpool City Churches Act of 1897 which brought about the closure of St John's Church and St George's Church. A letter to the Rector of Liverpool from the Ecclesiastical Commission dated 20 May 1898 notifies him of the transfer of the endowments of those churches to the endowment of the parish itself as "compensation in respect of the additional cure of souls of the Districts of St George and St John Liverpool now restored to the Parish of Liverpool."[34] The Act allowed for the preservation of the registers of the two churches which were transferred to the Parochial Chapel of St Nicholas. Large safes were built in 1897 under the tower: they were later moved after the parish offices were built in the 1920s, where they remain today.[35] The Act also transferred the remaining corporation churches from Liverpool Corporation to the Ecclesiastical Commissioners.[36] The town had held control over its churches and the parish in various ways since the Reformation. We shall see below that the Municipal Corporations Act of 1835 had compelled the disposal of advowsons, and so the patronage of the town's churches were all moved to private hands, but it did not affect municipal ownership of church property. The Liverpool City Churches Act therefore brought about the final legal separation of city and parish.

Just a few years later came the Liverpool and Wigan Churches Act 1904 which permitted the sale of old churches and vicarages including St Paul's, and also All Souls' Eaton Street, St Thomas' (closed 1905), St Mark's (closed 1908), St David's (closed 1910). The provisions of the Act allowed the closure of churches over the following decades, including St Titus' (closed 1918), and Christ Church, Hunter Street (closed 1920). The Act also consolidated the position of more successful churches: for

The division of the parish into districts associated with different churches made the area manageable. St Stephen's was given its own district in 1863. *OLSN Archives*

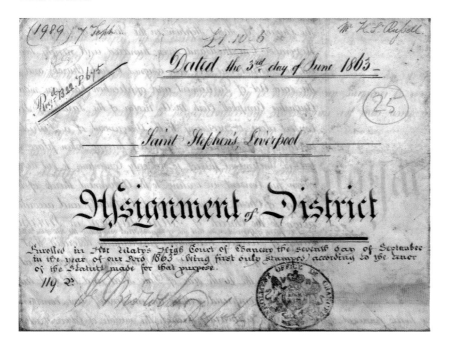

The earliest photograph of the Parochial Chapel, probably dating from 1871. *OLSN Archives*

example, the Church of St Anne was given her own parish, as were St Bride's and Christ Church (both 1904) and St Luke's.

The shift in population out of the city centre meant that as churches closed within the parish of Liverpool, they were opening elsewhere. The most direct link to illustrate this pattern is that of St Paul's. Since its consecration in 1769 it had seen the growth in residential population around it, but by the beginning of the twentieth century it was surrounded by businesses and warehouses. St Paul's closed in 1901, but the proceeds of the sale were used to fund a new church dedicated to St Paul in Stoneycroft (although £1,000 of the sale proceeds was given to the parochial chapel). This was designed by Gilbert Scott, who was by now engaged to build the new cathedral, and opened in January 1916.[37] But St Paul's was not the only instance. All Souls' Church in Eaton St, Vauxhall closed in 1923, but resurfaced in Springwood in 1927 as a separate parish. The new church, which remains at a busy intersection of roads, had the benefit of visibility, whereas its forebear is noted as being at the end of an insalubrious and narrow street, in an industrial area and facing the light-restricting retaining wall of the

Leeds–Liverpool canal, and with a notoriously dangerous street life around it.[38]

The Dead

The relatively small churchyard at St Nicholas' remained as a parochial cemetery for the town until it was finally closed in 1849. Although most did not, a few of the other churches within the parish had churchyards, but these were also filling up and further expansion was continually taking place. For example, in 1828 the corporation made a conveyance of land to the commissioners of St John's Church of a piece of land for a cemetery. In 1842 the vestry realised that St Mary's Cemetery was in a very poor condition and should be closed. They judged that when a new burial ground was found it should be in a less populous part of the parish.[39] With the closure of the churchyard at St Nicholas, the churchyard at St Martin in the Fields, Silvester Street, became the sole remaining parochial cemetery from 1849, but capacity within the town centre was coming to an end. There were other moments of crisis as well, such as the closure of the churchyard at St James' in 1862 after the discovery that bodies in were being exhumed to make way for fresh burials.[40]

In 1854 the corporation decided that burials should move out of the centre, which led to the closure of a number of churchyards, such as St Paul's and also the parochial cemetery at St Martin's which closed in 1856 but had its last burial in 1865. The corporation itself began a programme of building cemeteries: Toxteth Park Cemetery was opened in 1856, intended to serve the suburbs to the south; the first burial in Anfield Cemetery took place in 1863. Unlike Toxteth Park, Anfield was intended to serve the town centre. A parochial cemetery was still needed, though: whereas the prosperous citizens of Liverpool could afford to pay for their burial plot, the parish still provided for the burial of paupers. A parochial cemetery was "where all the poor inhabitants have burial ground gratis."[41] This was not entirely without cost, though, and some parishioners were appalled to find the rector claiming the burial fee for paupers in the parochial cemetery in 1854.[42] In 1849 the first expenditure was recorded for establishing a new cemetery in Walton, including £1300 on the boundary wall.[43] Areas of Walton Park Cemetery were given over to 'paid ground', but the majority was free, and the graves remained unmarked. The burial registers show a large proportion of burials from the workhouse and the prison. Walton Park

A plan of graves and vaults in the ancient Churchyard made *c.*1850, though the marked graves are all post-medieval.
OLSN Archives

The churchyard of St Nicholas' in 1846, just before the last burials took place. The tombstones were horizontal to create flagging. *OLSN Archives*

Cemetery is now closed to new burials, but remains part of the parish of Liverpool. The most visited grave is that of Robert Noonan, who wrote *The Ragged Trousered Philanthropists* under the pseudonym of Robert Tressell. He had no connection with Liverpool but was passing through on his way to Canada when he died of tuberculosis in 1911. With no money or local connections, he was buried in a paupers' grave (with thirteen inhabitants) which remained unmarked until 1977.[44]

With the need for city centre burials declining, but with space at a premium, these open green spaces became places of recreation. In 1880 a significant scheme was drawn up to create a walkway across St John's churchyard from William Brown Street to St John's Lane.[45] This was a precursor to the laying out of ornamental gardens in 1904, following the demolition of the church. Down the hill at the parochial chapel, a similar scheme took place, funded by a legacy from James Harrison whose shipping line occupied Mersey Chambers in Old

Churchyard. The clearing of the bodies from the churchyard of St Nicholas' began on 9 April 1884. A total of 1174 graves and 48 vaults were opened: the earliest of these was from 1750, and the latest was 1855. A small proportion of the bodies were claimed, such as in grave number 790 where a lead coffin was dug up containing the remains of Alexander Mason, a river pilot, from 1787, whose body was claimed by his granddaughter. Some of the work was gruesome: contemporary notes made by J. Hargreaves include the following description: "In some cases the flesh or other matter upon the bodies was very thick and one instance particularly, that of the body of a woman who had been buried about 83 years. The preservation of the body was most remarkable. It was attired in a white cotton gown with worked front and a hood. When the coffin was first opened the body was very wet and soft and of a purple shade or colour, but after being exposed to the air for a few hours it became quite hard and dry. The features were very distinct: she had evidently been a very stout woman. The greater part of the body turned black but the face and from the neck to the waist were of a purple and blue shade."[46]

A faculty of 1892 allowed this 'Ornamental Ground' and it was given to the care of the corporation, who still maintain it today.

Ministry to a City

Worship across the parish was not confined to the instruction of the Rector of Liverpool. The worship in the parish church and parochial chapel remained High Church in flavour, but largely not ritualistic. In the second half of the century there was a move away from reading the services from the reading desk, towards a more Catholic style of celebration, including the intoning of service. This occasionally brought objection and complaint.[47] There were occasional deviations from moderate ceremony, such as in May 1875 when the ritualistically inclined curate of St Peter's, the Revd George Burrows, officiated at Benediction of the Blessed Sacrament, with procession and incense, on the feast of Corpus Christi. It was scandalous enough that a report was published as far away as Sheffield, and the rector acted swiftly to forbid any repeat.[48] Other churches were distinctive within the ecclesiastical spectrum, such as the High Churches of St Martin's, St James-the-less (Kirkdale), St Catherine's Abercromby Square, and Christ Church, or the Low Churches of St Matthew or St Nathaniel.[49] Outside the parish, ritualism caused ecclesiastical reverberations on the national stage, particularly at St Margaret's, Toxteth, where the Revd James Bell Cox was prosecuted and imprisoned in 1887 for High Church practices.

By the Victorian period, an established expectation of worship in Church of England churches had developed. Each of the churches and chapels in the parish had a morning service beginning at some point between 10am and 11am (at St Nicholas' it was 10.45am, and at St Peter's it was 10.30am). Both the parish church and parochial chapel performed the greatest number of baptisms, and in 1843 both listed an afternoon service, which was undoubtedly just for baptisms. On the whole, the other churches did not advertise a weekly afternoon service, but given that the registers of St George's reveal just eleven baptisms taking place in 1843, perhaps there was no need. The majority, though, had an evening service at 6.30pm. Unusually, the Chapel of St Nicholas' was one of those listing no evening service at this time.[50] This may have been an omission in publication, because by the time the Registers of Services began in 1856 there are two services with a sermon every Sunday, and possibly more which were not recorded as the sermon was the primary focus of the register. Attendance was a concern, and in April 1879 the vestry passed a motion "that a committee be appointed with instructions to consider and report to this Vestry at an adjourned meeting to be held this day four weeks, the best plan or plans for securing a larger attendance of the parishioners and particularly of the working classes at the two parish churches of Liverpool."[51] Sadly the resulting plan was not recorded.

But for most churches the most visible ministry beyond the provision of worship was in the occasional offices of baptisms, weddings and funerals. The registers of the churches of the parish show thousands being baptised every year. There were, though, quirks to the pattern. Unlike today, there was no presumption that baptism should take place on Sundays and although the majority still did, at St Peter's Church the second most popular day in the mid-nineteenth century was Monday. In other churches there was no particular weighting towards an individual day, and the clergy were happy to baptise whenever the candidates were presented.[52] The registers of St Peter's and St Nicholas' suggest that the importance of going to the parish churches remained significant: throughout the century the pattern remained that, despite varying levels of population around each church, the principal churches of the parish remained most popular, perhaps because they lent a validity to the action. Furthermore, with the existing single parochial structure, families could choose to take their children to whichever church they wished. Even if they attended a district church, they might opt for the parish church for baptism.

For many years St George's church was the venue for the mayor's first service after being elected, but in 1863 the new incumbent, the Revd James Kelly, preached an anti-semitic sermon decrying the election of the first Jewish mayor, Charles Mozley, and labelling the councillors as apostates from Christ: from that moment the mayor and corporation ceased to attend St George's, a decision which was put in writing by Mozley and also his successor as mayor, Edward Lawrence. This was, ultimately, the beginning of the end for the church where congregations swiftly declined.[53] The place of the parish within the civic life of the town was unaffected. At the start of his mayoral year, Charles Mozley had processed to the Parish Church of St Peter and taken his seat for his inaugural service (as the Lord Mayor of Liverpool does at St Nicholas' today), and the following year the tradition continued. Despite what had happened the previous year, the incumbent of St George's seems still to have attended the Civic Service at St Peter's in 1864.[54]

A number of the churches also maintained schools, alongside the existing relationship with schools such as the Blue Coat School and the Moorfields Charity School. Even so, the provision of school places was woefully inadequate. The Revd Abraham Hume estimated in 1858 that there was a need for 76,467 school places, but only 44,767 were available, of which the Church of England provided 24,060 and the Roman Catholics 10,663.[55] What schools there were flourished as the Education Act 1870 gave them financial stability. Some of the schools survived well into the twentieth century, especially in areas of higher population density, such as Vauxhall and Kirkdale. St James-the-Less in Athol Street, which opened in 1866 and closed in 1967[56] or St Bartholomew's, Eaton Street, Vauxhall were successful examples of schools which served the communities around them. By the end of the century, the decline in population in some districts and the subsequent closure of churches had an impact on the management of education. For example, in 1898 the Charity Commission oversaw the transfer of the management of the National School in Great Crosshall Street from the minister and wardens of St John's to the minister and wardens of St Stephen's.[57] Similarly, when the Church of St Bartholomew closed in 1929 the school was transferred to the oversight of the parish church and eventually its name was changed to Our Lady and St Nicholas' School.

With a changing role within the city, and perhaps also conscious that a resident bishop meant that the parish of Liverpool was going to need a fresh identity with slightly less direct influence, the church looked for new ways to serve the city. St Peter's was forming an identity as the cathedral church, and although no one expected this to be the long term solution, its practical ministry as the church of the city had begun to transfer back to the original Chapel of St Nicholas. During Lent St Peter's put on special sermons on Wednesdays and Fridays, but in the 1880s these were poorly attended, one newspaper commenting wryly "It is a pity that no public announcement was made."[58] By contrast, St Nicholas' was becoming more confident in its city ministry, and in 1884 began a series of lunchtime Lent Addresses. Over the following century these attracted speakers from across the country, and an audience from across the city. In that first year a number of speakers took a week each, amongst the most notable being the Revd V.S.S. Coles, who spoke on St Luke Chapter 19 between 17 and 21 March. Coles is subsequently remembered as a hymn writer (including, in 1922, a patronal festival hymn for the parish church), but he was also an academic who joined the staff of the Pusey House, Oxford that year and later became principal. Another well-known speaker was the Revd Samuel Reynolds Hole, who spoke on Luke 15 on the 26, 27 and 28 March. Hole was appointed as Dean of Rochester in 1887. A similar pattern was maintained as the reputation grew, and those invited to speak included both bishops and more junior clergy, many of whom went on to more prominent posts. For example, in 1892 one week was taken by the Revd Richard Bullock, who was a well-known vicar of Holy Trinity, Leeds, before going on to be Vicar of Spalding, Lincolnshire; in that year another week was taken by the Revd John Diggle, the Rector of nearby Mossley Hill, who went on to be the Bishop of Carlisle.[59] The ability to attract speakers known nationally as well as locally remains a significant part of the church's ministry.

Although civic services remained at St Peter's until the end of the nineteenth century (certainly by June 1899 they had transferred to the chapel), other services for particular groups took place at St Nicholas'. For example, in October 1862 the rector's son, the Revd Edward Campbell, officiated at a service for the Liverpool Rifle Volunteers. Whilst indicating that Christianity generally prefers to avoid bloodshed, during the sermon he gave examples of when warfare is justified. At the end of the service the battalion marched from the church back to their barracks.[60] These became increasingly common, such as the annual Liverpool Postal Telegraph Messengers' Parade which began in 1895, or the Liverpool Tramwaymen in 1905.[61]

Endowment and Patronage

The frustration felt by the corporation in 1820/21 when they found themselves unable to control the performance of the clergy, despite holding the power of appointment of many of the churches in the parish, perhaps illustrated that the council was no longer the most appropriate patron of ecclesiastical livings. Whereas most parishes across the country had historic endowments or glebe, as well as tithing arrangements, the peculiar history of Liverpool's churches meant that the clergy were still directly funded by the church rate and the corporation, with limited assistance from the vestiges of chantry lands. Tithes had continued in Liverpool for some time as urbanisation continued, but by the 1730s they were contributing only £20 a year to the rectors' stipends, and in 1743 it was suggested that tithing should be discontinued altogether.[62] In addition, the rectors received the rents from a number of pews – the pew plans of the eighteenth century show that a significant proportion of the ground floor seating belonged to the incumbents – but this was balanced by the responsibility of the pew owners towards fabric and maintenance. The corporation therefore bore the financial responsibility for supplementing clergy stipends beyond what was raised from the church rate, but felt impotent at any control beyond appointing them. In addition, there was a shift of mood nationally, and whilst there were no serious moves towards disestablishing the Church of England, the repeal of the Test and Corporation Acts in 1828 admitted that members of the Anglican Church were not exclusively entitled to public office. In Ireland matters were coming to a head, and the Church Reform Act of 1833 (which was the immediate provocation for the beginning of the Oxford Movement, which subsequently affected the liturgical life of both the parish church and parochial chapel) reduced the number of Irish dioceses, and their financial cost, to a slightly more proportionate level. This was then followed by full disestablishment of the Church of Ireland in 1869. The growth of non-conformity in Liverpool (distinct from Roman Catholicism) was not as significant as in other cities, but the institutional bias towards Anglicanism was unsustainable.

The prevailing mood heralded a small crisis in Liverpool. The great defect of the establishment of the parish in 1699 was that no endowment was made for paying the clergy, and the subsequent building of such a large number of churches always depended on the willingness of the corporation to pay them. The introduction in 1834 of a Bill to abolish the church rates was therefore disastrous, because the council would have to find the money not just for the rectors, but also for the clergy of most of the town's churches. The mayor (John Wright) and others made immediate representation to Parliament, and they fought a strong case for a clause to make exception for the parish of Liverpool and at least to allow the payment of the clergy from the poor rate. As it happened, the Bill was dropped for broader political reasons, but the time had come for a new arrangement.[63]

The Municipal Corporations Bill which was brought before Parliament in 1835 was the catalyst for action. It stipulated that all stipends and allowances paid by a corporation to the clergy in the previous seven years set a precedent which became obligatory. Even though the last payment of £150 to the rectors had been in 1828, it fell within three months of the cut-off provided in the Act. Some provision was going to be necessary, but there was much local lobbying for a more generous settlement on the clergy. The churchwardens sent an address

The interior of St Peter's, pictured in the late nineteenth century when it was temporarily the cathedral. Note the bishop's throne on the south side.
OLSN Archives

to the mayor in June 1835 suggesting that the corporation took full responsibility for payments to the clergy which had previously been made by the parish. By and large, the case for this was accepted, but it was felt that a separate Act should make provision for a local matter, rather than encumber the Municipal Corporations Act with excessive detail. In October 1835 the council indicated that it was time for proper endowments to be made: a committee was formed which swiftly decided that an endowment should pay for the rectors and curates, and should entirely replace the amount raised by the church rates. In fact, after obtaining legal advice from London, it was clear that the corporation could not continue supporting the clergy financially as it had been, and the recommendation was that they raise a mortgage to endow the living properly. It was suggested that a variety of obligations were undertaken for both rectors and their curates, as well as clergy from the churches of St George's, St Thomas', St Paul's, St John's, St Anne's and St David's. The immediate plan was an investment in the railways, and in particular the Warrington and Newton Railway, in which they could secure some ownership of the assets.

This became rather a complicated case, and as soon as a resolution had been passed to raise a mortgage and make the investment, 125 burgesses signed a protest against the action and, upon that being dismissed, proceeded to get an injunction against the transaction. A counter-petition to the Rolls Court led to the injunction being dissolved in November 1835, and the following month the clergy of the town met at the Blue Coat Hospital and passed a resolution thanking the common council not just for building schools and churches in the first place, but also for securing "the independence of the Clergy by a sufficient permanent provision for those Churches which before were inadequately endowed." In fact the game was not over, and the opponents of the endowment returned to the Rolls Court claiming, amongst other things, that the original legal case was conducted by the old mayor and council, and not by the new corporation constituted under the Municipal Corporations Act. The case was paused for a while, whilst the council deliberated further, and in September 1836 the town clerk submitted a report which showed which churches produced an income from their pew rents, and which were wholly subsidised by the corporation. In the meantime, all payments from the corporation to the clergy had stopped, apart from the rather small amount which could be justified under the Municipal Corporations Act. This was unfair on the clergy, and brought them a degree of sympathy. Although the intricate legal wrangling continued, it was public opinion more than anything else which led the two sides to accept the services of a mediator.[64]

The obvious compromise was to reduce the costs which the council would have to pay towards the clergy, and a proposal to terminate the 'mediety' was acceptable to both sides. As we have noted in the previous chapter, it was always an anomaly that Liverpool should have two rectors with equal authority, and although the written record does not preserve any tension between them, it seems an unhelpful situation. Noting that the litigation in this battle had cost something in the region of £50,000, much of which latterly was born by the council, a conclusion was welcomed at a meeting of the council on 27 June 1838, the day before the coronation of Queen Victoria.[65] The resulting "Act for uniting the Medieties of the Rectory of Liverpool in the County Palatine of Lancaster and for the better Endowment thereof, and of certain Churches in the said Town" followed swiftly, and passed into law on 10 August 1838, though it only took effect upon the death of the Revd Jonathan Brooks in 1855, leaving Augustus Campbell as the sole rector for the remaining time of his 41 years as rector. Campbell was simultaneously Vicar of Childwall, which carried a stipend of nearly £1932p.a. (as opposed to Liverpool's stipend of £400p.a. plus fees), and he chose to live in Childwall Vicarage.[66]

The other consequence of the Municipal Corporations Act was the selling of the advowson (patronage). Although caught up in the great reforms of the 1820s, and 1830s, both the Tory repeal of the Test and Corporation Acts, and then the more extensive Whig reforms, the inclusion in the Municipal Corporations Act of a clause compelling local authorities to dispose of their advowsons was at the behest of the church. The newly extended franchise had a particular effect in more urban areas where the money of industrialisation was often held by non-conformists: whereas individuals who were not members of the Church of England were usually prevented from exercising their patronage, this was not the case where an advowson was owned by a corporation. The immediate consequence was that corporations with close links to parish churches (as well as Liverpool, these included Oxford, Norwich, Beccles, Bedford, and Helston) were obliged to sell them, but were then at liberty to take a broader view of religious affiliation. Within a short time this meant that in Liverpool the corporation decided that the Book of Common Prayer should no longer be taught in schools.[67]

The Ecclesiastical Commissioners had given notice to the corporation following the Act that they needed to dispose of the advowsons which they owned. The patronages of various corporation churches were sold at this time to leading figures in the town. For example, that of St Luke's was sold to another future mayor, Sir Joshua Walmsley (who served in office 1839–40). It was then sold to Charles Lawrence, a merchant who had been mayor in 1823, and who appointed his son, the Revd Charles Washington Lawrence, as the incumbent. The patronage remained in the Lawrence family for further generations.[68]

With the matter of endowment settled for the time being, the sale of the advowson of the parish itself was now possible. In April 1839 the patronage of the parish church was sold to John Stewart for £8150. Stewart was Mayor of Liverpool in 1855–6, the same year that the 'mediety' came to an end with the death of Jonathan Brooks. The remaining rector, Augustus Campbell, died in 1870, and Stewart promptly presented his own son, the Revd Alexander Stewart, to the Living. Within a year, John Stewart was dead, and the advowson passed to the rector himself. Although he was only the second rector not to die in post, Alexander Stewart decided not to retain the advowson so that he could appoint his own successor. The sale to the Gladstone family was apparently arranged through an intermediary, the Revd J. Bell Cox of St Margaret's, Toxteth.[69] William Ewart Gladstone, who himself had been baptised in the parish church and who had already been Prime Minister three times, wrote in his diary in 1889:

> 23 December *Having been led to entertain the subject of purchasing the important Liverpool Advowson, from intelligence brought by H. Drew, I this day consulted severally my wife, Stphen, & then Willy. All were warmly for it. So I sent further questions about it.*
>
> 31 December *Had H.N.G. for my envoy to Liverpool today respecting the Advowson. He steered his vessel admirably… After Harry had reported came the Tel. reporting acceptance of my offer of £7200 for this great advowson.*[70]

Gladstone still had another stint as Prime Minister to go, but he did not live to appoint the next rector, although the patronage has remained in the Gladstone family since that time. However, Gladstone did record his less than favourable view of the rector in a letter to his son, the Revd Stephen Gladstone, in March 1893.

> *However respected and respectable the Rector of Liverpool [Alexander Stewart] may be, he is not a man up to the mark which in my view qualifies for the Cathedral preferment in the gift of the crown.*[71]

It seems unlikely that Alexander Stewart ever knew of this letter, and he certainly did not stand in the way of a memorial service for Mr Gladstone, held in St Nicholas' on 24 May 1898, timed to coincide with Gladstone's funeral in Hawarden. The Bishop of Liverpool officiated at the service, and the Lord Mayor attended 'in state'. Another simultaneous memorial service for Gladstone took place at St George's Hall.[72]

As the corporation retreated from direct involvement in the running of the churches, further financial provision was necessary. The parish had relied on the church rate for some centuries, but the Compulsory Church Rate Abolition Act of 1868 brought an end to a guaranteed source of income. The hope it held out was in the voluntary tate, which was allowed by the same Act. This included the clause "It shall be

The Rt Hon W.E. Gladstone, who bought the advowson of Liverpool in 1890 shortly before his fourth term as Prime Minister.
Photograph by G. G. Bain, held at the Library of Congress, via Wikimedia Commons

lawful for all bodies corporate... who or whose cestuisque trust are in the occupation of any lands, houses, or tenements to pay, if they think fit, any church rate made in respect of such property."[73] Although this rate could be levied by any church, it remained more effective in urban areas. In Liverpool it continued to be a major part of the income of the parish until the 1990s, but in a different form remains a significant source of funds today. The final part of the settling of the endowment and income came in the Liverpool City Churches Act of 1897. Under the Act the corporation had to pay £95,000 into the endowment of the parish. In addition, the churchwardens (by which is meant the vestry) had to pay an additional £48,000 into the endowment, which brought an end to the ill-defined boundaries between church and vestry expenses within the parish.

Diocese and City

The growth and status of Liverpool was beginning to outstrip the church's provision for the town. The vast structure of St George's Hall, dwarfing the adjacent Church of St John, was completed in 1854, and the other monumental buildings were being constructed or planned. In March 1853 the vestry meeting asked the churchwardens to obtain plans and costs to build a new church in place of St Peter's "of such an architectural character as to its exterior as shall be a credit to the town of Liverpool." Just a few weeks later the discussion was re-opened with a fresh idea, that St Peter's should be left alone, but that "a Cathedral Parish Church" should be built on another site.[74] The people of the town were already envisaging that they should have a place of worship to rival other places in the country.

The Diocese of Chester was unmanageably large, and throughout the nineteenth century various bits were chipped away to join the Diocese of St Asaph, and the newly-formed Dioceses of Ripon and Manchester. Yet more parts were transferred to the Diocese of Carslile. There was, of course, pressure for the formation of a diocese centred on Liverpool, not least from the MP for the town, John Torr. The Additional Bishoprics Act of 1878 legislated for the formation of the Dioceses of Liverpool, Newcastle, Southwell and Wakefield, provided that an endowment of £100,000 could be raised to provide an income for the bishop of at least £3,500 a year. The Liverpool Bishoprics Fund had already been established in December 1878, and by 1880 it reached its goal. On 24 March 1880 the Diocese of Liverpool was created by

Order in Council (taking effect from 19 April), and the corporation successfully petitioned that Liverpool became a city at the same time. The first Bishop of Liverpool, J.C. Ryle, was an unexpected appointment by Disraeli just a couple of days before he left office on 21 April 1880. Ryle had just been appointed as Dean of Salisbury, but had accepted – along with most of the church – that his prospects of a bishopric were limited by his evangelicalism. It is impossible to know whether the appointment was an opportunistic and personal swipe at William Gladstone, a noted High Churchman, at the very moment when he took office as Prime Minister, or whether it was a genuine recommendation from Lord Sandon, the other MP for Liverpool alongside Torr, who felt that Ryle was the right man for the protestant flavour of Liverpool. Either way, Ryle was enthroned as the first Bishop of Liverpool in the Parish Church of St Peter – maybe only coincidentally the church in which Gladstone had been baptised – on 1 July 1880.[75]

The formation of a new diocese was an arduous task, but Ryle was able to use his power of patronage effectively to pursue his own agenda. By Order in Council on 21 July 1880 he was able to appoint sixteen canons, which he allotted to suitable candidates across the diocese, but the archdeaconries were always given to Evangelicals. Alexander Stewart, as Rector of Liverpool, was made an honorary canon immediately, a status given to all but two of his successors. In fact, Stewart slightly eschewed the title of canon, remarking, "There are a score of Canons of Liverpool but only one Rector."[76] Although he did not have the title, Stewart was also *de facto* Dean of Liverpool, but there was still no prospect of a cathedral. Progress for an appropriate episcopal seat had to wait until the second bishop, Francis Chavasse, whose energy brought about not just the site of the new cathedral and the finances,[77] but also the Liverpool Cathedral Act 1902 which designated St Peter's as the cathedral church until the first part of the new cathedral was consecrated. In due course, St Peter's would close, and its status as the Parish Church of Liverpool would be transferred to Our Lady and St Nicholas.

In the meantime, Ryle was creative in an episcopal ministry without an appropriate cathedral. The annual Diocesan Conference met at St George's Hall, and his first episcopal charge in October 1881 was delivered at both St Peter's and also All Saints', the Parish Church of Wigan. Despite fervent activity, church attendance across the new diocese did not increase at an impressive rate, although it was markedly better in middle class areas than working class ones. Gladstone – not yet the owner of the advowson of Liverpool, and probably still smarting at

Disraeli's appointment of an evangelical to the city of his birth – used Ryle's results in his first few years to oppose the Bishopric of Bristol Bill in 1884: "The religious Census of Liverpool, I do not hesitate to say, is a disgrace to Liverpool and to the country generally; and, considering that the Established Church of the country is *de facto* under a very heavy charge of duty with respect to these populations, it is a very great responsibility, I think, to interfere to prevent voluntary action for the purpose of doing something to mitigate this grievous deficiency which now exists."[78] This criticism would seem not to undermine Ryle's zeal, because he had already publicly stated that he was more concerned with spreading the gospel than with building a cathedral. Even so, in 1883 a committee had been established to decide upon the best location, choosing between St Peter's, Monument Place, St James' Mount, and St John's Churchyard (next to St George's Hall). Ryle's preference, leading to the Liverpool Cathedral Act of 1885, was for St John's Churchyard. The objection was that it would be overshadowed by the adjacent civic buildings, but in fact Ryle's understanding of the desirability of a city centre location was correct in providing the opportunity to engage with civic and commercial life. This cathedral was not to be, though. A recession, other pressing ecclesiastical demands, and an ageing bishop meant that progress was delayed by two decades, and when it resumed it was on the St James' Mount site.[79]

Meanwhile, Ryle showed very little interest in the pro-cathedral which he already had. It was not in very good condition: a report was read to the vestry in 1885 revealing that St Peter's was in a dangerous state and should be closed for safety until repairs had been completed, and the additional idea was mentioned that it might be better just to rebuild it with a more worthy building. No additional money was made available for the running of diocesan services except that which was collected during them, forcing the rector to contribute £150 a year from his own stipend.[80] Furthermore, although Ryle was expected to preach on the first Sunday of the month, except when he was on holiday, he often failed to do so for several months at a time.[81]

Our Lady and St Nicholas: From Chapel to Church

The pre-eminence of the parochial chapel was never lost and throughout the period it continued to receive more attention than the other places of worship. The most significant alterations to the building took place

in 1851–2 when the vestry authorised the churchwardens to spend
£200 from the church rate in re-pewing the chapel. More, in fact, was
done, including a new pulpit, choir stalls, and communion rails. The
west gallery was removed and a smaller organ gallery went in its place.
The font was also removed along with its cover, which was reputed to
be of carved wood, modelled after the spire of a Spanish cathedral.
The cover had supposedly been captured from a ship taken in the
Anglo-Spanish war of 1654–60. The new font was the gift of Robert
Hutchison, the town clerk, and survived the bombing of the Second
World War. It was placed in the narthex of the new church until it was
removed to the room under the tower in 2018.[82] The church narrowly
escaped disaster in February 1868 when a serious fire broke out in the

Canon John Kempthorne, Rector
of Liverpool, and the first of
six twentieth century rectors
who went on to be bishops.
Kempthorne became Bishop of
Hull, before twenty four years as
Bishop of Lichfield.
Photograph postcard by R. Brown,
Liverpool, on loan to author.

tower and spread along the roof. There was considerable damage from water and falling debris, but the interior largely remained intact, apart from the destruction of the organ. The building closed for worship whilst repairs took place.[83]

The popularity of the chapel as a place of worship is evident from the Registers of Services, which began in 1850. In the early years these did not record attendance figures, but the clergy made notes to indicate that the building was usually full for worship, unless it was raining. With the building in need of repair following the fire, the first suggestions were made at a General Vestry Meeting that the chapel should be properly rebuilt as the building was not handsome enough for the town. This proposal was withdrawn as there was insufficient enthusiasm for such an expenditure, but the idea lingered on.[84] In the end, the chapel was restored more modestly, and with a few enhancements to improve the lighting. In addition, of course, a new organ had to be built by Henry Willis. The restored building opened again in September 1868.[85]

The vestry felt bold enough in 1874 to have plans drawn up for a new gothic church in the finest perpendicular style of the later nineteenth century. The chosen architect, G.E. Grayson, had made a name for himself in the north west, and at the time was overseeing the building of All Hallows, Allerton, in the growing southern suburbs of the town. The desire for a new church was not entirely surprising as the existing building could hardly claim to be medieval, and yet its most recent iteration resulting from the rebuilding of 1775, lacked the architectural integrity of a wholly Georgian building. The churches which had been thrown up around the parish in the previous century were neo-classical (such as St Bride's or St Paul's), a Georgian blend of classical and gothic (such as St George's or St Thomas'), or just a modified gothic (such as St Luke's). In addition, the leading lights of gothic revival were creating shrines on the outskirts of the town which made the parochial chapel look undistinguished: G.E. Street's Church of St Margaret of Antioch was finished in 1869, and Bodley's design of St John the Baptist, Tuebrook, was completed in 1870. Grayson's design was slightly pedestrian, though more derivative of the Ecclesiological school than many of his other works, perhaps partly to complement Harrison's tower of 1815, which was retained in the plans. Alongside the church plans were designs for internal fittings, ornaments, and church plate.[86] Whether for money or taste, the designs were never built, and the hotchpotch of styles and history remained in place. Grayson made his impact on the site, though, and in 1878 Mersey Chambers was finished, to his design, overlooking the churchyard. Meanwhile, as in previous centuries, the existing building was merely updated, this time by the addition of a hot water pipe heating system in 1876.[87]

St Nicholas' combined the ministry of Civic Services, Lent Addresses, and oversight of city institutions with the everyday life of an ordinary parish church. The register of services shows the collections going to a mixture of local and national causes, many of which were religious in nature. For example, collections in May 1880 either went to the poor, or to the The Society for the Propagation of the Gospel in Foreign Parts (SPG). In other years charities included the Mission to Seamen, or the Ladies' Parochial Bible Mission. Music flourished, and a careful register of music was kept for many decades. The Willis organ was upgraded in 1909 with the installation of an electric motor in the room under the

PARISH
OF
LIVERPOOL.

NOTICE IS HEREBY GIVEN

That the ANNUAL GENERAL VESTRY will be held in Saint Nicholas' Church in this Parish, on Easter Tuesday, the Twenty-ninth day of March instant, at Twelve o'clock at Noon, to receive Summaries of the Churchwardens' Accounts for the past year ; to elect Churchwardens and Sidesmen of the Parish ; to receive a Statement of Expenses incurred by the Overseers of the Parish in making out a Valuation List under the Provisions of the Union Assessment Committee Act of 1862, and to authorise the charging of such expenses upon the Poor Rate ; to make a voluntary Church Rate for the ensuing year, and to determine as to its application ; and to receive certain Statements and Accounts made in pursuance of " The Charitable Trusts Act, 1853," and " The Charitable Trusts Amendment Act, 1855," with reference to the Parochial Charities.

Dated this Nineteenth day of March, 1910.

JOHN A. KEMPTHORNE, Rector } of the
HENRY STOKES } Churchwardens Parish of
E. J. M. PHILLIPS } Liverpool.

By the twentieth century the Annual Vestry Meeting had no real significance beyond the church, but was still advertised publicly (here in 1910) with enthusiasm.

Poster found in a Vestry Book held at Liverpool City Archives

tower, which necessitated a faculty for the removal of human remains
which seem to have accumulated there over the previous years. As well
as worship, the choir managed an annual outing: for example, in June
1894 they headed for Blackpool to experience the new tower, opened
just one month earlier, and proclaimed in the flier for the outing to
be four times the height of the church tower; in 1892 they headed for
Matlock, and later hung a photograph of the day in the vestry.[88]

St. Nicholas' Parish Church,
LIVERPOOL.

CHOIR EXCURSION
TO
BLACKPOOL,
ON WEDNESDAY, JUNE 13th, 1894.

This delightful sea-side resort is now attracting considerable
notice, in consequence of the erection of a remarkable structure
resembling the world-famed Eiffel Tower of Paris.   It is 500 feet
high—that is, more than four times as high as the Tower of
St. Nicholas' Church—and the ascent is made by means of powerful
"lifts."   The view from the top, on a clear day, is most extensive.

Should the weather prove unfavourable, there are innumerable
attractions under cover, in the Tower Buildings—there is an
Aquarium, an Aviary, the finest Zoological Collection in the
Provinces, and various musical performances at frequent intervals.

Dinner and Tea will be provided at the Clifton Hotel, on the
Promenade, facing the sea.

Train starts from Exchange Station at 10 o'clock, returning
at 7 p.m.   Saloon carriages have been engaged for the journey.

Any member of the Congregation, or friends of the Choir,
may join the party.

TICKETS { Including Railway Fare, Dinner & Tea, Admittance to the Tower Buildings, and Ascent of the Tower, } **10/-** EACH.

No Tickets will be sold after Tuesday the 12th, **noon.**

Apply to the Clerk, at the Vestry of the Church ; to members
of the Choir, or to

HENRY PEET,
CHURCHWARDEN.

97, MOUNT PLEASANT.

Victorian affluence
and mobility led
to outings, such as
this choir trip to
Blackpool in 1894.
OLSN Archives

CHAPTER EIGHT

The Great War and its Aftermath

The reshaping of the parish for the twentieth century was already underway by the time that war came. The city had continued to grow in population, but also in size, and the dispersal of population in suburbs and other centres of population resulted in a shrinkage of city centre residence. The work of the Liverpool and Wigan Churches Act 1904 was slow, as it depended on the resignation or death of incumbents of the affected churches before closures could take place. For example, the Revd C. A. Carter was in post at St Titus' at the time of the Act, but it was only on his resignation in 1918 that the church could be closed and its part of the parish of Liverpool was reallocated to St Martin-in-the-Fields, whilst its schools went to St Alban's, Bevington Bush.[1] All denominations were affected by the changes, and although the limited number of Catholic and non-conformist churches in the centre remained without significant change, there was a commensurate growth elsewhere.

Even as the number of churches diminished, the role of Rector of Liverpool was becoming recognised nationally as one of significance. In 1910 John Kempthorne was the first of six twentieth century rectors to be made bishops. He was appointed straight from Liverpool to the suffragan see of Hull, before being translated to the Diocese of Lichfield. His successor, Harold Bilbrough, moved during the war to be Bishop of Dover, before becoming Bishop of Newcastle. Meanwhile, with the building of a new cathedral underway – the Lady Chapel was begun in 1910 – it was time for the Parish Church of St Peter to go out of service. There was no significant congregation remaining: the life of a cathedral church was such that the congregation moved either to St Nicholas', or to worship in the building which was appearing at St James' Mount. This was all envisaged under the Liverpool Cathedral Act of 1902, and with the final closure of St Peter's, St Nicholas' once again became the principal church of the city, and for the first time its parish church. This was formalised by an order in council on 29 February 1916.[2] As the Parish Church of Liverpool, Our Lady and St Nicholas occupied a *primus inter pares* place amongst the other churches of the city and Diocese.

PARISH CHURCH, ST. NICHOLAS, LIVERPOOL

In 1916 the Church of Our Lady and St Nicholas once again became the Parish Church of Liverpool. *OLSN Archives*

The Great War

The beginning of the war initially made little impact on the life of the church, except for the reference in the Register of Services at St Nicholas' to a Day of National Intercession on Sunday 21 August 1914. However, St Nicholas' quickly found its role within the city as a place of memorial and remembrance for members of the city community. The first such event was a memorial service on 21 October 1914 for Captain Ambrose Grayson who was killed in action in France. Grayson had been a regular officer in the Royal Field Artillery before joining his family's ship-breaking company in Birkenhead. When war broke out, he rejoined his old regiment before going on active service. His memorial service was conducted by the rector, and attracted members of the business community.[3]

The war presented practical issues, such as when the organist of one church to the north of the city lost its organist to war service. The advertisement for a temporary replacement specified that the candidate must be "experience and ineligible for military service."[4] Those taken from the parish kept in touch: one member of the choir from St Nicholas' wrote to Charles Bridson, the organist at the parish church, from the front: "I managed to attend a Communion Service on Easter Sunday. Such a novel one. It was held in a wood and the men stood round. The altar consisted of a corned beef box and a biscuit tin box. Heavy firing was in progress on both sides; the heavy guns making a continuous roar. While receiving communion a Fritz plane flew over, and we had an anxious moment. Still I enjoyed the service immensely, and I have not had an opportunity since then."[5]

The practical need for supplementary liturgies and prayers was provided nationally by the Church of England, and copies were supplied for churches (those in St Peter's and St Nicholas' survive). In addition, there was the frequent congregation singing of the 'War Litany'. Other national initiatives filtered into Liverpool life, such as the "Special War Intercession" on 4 August 1915, and on 2 January 1916 there was a Solemn Day of Penitence and Prayer at which a pastoral letter from the bishop was read in place of a sermon.[6] Gradually church life adapted to the new needs, such as taking regular collections for the Red Cross, beginning on 31 December 1916.

As the new parish church, St Nicholas' had an increasingly civic role to play. One 14 June 1916 there was a memorial service led by the Bishop of Liverpool for those who died in action in the Battle of Jutland on 31 May.[7] On 23 July there was a Civic Guard present as the rector preached on "Our Part in the War", and a month later, on 24 August, the bishop preached at a memorial service for "the Officers, NCOs and Men of City Battalions" (i.e. the King's Liverpool Regiment). Reflecting the mood of the nation, in April 1917 there was a service to commemorate the USA joining the Allies at which the rector officiated and the bishop again preached. And just as the first memorial service of the war, for Capt Grayson, was particularly directed at the business community, so the last memorial service before the Armistice was for members of the British American Tobacco Company, which was based in Kirkdale.

Throughout the Great War there was also an attempt to maintain the normal pattern of events. An annual fixture at St Nicholas' was the 'Liverpool Diocesan Lectures' which were often part of services led by the bishop or archdeacons. The first reference is to a lecture on 19 June 1916 by Canon Scott Holland, the Regius Professor of Divinity at Oxford, with the title "The Real Problem of Eschatology." However, later in the war a more accessible and pertinent lecture was given on 9 June 1918 by E.W. Barnes, the liberal theologian who later became Bishop of Birmingham, on the subject of spiritualism.[8] This, at least, was 'of the moment', as a wave of interest in spiritualism struck a nation which was grappling with collective grief. The Lent Lectures had by now become part of the life of the city, and a pamphlet was printed every year and distributed across the business community. The introduction to the pamphlet in 1915 began: "The Rector sends this list to the business men of Liverpool in the hope that the Services set forth in its may be of some to them. It is under strange conditions that Lent begins this year, unlike anything known in previous years." The main series always took place at St Nicholas', but a token selection of talks from the rector were delivered at St Peter's. The Lectures remained, until the beginning of the twenty-first century, predominantly ecclesiastical in their tone, but the flavour of the moment was still captured. In 1915 the Bishop of Lichfield spoke in the first week of Lent on "Some directions of National thought and purpose"; in the second week the rector, Harold Bilbrough, spoke on the subject of "The Christian Soldier". Over the course of three days his topics were 'His Enlistment', 'His Uniform', 'His Equipment'. By 1917 there were still services listed for St Peter's, but talks were restricted to short addresses by the rector as a part of acts of worship. Meanwhile, St Nicholas' Lectures were beginning to attract ecclesiastical luminaries: in that year Charles Gore, the Bishop of Oxford, spoke on Ash Wednesday and the following two days; Canon Henry Scott Holland returned later in Lent, and S.C. Carpenter, a well-known churchman who became Dean of Exeter, came for Holy Week.

Two Memorial Services: Lord Kitchener of Khartoum and Noel Chavasse VC and Bar

As a city which flourished through Empire, Liverpool was ready to recognise the heroes of the age. Herbert Kitchener, later Earl Kitchener of Khartoum, had made his name as a soldier in the Boer War and had gone on to command the British Army in India. With no particular connection to Liverpool, Kitchener had been made a Freeman of the City in 1902, reflecting his status as a national hero. When the Great War came, Kitchener was not only brought into Asquith's Cabinet as Secretary of State for War, but he also became the public face of the war, with his distinctive moustache twitching out of recruitment posters. Kitchener died on the evening of 5 June 1916 on board HMS *Hampshire en route* to a mission to Russia to bolster the eastern front. His ship struck a mine and sank swiftly just off the Orkney Islands.

Kitchener's death had a profound effect on the nation, and in Liverpool the bishop and the rector swiftly organised a memorial service to which the Lord Mayor and the leaders of the council led the civic leaders on the afternoon of 7 June 1916. Before the procession

The civic and military procession into the parish church for the memorial service to Earl Kitchener of Khartoum, 7 June 1916.
Copyright Liverpool Echo

Captain Noel Chavasse,
VC and bar. Chavasse
was the son of the Bishop
of Liverpool, and his
memorial service took place
at Liverpool Parish Church
in August 1917.
*Liverpool Scottish Regimental
Museum Trust, now in the
collection of National Museums
Merseyside*

began, the Lord Mayor said in the council chamber, "The Empire has lost a great man, the Army has lost its vitalising head, and the people have lost their national hero." The procession itself was an impressive affair: it was headed by two mounted police officers, followed by the state carriage drawn by four horses and containing the Lady Mayoress attended by two footmen. Behind came the Lord Mayor on foot, with other leading councillors, followed by members of the consular corps. It was reported that the procession took the whole length of Water Street. When the carriage reached the Dock Road the procession filed up through the gardens and in through the south door into a church which was already full. The Town Hall had even managed to find a distant relative of Kitchener who lived in Liverpool to represent the family.[9]

With more immediate connections to Liverpool, the memorial service for Noel Chavasse, the son of the Bishop of Liverpool, was a more emotionally-charged event. Born in Oxford in 1884, Noel Chavasse moved to the Bishop's Palace in Abercromby Square in 1900 when his father was installed as Bishop in St Peter's Church on 31 May. He completed his education at Liverpool College before going up to Oxford to read medicine. His training as a doctor was punctuated by representing Great Britain in the 400 metres at the Olympic Games of 1908, but after qualifying in 1912 he worked in Liverpool, signing up in 1913 as a member of the Royal Army Medical Corps attached to the 10th Battalion of the King's (Liverpool Regiment), the Liverpool Scottish.

Chavasse was held in very high regard by all those who served with him: it was not just that he was skilled and experienced, but also took tremendous care of those around him. The letters he wrote to the families of the dead and wounded were not short and perfunctory, but showed great compassion. He wrote to the mother of a stretcher bearer: "I am afraid that the wound is a serious one and it will keep it lying up for a long while. You will no doubt hear from the hospital telling you more about it. I shall make enquiries myself and will try and keep you posted." but the letter went on for another 400 words, describing what had happened.[10]

Before the actions which led to Noel's Victoria Cross decorations, he had been awarded the Military Cross. Following his actions tending to the wounded on 9 August 1916 at Guillemont he was awarded the Victoria Cross. Remarkably, the following year he was awarded a second. The Battle of Passchendaele, also known as the Third Battle of Ypres, was one of the most intense offensives on the Western Front. It started on 31 July 1917 and over the succeeding months each side lost over a quarter of a million men. Noel's second Victoria Cross was won over the first three days of action.

A memorial service for Noel was quickly suggested, but the service which took place on 29 August was for all the dead from the Liverpool Scottish. In August 1917 alone, about 250 men had been killed or wounded or were missing in action. It was titled 'A solemn memorial service in remembrance of the officers and men of the Liverpool Scottish Regiment who have laid down their lives for King, Country and Righteousness.' No one was under any illusion, though, that this service was primarily about Noel, and in fact the *Liverpool Echo* advertised it as the "Captain Chavasse Service".[11] Bishop Chavasse had hoped to hold the service in the Lady Chapel of the cathedral – the only part of the building which was complete – but it did not have the capacity for the crowds expected. The Parish Church of Liverpool

In Memoriam.

The Church of St. Nicholas, Liverpool.

Solemn Memorial Service,

in remembrance of the

OFFICERS AND MEN

of the

LIVERPOOL SCOTTISH REGIMENT

who have laid down their lives for

King, Country and Righteousness,

WEDNESDAY, 29th AUGUST, 1917, at THREE p.m.

Voluntary offerings in aid of the Cathedral Memorial to Officers
and Men of the Army and Navy who have fallen in the Service
of their Country.

The war brought many memorial services to the parish church. Although this service was for the officers and men of the Liverpool Scottish Regiment, the focus of the service was Captain Noel Chavasse. *Liverpool Scottish Regimental Museum Trust*

was the obvious location. The Archdeacon of Liverpool officiated at the service, and the preacher was Canon Lancelot, who had been Headmaster to the Chavasse boys when they were at Liverpool College. The hymns, though, were the choice of Noel himself. Canon Lancelot told the congregation in a packed church:

> *It is no wonder that the King felt that the whole army would mourn the loss of so brave and distinguished a brother, or that his brigadier declared him to have been the most gallant and modest*

*man he had ever met, or that the major-general commanding his
division should say that his devotion was magnificent, or that the
whole battalion smothered in mud as they were and ready to drop
from exhaustion, insisted on parading for his funeral… See what
the Christian faith can do for a man. He might have been a great
surgeon, he might have been a really great clergyman and medical
missionary, such was the vision that floated before his mind from
boyhood; but he was already a great Christian.*[12]

Armistice

After four years of war, the Armistice was greeted with both relief and
celebration, and the parish church marked it in both civic ceremony
and parish religion. There was sufficient warning for a Civic Service of

The Lord Mayor and other dignitaries processing into St Nicholas' for the Civic Armistice
Service on 12 November 1918.
OLSN Archives

Thanksgiving to be planned, and on Tuesday 12 November 1918 the Lord Mayor and council assembled at the Town Hall at 11.45am and processed down Water Street and along the Strand to the parish church. The service itself, taken by the rector, Guy Hockley, was largely spoken, but with a sung setting of Psalm 150, and the hymns *All People that on Earth do Dwell, O God, our Help in Ages Past*, and *Now thank we all our God*. The bishop preached a sermon which reviewed the previous four and a half years of war, whilst also reminding the congregation of the need for forgiveness. As soon as the service was over, the procession formed up again and moved up Chapel Street to the Exchange Newsroom where another, shorter, service took place.[13] Although the church could only accommodate 1,300 people, it was estimated that 2,000 people were present.[14] Earlier that day, there was a sung service of Holy Communion at 10am, advertised in the press and presumably aimed at the city communities, though the main parish acts of thanksgiving and celebration were the following Sunday. The rector officiated at all service, and at Evensong the by now familiar War Litany was dropped in favour of a *Te Deum*, three verses of *God Save the King*, and a procession, before the Hallelujah Chorus was played as an organ voluntary.[15]

The role of the church in the memorialisation of the war had already begun. In 1917 a 'War Shrine' was dedicated outside St Peter's Church with a copy of the painting 'The Great Sacrifice' and a roll of those from the parish who had lost their lives.[16] Immediately after the war, an annual civic Armistice service started, and even after the erection of a cenotaph at St George's Plateau this continued to take place at the parish church every year, attended by the Lord Mayor and other dignitaries. Wreaths, though, were laid at St George's Hall[17] The addition of a Hall of Memory at the Town Hall, opened by the Prince of Wales in July 1923, gave an additional focus for remembrance. Names associated with the Great War continued to call and lay wreaths, including Lady Haig (widow of General Haig) in 1929 and Admiral Jellico in 1930. In 1932 it was decided to begin an annual 'Garden of Remembrance' in the churchyard on Armistice Day, just two years after the British Legion's 'Field of Remembrance' first started outside Westminster Abbey.[18] Other regimental services continued to take place, just as they had done during the war. The Liverpool 'Pals' (King's Regiment) had a service in August 1916 whilst the Battle of the Somme was underway. Immediately after the war they were deployed to the conflict in Russia, from which they returned in September 1919: on 7 December they had a regimental memorial service at St Nicholas'.

The continuing need for memorials persisted. Ten years later the same arrangements were taking place, with the Lord Mayor and council members attending a special Armistice Day service at the parish church, in addition to events at civic buildings.[19] However, it was also felt that a permanent war memorial was needed within the church itself, and from a variety of option it was decided that a war memorial chapel should be created in the south east corner of the church, using pilasters from the now-demolished St Peter's to create a screen to separate it from the main body of the church. The High Altar, which was a small Chippendale table, would have its larger false top removed and it would become the altar in the chapel, and a new High Altar would be given to the church, which would cover the entire width of the east window. At a time in church life when there was a conscious Catholicisation of ritual and practice at the parish church, including sending delegates throughout the 1920s to the Anglo-Catholic Congresses in London, the provision of a new large altar was a useful by-product. The faculty was granted in October 1930, and work began immediately.[20]

The Lent Addresses, started in 1884, continued every year throughout the war. In 1915 the first week was given by Kempthorne, formerly Rector of Liverpool but now Bishop of Lichfield.
OLSN Archives

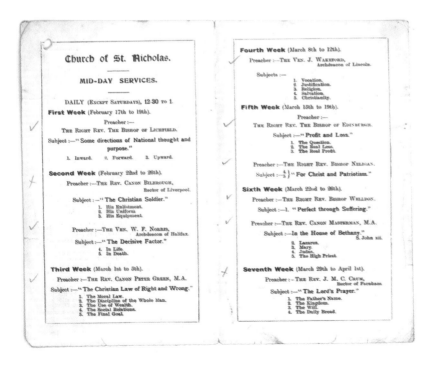

Parish Life

The Parish Church of the city continued to be well-used by the civic community, but was increasingly ecclesiastical in its interests, particularly because the clergy were often known across the Church of England. So, for example, the list of services in October 1922 included the Lord Mayor's Civic Service, and then within a few days an anniversary service and meeting of the English Church Union; later in the month there was an address and collection on behalf of the Universities' Mission to Central Africa. In the same month, Canon V.S.S. Coles, now a friend of the parish for some decades but also now a noted hymn writer, published his Patronal Hymn for the Parish,[21] which included the bespoke verse:

> *Here the shrine in which they worshipped,*
> *Here the Chapel by the sea;*
> *Nicholas, their chosen patron,*
> *With Our Lady of the Quay,*
> *He, and Mary at his side,*
> *Magnifying, magnified.*

Alongside the continuing contribution to the life of the city, St Nicholas' began to adapt to the expectations of a parish church with many of the attributes which would be found in the suburbs. The building lacked versatility for parish activities, and so 87 Tithe Barn

A notice
from
the Lent
Addresses
between the
wars.
OLSN
Archives

The interior of Our Lady and
St Nicholas at the beginning
of the century.
OLSN Archives

Street was rented as a 'parochial institute'. The St Nicholas' Institute
became, in effect, the church hall, with activities taking place mainly
in the large recreation room. It was here that young people's groups
met, including a "Girls' Club" which continued to meet throughout
the war. A skirmish with the owners meant that it was almost lost: in
1920 it was proposed to increase the rent by 25 per cent, and when
the church balked at this amount a notice to quit was duly issued on 4
March. Within days the church offered to buy the property for £2000,
short of the £2250 which was being asked. Guy Hockley, the rector,
wrote a long letter, listing the activities taking place in the institute:
"The numerous clubs and classes, and other organisations for men
and women, for lads, for girls, and children, need these rooms every
day of the week." He offered £2150, which was accepted. The money
was hastily pulled together, and scribbled notes of donations received

show the support of anonymous donors, as well as prominent names from the city, and institutions such as the corn and cotton markets. The building was indeed well used, and illustrates the residential nature of the city centre at this time. Every day there was a two hour slot labelled "Dinner Hour Girls", but throughout the day there were Girls' Clubs and Boys' Clubs, as well as Mothers' Meetings and District Visitors' Meetings, and something intriguingly called the "Junior King's Messengers' Club."[22] By 1934 the parish also investigated obtaining a 'Dancing and Music Licence' for the institute.[23]

Although the plans to rebuild St Nicholas' in 1874 had not come to fruition, the shortcomings of the building became increasingly evident as the church attempted to fulfil its civic role while also competing for

The interior of Our Lady and St Nicholas at the beginning of the century.
OLSN Archives

attention with the cathedral. In 1924 plans to extend the church were drawn up by the London church architect J. Harold Gibbons, who was at the beginning of some of his major church commissions. His plan was to extend to the east and create an apsidal sanctuary with an adjacent chapel to the south. The main entrance to the church, reached through sweeping steps from the Strand, would be through the tower. Filling the site to the north against the churchyard walls would be meeting rooms, lavatories and vestries. Inside, Gibbons enlisted the help of Giles Gilbert Scott, the architect of the new cathedral, whose plans show not only elaborate woodwork, but an ostensibly Catholic arrangement, with an altar and reredos behind a rood screen with carved crucifix and saints.[24] For whatever reason, these plans were never realised, but a more modest extension was built instead, using only the plans for vestries and rooms on the north side of the church, which later survived the bombings of 1940/1. The main body of the church had survived for centuries by being rebuilt or restored, and this continued: in 1931 the iconic weather vane had to be taken off the tower for safety reasons. It was restored and reguilded, and the rector made a public appeal for £500 to fund it.[25]

Guy Hockley was a popular rector and the last to have known W.E. Gladstone personally, from when he was curate of Hawarden in 1893. When he moved in 1925 to be Archdeacon of Cornwall the search for a new rector was undertaken by the patron, Albert Gladstone, the grandson of the Prime Minister. In September 1925 he approached John How, the Diocesan Missioner in Manchester. How refused, and the offer was eventually made to the Revd C.P.S. Clarke from St Andrew's, Shaftesbury. Clarke wrote enthusiastically to the parish community in December 1925 looking forward to his arrival, before withdrawing on health grounds just a few weeks later.[26] Gladstone returned to John How in January 1926. How's bishop, William Temple, knew Liverpool parish already, having first delivered Lent Talks in March 1919 on the subject of 'Religion and Reason'. Temple encouraged How to accept the post, writing that the Rectory of Liverpool "could only be put aside with the very greatest hesitation."[27] Other friends knew the parish as well: John How had been part of a nascent religious order in Cambridge at the beginning of the century with Spencer Carpenter, who had given Lent Addresses in 1917.[28] How was instituted as rector in May 1926.

A snapshot of Liverpool parish at this time was given by Michael Ramsey, later Archbishop of Canterbury, who was ordained into a curacy in the parish in 1928. A handwritten note on Ramsey's licence stipulated that he had to live within one mile of the parish church, but

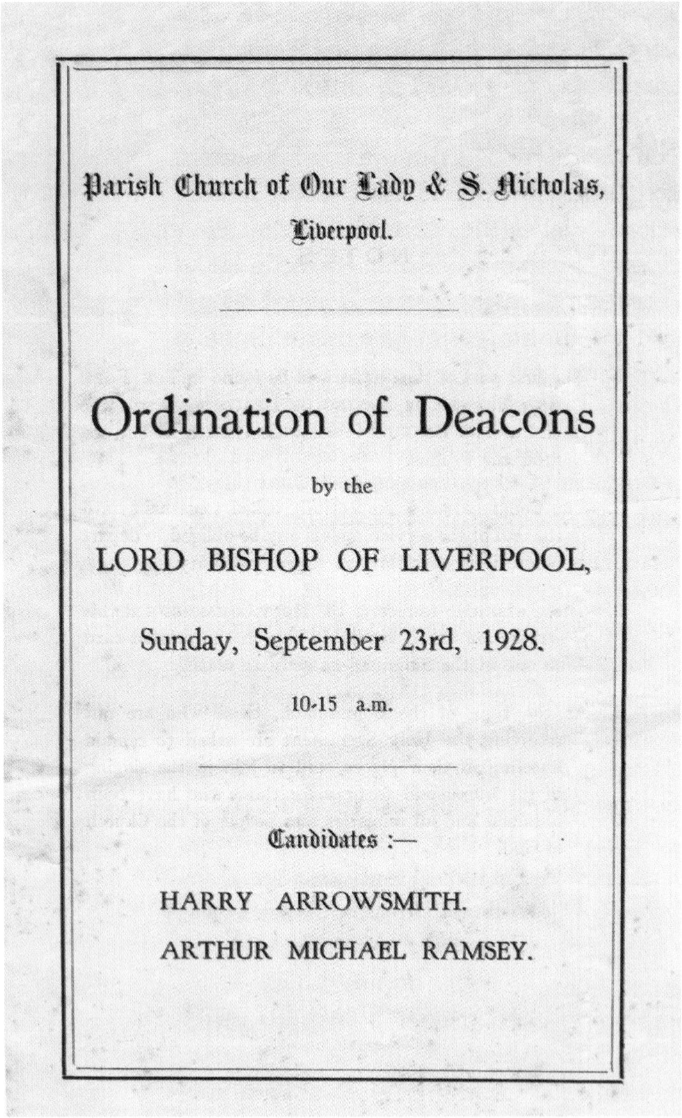

𝔓arish 𝔆hurch of 𝔒ur 𝔏ady & 𝔖. 𝔑icholas,
𝔏iverpool.

Ordination of Deacons

by the

LORD BISHOP OF LIVERPOOL,

Sunday, September 23rd, 1928.

10-15 a.m.

𝔆andidates :—

HARRY   ARROWSMITH.

ARTHUR   MICHAEL   RAMSEY.

1928 Order of Service
for the Ordination
of Michael Ramsey,
later Archbishop of
Canterbury.
OLSN Archives

in fact he was unable to find anywhere closer than St James' Road, close to the new cathedral. It seems to have been an unsatisfactory lodging house, from which he eventually moved after a political disagreement with his landlady. The parish, Ramsey recalled, had only about 7000 residents, over half of which were Roman Catholic. They were predominantly working class, and mainly either dockers or caretakers. The Sunday congregation at the parish church was a mixture of these people, together with those who came in from elsewhere. The ministry was with residents, but also a broader ministry to the whole city. Ramsey was deployed to teach Bible classes, school classes, prepare people for confirmation, and visit the sick. However, there was a pervading sense of decline as well, whilst the new cathedral began to flourish. The Dean, Frederick Dwelly, and Canon Charles Raven were gifted preachers and teachers, and they proved a draw for many. Attendance at St Nicholas' was a concern throughout the 1920s, with frequent admonitions to the congregation in the parish magazine for not attending church more regularly. The relationship between parish and cathedral was not acrimonious, though. Not only was How a residentiary canon of the cathedral, but Ramsey invited Raven to preach at his ordination. John How was enthusiastic in his work, and in his nine years as rector of the parish he preached and taught and also organised a 'mission' to the city, with clergy and lay-workers working across the city for a fortnight in February 1935. This was planned as a sequel to the diocesan 'Merseyside Church Crusade' of 1933.[29]

Curate's Licence for Michael Ramsey.
OLSN Archives

Priory of the Society of the Sacred Mission

John How also developed the staffing of the parish which was now much reduced from previous years. The closure of several churches within the parish, albeit in response to changing demographics, led to a lessening of permanent clergy. How's response was to invite the Society of the Sacred Mission (an Anglican religious order founded in 1893, whose mother house was in Kelham) to found its second Priory House (the first was in Nottingham) in the parish of Liverpool.

How was very familiar with religious orders of priests: along with Edward Wynn, Eric Milner-White (later Dean of King's and instigator of the famous Carol Service), John How had founded the Oratory of the Good Shepherd in Cambridge in 1910. How had been the *de facto* leader of the order, which was later formalised when in 1919 they all made their full profession as members of the oratory and then in 1920 a permanent oratory house was established in Cambridge.[30]

Although How left the Oratory of the Good Shepherd in 1924, partly because of his call to the Diocese of Manchester by Temple, and partly because of his wish to get married,[31] he was experienced in the value of a college of priests living together. A Priory House at 5 Canning Place was bought by the parish in 1932 (by cashing its War Loan stock) and was established with the agreement of the Bishop of Liverpool, who wished to encourage clergy colleges within the diocese. In return for the accommodation, the society promised to provide two clergy for the benefit of the parish of Liverpool,[32] which also made an annual cash contribution towards this ministry. Although the house had its own chapel, the clergy remained linked to the parish church for the next decade. The prior, Fr Basil Oddie SSM was immediately licensed to the parish and became a member of the church council, but he also played a role in the diocese for many years, including becoming an Examining Chaplain to the Bishop of Liverpool in 1940.[33] The Priory House supplied curates to the parish church and to other churches immediately: amongst those ordained deacon in Michaelmas 1932 were the Revd L. Paul Hume SSM who served as curate at St Nicholas', and the Revd S.D. Short, who went to St Dunstan's, Earle Road. Within a few years others followed, such as the Revd Lewes Ward-Andrews SSM, who became curate of St Nicholas' in 1936.

The house itself was the financial responsibility of the parish, which over the next decade continued to debate the growing sums required to keep it in good repair, and occasionally looking for external sources of money to manage it. The house was not, though, appreciated by its residents, who described it as "that incredibly dreadful house, dark and rat-ridden, down in the docks of Liverpool."[34] Each priory house had its own rules, and the community of brethren had a common life alongside that which they led in their parishes.

The presence of clergy from Kelham was fortuitous in the growth of the Parish Eucharist (communion) at 10am. The Parish Communion movement had gained pace in the Church of England in the first half of the century, encouraging worshippers to attend communion services weekly, rather than in the more occasional manner which, even if not intended by the Book of Common Prayer, had become usual. Liverpool Parish Church, which had long been associated with the High Church wing, had been an early-adopter of the practice. The music registers indicate that from the beginning of the century Mattins had often taken second place to the Eucharist at 10am. The Parish Communion movement was championed by the Kelham community: it received its theological imprimatur from the publication of *Liturgy and Society* by Fr Gabriel Hebert SSM in 1935, followed by his edited collection of essays *The Parish Communion* in 1937. Liverpool Parish Church, as the host of the second priory, was at the forefront of this movement, and in 1934 the rector reported to the Annual Meeting that although the evening congregation had dwindled to its lowest ever level, the figures for both congregation numbers and collections at 10am were the most encouraging.[35] In the following year, the church council communicated to the patron that when a new rector was appointed he should follow the liturgy of the Book of Common Prayer with the various deviations which were allowed, that there should continue to be a daily celebration of Holy Communion, and that the Sung Eucharist on Sundays was a long-standing tradition, with vestments and the occasional use of incense.[36] The championing of the Parish Communion movement continued beyond John How's incumbency: in 1946 Fr Hebert SSM came to St Nicholas' and preached at a Saturday Evensong, before giving an address on the "Parish Communion" on the Sunday morning.[37]

David Railton

When Canon John How resigned in 1935 to become Vicar of Brighton (he later moved to become Bishop of Glasgow and Galloway) there was some difficulty in replacing him as rector: the church council was adamant that it should be given to someone from outside the diocese, but the post was subsequently offered to at least two people, who turned it down.[38] It was eventually given to the Revd David Railton, who had been Vicar of Shalford in Surrey since 1931. Railton was no anonymous country priest, but already familiar with Liverpool, and a known name in the country at large. He had been ordained in Liverpool in 1908 and he served as curate of St Dunstan's in Earle Road. In the 1930s he was developing his links with the Revd P.B. (Tubby) Clayton who had founded the Toc H network of rest houses for soldiers, and he visited Toc H in Liverpool, which was based in Gladstone House in Rodney Street. More significantly, Railton was famous as the man who initiated the Tomb of the Unknown Warrior in Westminster Abbey, and whose Union Flag was supposedly draped over the coffin as it was brought from the Western Front to Westminster Abbey. It was not an easy time to come to Liverpool city centre, as the trajectory of depopulation in favour of commerce which had begun in the previous century had progressed further.[39]

When Railton left Liverpool in 1942 he was described as "a popular figure in the city and diocese"[40] but he could be a difficult man who was in frequent conflict with his congregation. In his first few months he faced arguments within the church over both liturgy and music, and motions in the church council against the direction in which he was taking the church, followed by the resignation of the treasurer who subsequently left the church. Disagreement continued throughout Railton's time: in 1939 Mrs Railton (in her husband's absence from the meeting) tried to reclaim from the church council the costs which they had borne in providing advertisements for boards erected in the churchyard over the previous three years. Although the council eventually agreed to pay the Railtons the £19 they had spent, it was only after a vote of ten in favour, and five against.[41] The electoral roll of the church, which had grown under Canon How, also began to decline. More significantly, since the war the parish church had exercised a negligible role in the institutions of the city. With the demise of Select Vestries under the Local Government Act of 1894, the place of the rector and churchwardens was almost entirely within an ecclesiastical context. Unless the rector came with personal gifts which enabled him to exercise authority in the city, the city itself would make few demands on his time. The more outward-facing activities which took place in St Nicholas' Institute were no different in character from those found in any suburban church. That is not to say that Liverpool Parish Church was either introverted or ignored by the city, and the Rector of Liverpool continued to be a person of consequence. After

Mussolini's invasion of Abyssinia, the newspapers reported Railton's impassioned denunciation from the pulpit, stating that Christ's truth condemned the Italians who had broken their word to the international community: "Your word is a lie."[42]

However Railton handled the relationships which he inherited within Church life and within the City, he was sometimes also the victim of circumstances. Walton Park Cemetery continued to be a source of anxiety to the parish, and by the 1930s it was running at a loss and a drain on resources. When in 1939 the city corporation wanted to widen Hornby Road in Walton it negotiated the sale of a piece of the cemetery for £2,500 which Railton was content for the church council to use for the maintenance of the cemetery. A Consistory Court, in approving the sale, noted that the cemetery was part of the benefice, and therefore within the freehold of the rector, and any money resulting from the sale must be added to the endowment for the income of the rector. Although Railton arranged to pay the income on the money to the church council for cemetery maintenance, future rectors were not obliged to do so.[43]

Church Closures

The vast structure which had been the parish of Liverpool had, by 1914, largely been dismantled. Some of the former district churches, such as St Luke's and St Bride's, survived as separate parishes, but others which had achieved parochial status were beginning to disappear. Christ Church, Hunter Street managed only sixteen years as a parish in its own right before it closed in 1920.

The closure of the old Parish Church of St Peter should have been a momentous event, but in fact it slid out of existence almost unnoticed. The parish planned to keep some presence in the area with the opening of 'St Peter's Rooms' in College Lane which were opened on 3 April 1916.[44] The Register of Services show that worship continued regularly, even after St Nicholas' had become the parish church in 1916, but although precise attendance was not recorded, communicant numbers and collections were low.[45] The final service took place on 31 August 1919, and the church was then closed. Although the fittings were removed shortly afterwards, demolition did not take place until 1922. Between 1704 and 1853, 43,847 were buried in the churchyard: human remains which had not already been relocated to Anfield Cemetery in 1868 were now moved to Walton Park Cemetery.[46] The fittings within the church were relocated to other churches across the region where some of them can still be seen. For example, the wooden panelling in the sanctuary of St Cuthbert's, Southport, or the organ in St Bede's, Toxteth. An oak altar (communion table) was moved temporarily to a chapel within St Peter's Rooms.[47] It seems unlikely that this is now the same altar today in St Peter's Chapel, as a church guide from the early 1930s suggests that the surviving altar had been the High Altar of Our Lady and St Nicholas until it was moved to a side chapel in 1931.[48]

Most of the furniture moved to the parish church was destroyed in the Blitz. Symptomatic of the growth of retail in the city centre, the site was sold to Woolworth's, and the proceeds went towards the building of the cathedral.[49]

The separation of church and corporation under the Liverpool City Churches Act 1897 had been thorough. The previous obligation for maintenance of the corporation churches passed from the Corporation of Liverpool to the Ecclesiastical Commissioners; similarly, those churches which were previously maintained by the churchwardens were also now subject to the commissioners who had established a Building and Endowment Fund for Liverpool. As churches within the city were closed, the proceeds were directed into the fund so that new churches could be built and endowed as the metropolitan area increased. By the Liverpool City Churches Act 1897 (Amendment) Measure 1938 a final step was taken which allowed the fund to be used for building churches outside of the boundary of the city of Liverpool, where the displaced urban populations were now settling.[50] The city had ceded final control of and responsibility for its parish some four decades earlier, but on the eve of the Second World War the church claimed its right to plan ministry in the area and deploy buildings and resources as it saw fit.

CHAPTER NINE

The Blitz and Rebuilding

As war came again, David Railton's fame from the Great War meant that he was bound to look for activity in the war effort. The family spent the summer of 1939 in Scotland, but Railton returned to Liverpool swiftly. Mrs Railton did not feel able to return and remained in Scotland for the duration of the war. Railton wrote at once to the War Office offering his services as an Army chaplain, but a letter of 12 September 1939 rejected his application on grounds of age (he was 55).[1] There was much to do in Liverpool: when the last of the curates from the Society of the Sacred Mission left in October 1940 it was noted that they had regularly visited the children of the parish after they had been evacuated to Chester, going to their billets and then reporting back to the children's parents in Liverpool.[2] Church life continued as before, but with minor adjustments for wartime: Evensong, for instance, was brought forward to 3pm because of the blackout.

The Blitz

The Battle of the Atlantic brought Liverpool to the front line of the Second World War. For many months enemy bombing of Liverpool had been intermittent, but on the night of 20 December 1940 fifty bombers raided Liverpool for nine and a half hours. Although newspaper

The Revd David Railton in the bombed church in December 1940.
Courtesy of the Railton Family Archives

reports were limited in the detail they gave about the damage, a significant number of notable buildings were hit: the Town Hall, municipal buildings, the Cunard Building, and also Liverpool Parish Church.[3] It suffered a direct hit from an incendiary bomb. In 1943 the church decided to chronicle the war in a log book, to be kept by parishioner Eileen Vaughan (1905–2006), but with a joint responsibility for providing the material.[4] She recalled in the log: "Four days before Christmas in 1940, we heard that our Church, St Nicholas, at the Pier Head had been damaged, so on the Saturday morning I went through all the glass and rubble to see what had happened. When I got there I saw that it had been hit by incendiaries and was still burning because of the lack of water but the walls and tower were still standing. No one was allowed near the church but outside the gates were the churchwardens and many of us were in tears."[5] In fact there had been frantic activity as the bombs fell to salvage what was possible: Railton was on the scene early as the fire took hold of the nave and, under the spray of two hoses, climbed the gallery and made his way to the sacristy where he rescued the church silver. When the flames had died down Railton went in again and rescued the cross from the High Altar, and the firemen removed the Altar from the Lady Chapel,[6] After the ruins had cooled, Railton went back into the church and formed a cross from the fallen roof beams, which he then placed in the sanctuary, just as the provost of Coventry Cathedral had done about five weeks earlier.

Although the tower was fairly unscathed, and the vestries and rooms from the 1920s' extension were saved, the nave was gutted and the roof had fallen in, leaving the church unfit for use. The following evening a further tragedy took place as the St Nicholas' Institute was bombed. Eileen Vaughan's diary reports: "I made my way on Sunday morning to the church hall in Tithebarn Street, where I thought a service might be held, but when I arrived there, that too had been destroyed on the Saturday night. One of our Curates was there, so the two of us trudged

Looking towards the east end and sanctuary following the bombing in December 1940.
OLSN Archives

sadly to their Priory in Canning Place and had a short Communion Service there." By March 1940 it was agreed that the institute was of no further use and was cleared of all church property.[7]

St Nicholas' was not the only church in Liverpool to be damaged or destroyed. A number of the churches which had once been in the parish, but had since been given parochial status of their own, were hit. Most of these were hit during the aid raids of May 1941. Amongst these churches, St Martin-in-the-Fields was destroyed, as was St Michael's, Pitt Street, St Catherine's, Abercromby Square, St James-the-Less in Stanley Street, and St Luke's in Bold Street. Holy Trinity, St Anne St (by now also a separate benefice, and united with St Mary Magdalene, Kempston St in 1929) was damaged but not beyond repair. It was restored and rededicated in 1950 before its final closure in 1968.[8] St Silas', Pembroke Place, became a parish in its own right (along with St Columba and St Simon) in 1930, but was hit by bombs in 1941 and demolished in 1942.[9] Church House in South John Street, the offices

The same view in September 1941 following the second bombing in the May of that year. *OLSN Archives*

of the Diocese of Liverpool, was also severely damaged that month, although the new cathedral had a lucky escape with only minor damage and the loss of a number of stained glass windows.[10] St Nicholas' Church had a second bombing on 5/6 May 1941 which destroyed much of what remained of the building, leaving just the tower, the walls, and two vestries.

It was not just the Church of England which suffered. Holy Cross Catholic Church, in Great Crosshall St, was an Edward Pugin building opened in 1860 and destroyed in the Blitz. A new church reopened in 1954 and continued until its closure in 2001. The first Catholic church in Liverpool, St Mary's in Edmund Street, had been rebuilt from the Warehouse Chapel into a fine building by A.W. Pugin. This was moved in 1885, brick by brick, to Highfield Street to make way for the railway, but was destroyed in the Blitz. The replacement church was opened in 1953.[11]

The human toll was worse, of course. In Liverpool in May 1941 alone there were 1453 people killed and 1065 seriously injured.[12]

Most of the congregations found somewhere new to worship. St Martin-in-the-Fields transferred its services to St Alban's, Bevington, though this was also damaged by bombing in 1941. Although a temporary church was built, the parish was merged back into Liverpool parish in 1947. In May 1949 the church of St. Martin-in-the-Fields was permanently closed and its parish also merged back into the parish of Liverpool. St Michael's, Pitt Street was destroyed in the same month. St Luke's in Bold Street moved to the British Legion in Leece Street, but the church was never rebuilt. Services at St Nicholas' moved first to St Paul's Chapel in Church House, and then after it was bombed they moved to the Chapel of the Mersey Mission to Seamen in Hanover Street.[13]

Life in the Ruins

David Railton had to manage the salvage and set the course for the continuation of a parish without a church, but he was also looking for more active war-work. Denied a place in the army chaplaincy, he became Padre of Toc H in Liverpool in June 1941[14] and after resigning as Rector of Liverpool in 1942 he was given a role in the RAF. Although he undoubtedly provided leadership and stability after the bombing, his relationship with his parishioners was often still tense. Some of the decisions were easy: for example, the bells were removed to Taylor's of

Loughborough for safe-keeping during the War.[15] Other decisions merely fuelled division: Railton set about disbursing the vestments and other furnishings which had been rescued amongst other churches, but had failed to consult before doing this, saying that he had not thought he needed the consent of others. Railton was instructed to supply a list of these 'loans', with signed receipts, within a week. At the same meeting Railton announced his resignation, which he had already submitted to the bishop.[16] The following day, Ambrose Reeves, the Vicar of St James' Haydock, was introduced to the churchwardens as the next Rector of Liverpool. Railton was diligent in the final demand made of him, and at the Easter Vestry Meeting he produced receipts for the items he had lent, including from HMS *Eaglet* (the receipt survives, as well as a transcription in the Church Council Minutes) who borrowed a selection of altar furniture and linens, as well as cassocks, surplices and ruffles and some flower vases for the use of the Royal Navy in the War.[17]

Ambrose Reeves was inducted as Rector of Liverpool in a marquee set in the ruined church in June 1942, with the ringing of handbells by the bellringers in celebration.[18] Without a functioning building, and with limited other resources, the question of staffing was bound to be raised. The last curates had left just weeks before the first bombing in 1940, and the church council asked Ambrose Reeves at their first meeting with him on 20 March 1942 whether he would ask the Society of the Sacred Mission for assistant clergy. Reeves had anticipated the question and had consulted both Fr Oddie in the priory house and also the bishop. With Fr Oddie he had agreed that the former situation led to divided loyalties for the curates towards parish and their community, which was unsatisfactory. With the Bishop he had agreed that a city centre church was not a suitable training parish for new clergy, but that at a later point the diocese guaranteed to provide assistant clergy if required.[19] This was the end of the priory house as a parish resource: the priory house remained in Liverpool until 1946, where the SSM clergy had continued to minister to students, nuns and hospitals, but their eventual departure was to enable the community to start a new house in Australia.[20] In fact the Revd Leslie Evans was appointed as assistant priest of the parish church almost immediately and began work in September 1942. In 1944 the Revd John Montague arrived in Liverpool as Secretary of the Students' Christian Movement at Liverpool University, and joined the staff of the parish church, and at the same time plans were made that a priest from the Gambia should come to Liverpool in 1945, the beginning of a succession of assistant clergy from West Africa and Burma.[21]

Meanwhile, ministry in the city continued. At his first meeting of the church council, Reeves outlined his vision for the work of Liverpool Parish Church. As well as arranging the service times to suit civic services at 11am, much of the detail was geared towards ministry with children. At following meetings Reeves also addressed the need to build links with the business community as soon as there was a building from which to operate, and in September 1942 permission was given to build a temporary church to seat 200 people within the ruins, but using the space under the tower as a sanctuary. This was blessed on 6 March 1943.[22] The need for a place of worship was paramount. The church's electoral roll stood at 210 at the Annual Meeting in 1940; by 1943 the roll stood at only 58.

As soon as the temporary church was operational, the activity of the church increased. The first significant event was a Service of

Before the first temporary church was built, services resumed under the tower with the congregation standing in the ruins.
Copyright Liverpool Echo

Thanksgiving for the Merchant Navy and Royal Navy, broadcast on the BBC on 11 July 1943. The Parish Eucharist was brought forward an hour to enable the regular congregation to receive communion before they were joined in the building by civic leaders. The Ven Thomas Crick, Chaplain to the Fleet, preached the sermon to a congregation of civic dignitaries, shipowners, underwriters, and seafarers' organisations.[23] This was the start of regular engagement with the BBC,

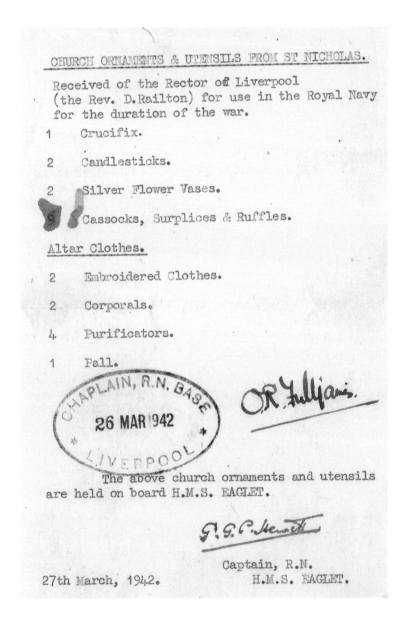

The Parish's contribution to the war effort included the loan of vases to the Royal Navy.
OLSN Archives

Parish Breakfasts were revived in 1942, sometimes with more than one sitting.

The Revd Ambrose Reeves presiding over a more sombre Parish Breakfast
in January 1944.
Both images: copyright Liverpool Echo

including in January 1948 when Reeves gave his first broadcast address on the Overseas' Programme: he continued to broadcast addresses throughout his time in Liverpool. In November 1943 the full array of lectures, meditative services, exhibitions, films, and music recitals were resumed. Ambrose Reeves was also active in the city, including the chaplaincies of both the Royal Court and Empire theatres, as well as Josephine Butler House. His curate was a Sea Cadet chaplain, and various clergy and lay parishioners ran a number of groups catering for different groups within the parish.[24] Civic occasions were still marked in the ruins, the most significant being the end of the war. The nation had known for some days that Victory in Europe would be proclaimed on 8 May 1945, so the church had time to advertise 'Special Services of Thanksgiving for the cessation of hostilities in Europe and of Prayer for our national life' on VE Day at 11am, 12.25pm, 1pm and 1.25pm.[25]

Within the congregation, the Parish Breakfast became an important part of communal life. After an average attendance of about seventy people at the service, a considerable number of them gathered in one of the surviving vestries for a communal meal, which Reeves explicitly linked to the food shared at gatherings of the Early Church.[26] The normal work of the church was also able to continue: the font salvaged from the bombed church was installed in the temporary church for baptisms, and the provision of a roof meant that weddings could legally resume at St Nicholas'.

The Dock Strike

The Rector of Liverpool continued to have a considerable ministry outside the church, and in the 1940s this was most evident in Ambrose Reeves' role in bringing the dock strike to an end. Dock strikes were not unusual, but the scale of the strike in October 1945 was considerable. In Liverpool alone at the start of October there were 14,000 dockers on strike, and initially unrelated but parallel strikes took place in Hull and Londonderry.[27] Within days it had spread to Glasgow as well. Reeves was prompted into action by Fr Edward Talbot CR, and together with Fr John Fitzsimons from the Archdiocese of Liverpool they met with the Strike Committee, the Trade Unions, and finally with Sir Reginald Hodges, the Regional Port Director of the North West, and also manager of the Mersey Docks and Harbour Board. The meetings all took place in secret as Reeves and Fitzsimons looked for common ground. The perceived integrity and impartiality of the clergy meant that they were the ideal mediators, but Reeves' main triumph was in finding a way in which both sides could back down sufficiently to enable proper negotiations. By this time there were 43,000 dockers on strike, and Reeves drew up a document which allowed movement by everyone in all the affected ports. Most importantly, the dockers felt that they had an ally in Reeves.[28]

Reeves was clear that his intervention was the fruit of pastoral ministry, and that Christian faith enabled the kind of leadership which was not available elsewhere. Amongst his reflections he wrote:

a) I believe that effective action by the Church in situations such as this cannot be done from central offices but by individuals who have a pastoral responsibility for the people concerned and who themselves, while acting as individuals, do so with a deep sense that they are acting out of the rich community life of the Church.

b) As far as the Clergy are concerned this experience has shown me that in approaching any such confused and tangled situation we need a new humility. So often people expect us to have the answer and instead of admitting that we do not know the answer, we give them what they expect. In this particular situation we had no answer but because we tried to act in faith the answer was given.

c) It became clear to us that the issues involved in this dispute were primarily theological and demanded from us some clear understanding of the Christian doctrine of man if our work was to be at all effective.[29]

Reeves encapsulated in these thoughts his model of ministry in the city. He realised that the church had no authority beyond the results it could deliver, but that those results were founded upon personal relationship and a model of listening and servant leadership which did not come easily to the employers at that time.

Post-War City Ministry

The resources of the parish were severely depleted by the end of the war. There was not just a shortage of money, and a small temporary church in which to conduct services, but the loss of the St Nicholas' Institute meant that, for the first time since 1704, the activities of the parish were restricted to one site in the city. In addition, although there were still assistant clergy, there were also the additional districts of the parish which needed attention following the destruction of other churches. St Catherine's in Abercromby Square was the most immediate area of activity, and as the war ended it was suggested that the vicarage of St Catherine's be converted into a clergy house.[30] At the same time, the Society of the Sacred Mission withdrew entirely from Liverpool and St Nicholas' House, their priory in Canning Place, was sold to the Diocese of Liverpool for £1000 for use as the office of the Diocesan Registrar.[31]

With the exception of Reeves' engagement with the Dock Strike, a focus on the worshipping life of the parish often took priority over a wider ministry to the city in much of this period. Making worship available across the parish remained a priority, and in 1948 three open-air Good Friday services were held in Ranelagh Street, St George's Plateau, and at the Pier Head, with a range of lay and ordained, male and female speakers.[32] Film 'exhibitions' and music recitals continued as popular ways of engaging the public, but with poor parish infrastructure the opportunities were limited. With the parishes of St Alban's, St Martin-in-the-Fields, and St Matthias now gone, the population of the parish was 41,000, in addition to the parish of St Catherine's, Abercromby Square, which was being annexed.[33] Particularly in the Vauxhall area to the north of the parish, there was a need for active provision for both worship and social outreach amongst a population largely in lower socio-economic groups. St Bartholomew's School, now lacking any other parish association, was insufficient for the need, and Reeves engaged in discussion on rebuilding. In addition, he wished to convert the former St Martin's School (which housed the congregation of St Alban's Bevington, until their parish was subsumed back into Liverpool) into a 'Liverpool Parish Church Family Centre' with the plan "to combine the service of the parishioners during their leisure hours with the worshipping life of the Christian community centred in the Parish Church."[34] In fact the family centre never came into being, as the school was not appropriate, and there was no money for acquiring other premises.[35] Developing St Bartholomew's School did proceed as planned, and in 1950 it was renamed the School of Our Lady and St Nicholas.

However, the success of the visible ministry the church still exercised in the city is evident from the collection of the Voluntary Rate. Following the Compulsory Church Rate Abolition Act of 1868, the parish church had continued to levy a Voluntary Rate under the Act, based on an increment to the statutory rates. Although this had received less attention during the war, renewed energy went into collecting the rate whilst reconstruction was underway. In 1947 around four thousand letters went out to businesses within the city with the expectation of raising £700; by 1952 this was over £1000.[36] The link to the city was fairly universally regarded, and in the church there was said to be "a long recognised bond between the religious and commercial activities of the city, and a symbol of tradition, respect for which is not confined to any particular section of the community."[37] The business community contributed financially to the rebuilding of the church, and when the building work was underway the heads of the main business houses were invited to view the construction alongside civic dignitaries in June 1951.[38]

The loss of Ambrose Reeves as rector after a relatively short time was inevitable. Reeves left Liverpool to be Bishop of Johannesburg in 1949 and was replaced by Robert Nelson. There was a seamless transition, and Nelson made no attempt to redefine ministry in the parish, or to change the direction of the rebuilding of the church. Civic ministry continued to increase, even amongst the scaffolding of the new church. For example, on the day of George VI's funeral at Windsor on Friday 15 February 1952 the parish church held services of Holy Communion at 7am, 8am and 9.30am, but the main event was a memorial service for the convenience of city workers at 1.15pm.[39] Although the main civic memorial service took place at the cathedral on that day, about 2300 people attended the service at St Nicholas': although the service was led from inside the partially built church, it was also broadcast to the people in the gardens outside.[40]

Building a New Church for Liverpool

The first donation towards the new church came as Railton stood watching flames engulf the old church. A man stood with him and handed over his card, on which he had written an offer of £50 towards rebuilding.[41] However, planning for a new church began in earnest in March 1944 when the church council agreed that it was time to appoint an architect and move forward, as well as form an advisory committee from across the city institutions to get broader support and financial help.[42] By the Annual Meeting of 1945, in the final days of the war, the rector was able to report that the year would be "a momentous year in the long history of our ancient parish church, for the decisions which will have to be made by the Parochial Church Council will have far-reaching effects on the life of the Church for at least the next hundred years. Already the outline of reconstruction has been sketched."[43]

In fact the progress of rebuilding was slow as the church took its place in the queue of reconstruction. Reeves received a letter from the government informing him that the building of a permanent church would be delayed owing to the need for housing nationally.[44] However, there was also a wish to press ahead with drawing up initial plans, and the first architect appointed for the task was W.A. Forsyth (1872–1951), who was already engaged on enlarging Blackburn Cathedral.[45] By June 1947 plans had been drawn up for a new building: of note was the change in orientation, with the High Altar at the west end, and also the relocation of the choir stalls so that they were behind the congregation. Although it was anticipated that the surpliced men and boys choir would continue, it was envisaged from the start that a mixed choir might be

Service in the building site of the new church to mark the funeral of George VI in February 1952. Around 2300 people attended services that day. *OLSN Archives*

appropriate for some civic events.[46] Structural investigation revealed
that the foundations of the old church were sound and could be re-used.
It was envisaged that the stone from the old customs house, which was
also a victim of bombing in 1941, and which was finally demolished
in 1948, would be used in the rebuilding of the church, although this
plan was later abandoned and fresh Stanton stone from a quarry in
Macclesfield was eventually used.[47] All of this was, of course, dependent
on the War Damage Commission's arbitration of the compensation
which would be awarded, and consequently the additional funds which
the parish could raise. The commission resolved the compensation for
the loss of the Church Institute in Tithebarn Street more quickly, and
in 1948 made a payment of £1,100 to the parish, most of which went
towards the building of the new church. But contributions towards the
rebuilding also came from across the world, from a generous amount
from the Church of New Zealand, to whose Archbishop the church sent
profuse thanks, to three sets of vestments made by ladies in Princeton,
New Jersey.[48] In addition, a public appeal was launched for £25,000 by
a committee chaired by Frederick Bates, the chairman of the Cunard
White Star shipping company.[49] The building contract, when it was
eventually signed with William Thornton and Sons, was for £125,145.[50]
The gifts continued throughout the building, from the sole stained glass
window in the church, which was given by the designer and maker,
Harcourt M. Doyle ARCA, to the large collection of church plate
which was donated from the Royal Liverpool Seamen's Orphanage
Institute.[51]

The practicalities of the new building occupied much ecclesiastical
energy, but exceptional times enabled swift decisions. As the remains
of the old church were demolished in 1948, coffins found in vaults
were swiftly removed to Walton Park Cemetery without the need for
further permission. The following year the Bishop of Liverpool laid the
foundation stone of the new church on 14 May 1949. The temporary
church within the old walls had also been demolished, and a second
temporary church was built in the church gardens. Building began
with enthusiasm, though with constant attention to the detail. The
designs were revised throughout the building, such as abandoning
the plan for stone screens for the chapels, and placing the font near
the main doors, but essentially Forsyth's plan for the new church was
executed, but from early 1950 one of the partners in his architectural
practice, Edward C. Butler, had already taken practical oversight of
the project. Forsyth remained engaged in the building but visits to
Liverpool were made by Butler alone, and when Forsyth died in 1951

Butler became the sole architect. The church council continued to take a details interest in the plans, which were often shown to them. Sometimes this was for financial decisions, such as whether the bells should be recast or the old ones just rehung (they chose recasting, though payment was not immediate and only due within five years of the consecration), and sometimes aesthetic ones, such as the design of the canopy over the High Altar.

The new church maintained links with the past, as well as with the old seafaring associations. One of the chapels was dedicated to St Peter, with the altar which may have been the High Altar at St Peter's until 1931. This was the Merchant Navy chapel, and the bell of the Cunard tender SS *Skirmisher* was presented to the church to sit in this chapel.

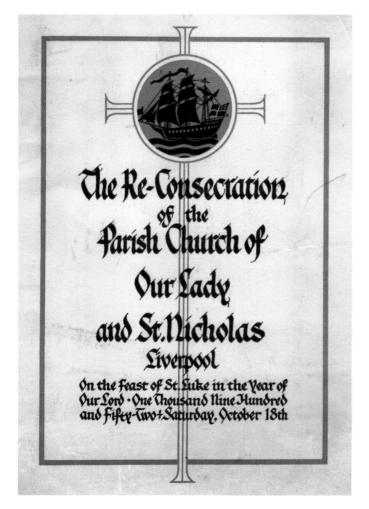

The Re-Consecration
of the
Parish Church of
Our Lady
and St. Nicholas
Liverpool

On the Feast of St. Luke in the Year of
Our Lord · One Thousand Nine Hundred
and Fifty-Two † Saturday, October 18th

Order of Service for the consecration, 18 October 1952. *OLSN Archives*

The civic party is greeted at the door of the church by the Revd Robert Nelson and the churchwardens at the start of the consecration service. *OLSN Archives*

What is now the Maritime Chapel was consecrated as the Chapel of St George as the Royal Navy chapel. So both chapels recalled the earlier principal churches in Liverpool alongside St Nicholas', though this was not entirely by design as the Royal Navy had requested the dedication to St George.[52]

The rebuilding of the church gave great impetus to the rebuilding of the parish structures and activities. From 1950 onwards there was much activity in the development of children's groups, youth groups, church music, and church outings. There were quiet days and discussions. There was a sense that the church had a part in play in wider society. In the first issue of the new parish magazine, the anonymously-written 'Topic of the Month' in January 1950 was of the place of the church in a welfare state, and there was a discussion on how society had to be reformed in order for the welfare state to be successful.[53] The reconstruction of the parish was innovative and dynamic and paraded as an example to others, particularly the establishment of 'guilds' for young people which met on Sundays and weekdays, so that there was no sharp distinction between the religious instruction of Sunday School and the secular entertainment of a youth group. The other area which continued to gain attention was the ethnic diversity of the congregation. Ambrose Reeves' connections with Africa were perpetuated, which led to a continuing stream of African priests serving the parish, alongside a noticeable growth in black members of the congregation. In this respect the parish church was ahead of its time, and *Church Times* noted that the work of the church in breaking down "colour prejudice" was well known.[54] The Lent Talks continued throughout this period, though marketed as the "Lent Lunch House Services." The speakers were not quite the ecclesiastical luminaries from before the war, but they were largely from outside of the city, and they were popular with city workers.

Consecration

The blessing of the finial cross by the Bishop of Warrington and its fixing by the Lord Mayor on 1 May 1952 marked the completion of the stonework. Although the initial consecration date for the new Church was to be the 11 October,[55] the final date was set for Saturday 18 October of that year. We cannot know if this date was chosen in the knowledge that from at least Tudor times it was the beginning of the new civic year for the town of Liverpool, on which mayors and churchwardens were elected, along with the clergy. The ceremony took place in the presence of the Princess Royal (daughter of George V), and various liturgical opportunities were taken by the Bishops of Liverpool, Warrington and Plymouth, and the Assistant Bishop of Birmingham. Charles Gladstone, the grandson of the Prime Minister and now patron of the benefice, stood alongside the Princess Royal as she opened the door to the Bishop of Liverpool, the Rt Revd Clifford Martin, who had knocked on the main doors with his crozier. After the prayer of dedication there was a fanfare from trumpeters from the King's Regiment (Liverpool) before the congregation sang Psalm 150. The consecration followed, and the altars were uncovered and frontals and candles put on them.[56]

The splendour of the consecration service was set within a festival which celebrated the work of the parish church within the city of Liverpool. The following day the Bishop of Warrington presided at the first Eucharist in the new church, and his predecessor preached at a Festal Evensong. Over the coming days there was a procession of bishops, deans and archdeacons into the pulpit. More importantly, the relationship of the parish with the city was demonstrated over the following week with special services for shipping companies (20th), banks (21st), the chamber of commerce (22nd), Rotary clubs (23rd), the Mersey Docks and Harbour Board (24th), a civic service for the Lord Mayor (26th), the trades' unions (27th), the insurance companies (28th), and the staff from hospitals (29th). The church had been built with a seating capacity of 475, but at some of these services there were considerably more: whilst there were only one hundred people at the trades' union service, there were five hundred from the banks, and six hundred from the insurance companies. In addition there were extra services to celebrate historic and present relationships, such as with Walton Church, from which the Parish of Liverpool had been carved, the Diocese of Chester, within whose territory it once sat, and also the local deaneries. Alongside these services the Consecration Festival also included music recitals and a theatrical performance.[57]

Although the new church was publicly open, in fact it was far from complete. Over the next few years there was still much practical work to be done. There was detailed work outstanding, such as the electrical wiring in the tower, but also more significant issues such as the installation of effective boilers. By the end of 1953 the parish was still in dispute with the War Damage Commission: this meant frequent journeys to London by Robert Nelson, and the engagement of various quantity surveyors alongside the architect. In 1954 it was decided to approach Sir Malcolm Trustram Eve (later Lord Silsoe) for his assistance in settling costs. Eve was the First Church Estates

The Liverpool Blitz memorial, unveiled by the Duke of Edinburgh on 7 July 2000. *Author's collection*

Commissioner, but had previously served as the first chairman of the War Damage Commission. By the middle of 1955 the matter was sent to a deputy commissioner of the War Damage Commission, with all parties agreeing to accept his adjudication. The decision fell against the church, which had been hoping for 170 per cent of the valuation of 1939, but were awarded 140 per cent.[58] Meeting the liabilities was the next challenge, and a restoration fund was launched in 1957.

The consecration of a new parish church was heralded as a great event for the city, and reinforced the received understanding that the relationship between the two was unusually close. However, despite the enthusiasm and support, there were no institutional links remaining between city and parish, and the influence of the parish was increasingly through the person of the rector. The Festival of Consecration explicitly proclaimed the relationship to be based on invitation rather than right, but Nelson realised that some significant work needed to take place to start building the worshipping life of the parish. In 1951 he proposed the idea that about six months after the consecration there should be a Parochial Mission. The preparation would begun with visiting across the parish for six months, followed by members of the congregation taking responsibility for particular areas. There would be a Chief Missioner, and Nelson proposed Fr Mark Gibbard from the Society of St John the Evangelist (Cowley Fathers) as an appropriate leader.[59] Although the consecration date had moved, the mission took place as planned six months later, starting on 19 April 1953, with the title "The Key to the Future."[60] The building and extension of every church on the site since the thirteenth century had been a response to the needs of worshippers. As the most recent building was opened and consecrated, the challenge was to find worshippers for the building.

CHAPTER TEN

The Church since the War

The consecration of the rebuilt church in 1952 provided fresh possibilities for ministry, but it was also consolidating the provision which the Church of England could make to a city in the midst of reconstruction. The shrinking of the city centre population had been underway since the start of the century, and the various churches and parishes were gradually subsumed back into the one parish of Liverpool. The result of wartime bombing had hastened the end of some parishes, such as St Catherine's, Abercromby Square, but other amalgamations took longer. In 1937, the parish of St Stephen (Byrom Street) was merged with the parish of St. Anne. The living of St Anne's fell vacant in 1956, and the church demolished in 1967, but it was not until 1970 that the parish of St Anne, Richmond with St Stephen was united with the parish of Liverpool. Also to the north of the city, St James-the-Less was destroyed in bombing, and worship continued in the parish hall. By 1957 the average congregation had fallen to ten: the parish was divided up between neighbouring areas, in particular St Athanasias and the parish of Liverpool.

The parish church was the only church in the region with a national profile, and this was reinforced not just by the frequent visits and talks by episcopal luminaries from across the Church of England, but also by radio and television broadcasts as well as print media. The work of the parish was highlighted in the first edition of the short-lived

Church Illustrated in January 1955, eclipsing the well-known evangelical leader the Revd John Stott at All Souls' Langham Place who made it into the second edition. Continuing the broadcasting work of Ambrose Reeves, Robert Nelson was a regular radio broadcaster, but a more significant 'first' came on 1 November 1953 when Liverpool Parish Church was chosen by the BBC for the first television broadcast service of Holy Communion. The rector presided at the service for All Saints' Day, and the Bishop of Liverpool preached. There was considerable discussion beforehand about whether members of the congregation should be shown receiving communion, and everything was carefully rehearsed. There was, of course, dissent: newspapers across the country reported general approbation, but also those who felt that broadcasting had gone a step too far.[1] Although the television cameras did not appear again on a Sunday morning, services continued to be broadcast, such as the Parish Eucharist on 29 September 1957, which went out on the Home Service (North).[2]

The first televised service of Holy Communion, 1 November 1953. *OLSN Archives*

The pattern of ministry to the city was now well-established. Talks, sermons, music, and theatrical performances complemented the daily acts of worship. Although the liturgy for the broadcast service on All Saints' Day 1953 was strictly according to the Book of Common Prayer, the liturgy of the parish church pushed forward the growing Catholicisation of the Church of England, seen most obviously in Holy Week which, by 1955, began with the distribution of palms and a procession, and went on to include the Three Hours Devotion on Good Friday, and the lighting of the Paschal candle on Holy Saturday after Evensong. Preachers in Holy Week of that year included the Primus of Scotland (the successor in post to the former rector, John How) and Ambrose Reeves, Bishop of Johannesburg, the previous rector. Robert Nelson was clearly superb at producing events for the parish, and 1957 posed a possible date for the seven hundredth anniversary of the parish, and therefore an opportunity for another festival, which included the usual array of local bishops, as well as visitors such as Fr Trevor Huddleston CR.

Daily Ministry

The daily pattern of the parish and its clergy was directed by the rector, who oversaw everything. There were four full time curates (Neil Humphreys, Christopher Hodgson, Frank Telfer, and Roy File) and on Fridays the curates reported back on everything they had done and the visits they had achieved. Pastoral problems were discussed, and curates felt mildly relieved when the rector decided to deal with a problem personally. One curate from that time, the Revd Frank Telfer, was drawn to the Parish of Liverpool: when he first visited the parish church before ordination he knew he wanted to be in the 'atmosphere' of St Nick's. "It was serious without being solemn. It wasn't the middle classes 'doing something' in the slums." Telfer recalled working with Robert Nelson: "I've never met anyone like him. He was very kind, especially because my mother was ill… He tried to get help from doctors he knew." After Telfer's first sermon Nelson said, "I think we should have a chat about sermons." He then wrote out a sheet on how to construct sermons. Occasionally Nelson would invite curates for a drink in one of the pubs by Exchange Station. Telfer recalled that Nelson once had to get him up on a Sunday morning when he overslept by throwing stones at the window: "He wasn't angry, but he said that perhaps I should do some extra visiting that afternoon."

Canon Robert Nelson with a parishioner in the church office in 1954. *OLSN Archives*

In theory all the clergy said Morning Prayer together, but in practice they were often absent for different reasons. Fridays were different: they all had breakfast together (in the church kitchen), and then went to the school where they all did some teaching. Then they came back for a staff meeting before going out to lunch, often in restaurants on Chapel Street on the ground floor of offices. There was no work done over lunch, but this was a time for socialising with each other. The curates had one morning 'working' in their lodgings every week – reading or writing, or at least something productive – and then they would be out working in the parish. As well as the daily Eucharist in church, there were Eucharists in other places at which they all took turns. The furthest was the girls' school in Huyton, where the rector was chaplain. There was also work in hospitals, or in the Eye Hospital, as well as lot of visiting: in addition to those who lived in the parish, members of the congregation were visited: if you lived in West Kirby then it was expected that you would only get one visit a year. If the clergy encountered people who needed feeding, then there was an arrangement with a café on the Dock Road: the clergy either went with them or sent them with a letter. This was not an ecumenical age, but the barrier was education as much as religion. The clergy of the parish church were largely products of Oxford and Cambridge, and they found they had little in common with the Catholic clergy they encountered, unless they met a priest from a Catholic Order in a hospital, in which case there was some conversation to be had. It was no surprise that Robert Nelson, like his predecessors, was called to the episcopate, and in 1958 he was appointed Bishop of Middleton. Frank Telfer had originally been invited to consider a curacy at St Mark's, North End (Portsea) but had turned it down as he felt it was harder work than he could manage. One Sunday in 1958 he was celebrating the Eucharist in Liverpool and turned around to see the Vicar of North End in the congregation: "Aha! The next Rector!"[3] Pepys was instituted as Rector of Liverpool on 23 June 1958.

The Samaritans

On 18 November 1958 the Revd Chad Varah visited the parish church to discuss the possibility of starting a branch of the Samaritans.[4] The driving force behind this was Christopher Pepys, and as well as his personal commitment to the Samaritans, he was exploring what distinctive ministry the parish could develop within the city. He recorded at a church council meeting two years later: "It was not a Diocesan venture nor an Ecumenical gesture, but the work of the Liverpool Parish Church."[5] However, the momentum for the establishment of a branch gathered pace following the devastating news of 3 June 1959, when Robert Nelson took his own life, just a little over a year since becoming Bishop of Middleton. Pepys spoke to members of the congregation about how forming a branch of the Samaritans could be part of the healing of a congregation which was in shock and grief. The branch opened in the basement of the church in 1960: it started with 25 volunteers and was a night service 7pm until 7am. The *Daily Mirror* proclaimed: "Britain's eight millionth telephone was yesterday presented free of charge to the 'Good Samaritans' of Liverpool Parish Church. It will be manned day and night by a group of volunteers who offer aid and advice to distressed and suicidal people."[6]

There had to be two people on duty, and volunteers used to sleep on camp beds whilst waiting for calls on the one Bakelite telephone which had the telephone number MAR9000. In the daytime Pepys and a curate took any business which came in, but within three years the branch offered a drop-in service.[7] Every call which came in was meticulously recorded: entries in the log revealed people with practical difficulties as well as emotional ones. For example, entries from December 1962 included: "x rang up. Wanted accommodation for night. Very little money. Tried Salvation Army hostels, YMCA and David Lewis hostel – all full. Got him in at Belmont Rd Reception Centre. He seemed grateful." Another read, "A man rang up. Wanted someone to talk to – feeling fed up and depressed with work and broken engagement."[8]

Before long the branch acquired a van so that they could start going out to callers. Initially these visits were undertaken alone. On one evening one of the curates, Fr Cyril Telford, was sent out on his own in the van to a report of a domestic dispute in Speke. When he knocked at the door a man hauled him into the house and sat him down on the seat with the man's wife and three children, and then continued threatening them all with a carving knife. Fr Telford managed to calm the situation down, but it was a lesson that people should be sent out in pairs.[9]

The Samaritans became the defining feature of Pepys' ministry in Liverpool and he maintained the connection at a national level after he had left Liverpool to become Bishop of Buckingham. He was ideally suited to the work. One of his curates, Keith Lightfoot (later Dean of Waikato in New Zealand), wrote of him, "He was a good listener – to God and to his fellow men. He was able to be both involved and detached; to identify himself with those who were suicidal or broken in spirit and to bring into that relationship strong compassion, going where people were, without judgement."[10]

Shops and Theatres

The decline of a residential population turned the attention of the parish to those who were left in the city centre. Ministry to the theatres had begun after the war. As early as 1954 there had been a special Evensong attended by members of the casts of the Empire, the Royal Court, and the Playhouse, with the readings given by the cast of a pantomime.[11] Work with the theatres became rather more prominent when Edwyn Young became rector in 1964. He came with considerable experience of ministry to the stage when he was Rector of Stepney, when he also served as chaplain of the London Palladium and was a member of the Actors' Union.[12] Within months of his arrival he arranged a service on the stage of the Empire Theatre with the Bishop

Canon Edwyn Young with the staff of Richards Shops. *From Edwyn Young*, No fun Like Work, *1970*

of Liverpool, and popular performers Jimmy Tarbuck and Frankie Vaughan. Young spent much time with actors at the theatres, but also encouraged actors into church whenever he could, both for regular services, and for baptisms and weddings.[13]

Under Edwyn Young one of the curates gave a report at each church council meeting to explain their work in the parish. As well as work in hospitals and schools, Fr Nicholas Bury (later Dean of Gloucester) spoke of his chaplaincy to the department store George Henry Lee Ltd.[14] The following month Fr Christopher Smith included in his report visiting clubs as well as Owen Owen's store.[15] All the clergy took an enthusiastic role in this work, realising that shops gave them access to many more people in one location than most other areas of ministry. There were over two thousand people employed by Lewis', and Edwyn Young's appointment as chaplain meant that his photograph with some notes about him went up in the canteen and he had open access to the shop. Spending two hours a week there meant that he was soon well-known, and he knew them.[16] This ministry across the retail district remained an essential part of the work of the clergy for the rest of the century. Today the need is just as great following the growth in Liverpool as a retail destination: the rector is Chair of Trustees of Mission in the Economy, a charity which provides chaplaincy in the city centre and elsewhere in

Merseyside, including for Merseyside Police which has its headquarters in the parish.

Serving the City

Although the population of Liverpool has remained smaller since the war than throughout the industrial period, the city centre has continued to be redeveloped. The parish contains retail and commercial districts, as well as visitor attractions. The streets closest to the parish church are largely those of the business district, and the number of people working nearby has continued to increase. Whilst the bombsite of the old Peter's Building, on the corner of Rumford Street and Tithebarn Street, remains as an undeveloped car park, the use of available space has changed the landscape around the church considerably. The historic Old Churchyard, largely unchanged in its layout for centuries, was

Regular civic and maritime events are still at the heart of ministry. In 2016 the Liverpool Pilotage Service celebrated their 250th anniversary at a service during which they received the Freedom of the City. *OLSN Archives*

redeveloped in 1982 with a new courtyard between the church and the office accommodation called St Nicholas' House.[17]

As in previous centuries, connections and influence were vital for the parish. A year after his institution as rector, Donald Gray set up the Rector's Advisory Committee in December 1975. The first chairman was Sir Douglas Crawford, appointed the previous year as the first Lord Lieutenant of Merseyside. Another founder member of the committee was Henry Cotton, who later became the third Lord Lieutenant. Crawford summarised the intention that it should be "a group which would offer advice to the Rector of Liverpool on matters relating to the activities of the Parish Church in the city." The first meeting discussed a variety of matters, from an 'Industrial Harvest' celebration for the city, to the plausibility of continuing lunchtime recitals.[18]

The involvement of the Lord Lieutenant of Merseyside in the parish church has been considerable since the formation of Merseyside as a county in 1974. The first four Lord Lieutenants all chaired the Rector's Advisory Committee, and even after the committee came to an end shortly after Nicholas Frayling's departure, a strong link remained. The connection of the Rector of Liverpool with the institutions of the city often sees the Parish Church of Liverpool as the focus for celebrations and commemorations in the county, and the parish works in collaboration with the Lieutenancy and Liverpool Town Hall to develop civic life. Since the formation of the county, the rector has often served as chaplain to the High Sheriff of Merseyside, and from civic functions to royal visits is often at the forefront of representing the city.

Many of the ways in which the parish served the city were long-established. The most enduring of these was the Lent Talks. Immediately after the war these remained in the format of one speaker making repeated appearances. For example, the Revd Edgar Bell privately printed the addresses he gave on Fridays throughout Lent in 1953. Within a few years a new pattern developed, with a different speaker every weekday during Lent. The programme in 1960 included nine bishops, and a clutch of deans and archdeacons. And so the tone was set for the following decades as senior clergy from across the country boarded trains for Liverpool to speak for twenty minutes at the lunchtime service, followed by lunch with the rector and selected guests. Edwyn Young commented, "a Bishop a day keeps the devil at bay."[19] Successive Archbishops of Canterbury came, including the former curate, Michael Ramsey, in 1974, George Carey in 1993, and most memorable Robert Runcie in 1982 who came to speak on the subject 'In Church and State'.[20] Runcie's appearance was just two months before the visit of Pope John Paul II to Liverpool, and tensions were mounting with the Orange Order and other protestants who objected to the papal visit and to the obvious rapprochement between the denominations. Two days before Runcie was due to speak, Archbishop Derek Worlock had given the Lenten Address and had been interrupted by shouts of "No Pope" before the protesters walked out, with accusations of punches thrown on the way.[21] Disruption was therefore predictable, and as Runcie got up to speak, the protestors outside the church had made their way inside and began chanting "Runcie out" and "Traitor" whilst waving placards. Runcie could not be heard, and so returned with the rector, Donald Gray, to the altar to kneel in prayer. The congregation in the church tried to drown the noise of the protesters by singing the hymn *City of God*, although when Runcie eventually gave up and left the building the protesters sang *Land of Hope and Glory*. The following day the Bishop and Archbishop of Liverpool issued a statement: "None who witnessed the ugly scenes in Liverpool Parish Church will wish to see any return to the disputes of former days. There must be no going back, and no retaliation."[22]

The Lent Talks declined after the departure of Nicholas Frayling as rector for a variety of reasons, some of which were out of the control of the church. Changing working patterns meant that city workers often no longer had a lunch hour. The timetabling of many events had for many decades worked around every grade of employee having an hour's break either at 12 noon or at 1pm. On some days there were two lunchtime Eucharists, at 12.05pm and 1.05pm, which allowed people to get to the church as soon as their lunch began. It was not just Lent Talks which were structured around lunch: for example, on 10 December 1970 the William Morris Singers performed in "Lunch Hour Music Recitals" at both 12.25pm and 1.25pm, and in February 1971 the Liverpool Lieder Circle performed at the same times.[23]

Changing working patterns and the declining culture of public lectures meant that the Lent Programme was relaunched in 2015, mainly as early evening events which lasted longer and included refreshments. They were no longer every day in Lent, but focused on fewer events which have included both speakers and musical performances. Although some church people have continued to be part of the programme, including both the Bishop of Liverpool and the Catholic Archbishop, other speakers have included authors, politicians, and actors. In 2019 the Archbishop of York presided and preached on Ash Wednesday, but two days later also spoke to fifty invited guests from the business community over breakfast. This echoed an earlier regular feature of city ministry: Nicholas Frayling had begun regular 'City Breakfasts' which met by invitation to hear a guest speaker. The initiative had come from an idea presented at the Rector's Advisory Committee by Jim Fitzpatrick, the chief executive of the Mersey Docks and Harbour Company, who felt that the city connections made by the Lent Addresses could be perpetuated throughout the year. The series attracted local and national speakers, and an invited audience of around sixty people would gather just before 8am for a breakfast and a talk, with the aim that they should be away by 9am to start work.[24]

In the eighteenth and nineteenth centuries the rector held a role within the city – mainly through the Vestry Committee – which was quite divorced from the worshipping life of the church. In the twentieth and twenty-first centuries the pattern was repeated, though largely through the charitable and voluntary sector. As the power and financial authority of the church decreased, the parish maintained its significance in the city through trusteeships and personal influence. For example, Nicholas Frayling chaired the Welfare Organizations' Committee of the Liverpool Council for Voluntary Service (LCVS), which met monthly and brought together the leaders of key charities from across the city. Today the tector is a trustee of about a dozen charities and has significant relationships with other city organisations; he also leads on civic and interfaith work for the Diocese of Liverpool. The church is a member of the Liverpool and Sefton Chamber of Commerce, and has formed a number of partnerships with companies and charities. To support this work, the Voluntary Rate continues to provide a mechanism by which companies within the parish can contribute financially towards a city-wide ministry.

The Structure of the Parish

Throughout the post-war period there was some fluctuation in the size of the parish. Churches which had once been part of the parish but had since gained their own parochial status continued to close and be joined to other parishes, including St Jude's in Hardwick Street, which finished in 1965 before being demolished in 1966 to make way for the Royal Liverpool Hospital; St Anne's in Richmond Street closed in 1970, and was joined back with Liverpool parish. Later, in 2004, there were further changes to the boundaries of the parish which moved much of the Vauxhall district to the neighbouring parish of St Athanasius, Kirkdale. The effect of this was to reduce the social and economic diversity of the Parish of Liverpool at a time when the city centre was becoming increasingly affluent. The increasing opportunities for work within the city centre meant that there was some benefit in focusing the work of the clergy, but there was also clearly a loss for the parish, as the church became cut off from the more deprived residential districts of the city. The new boundaries left the parish with the thin strips of now-deserted docks which are only just beginning their redevelopment in 2019, necessitating new ideas for ministry in previously unpopulated areas.

The unusual pattern of work in the parish, with the extensive civic roles of the rector alongside the demands of normal parish life, led to the formation of a Team Ministry in 1990. This ecclesiastical device enabled more experienced priests to be appointed as assistant clergy, rather than those newly ordained. With Nicholas Frayling as the team rector the system worked well, with team vicars overseeing the traditional aspects of a parish church, and Frayling free to concentrate on civic work. The experiment was short-lived, partly for financial reasons, and the final team vicar left in 2006. Dissolving the Team Ministry gave the then Bishop of Liverpool an opportunity to address the issue of patronage. Since 1968 the advowson had been in the hands of Sir (Erskine) William Gladstone, the great grandson of the Prime Minister, and now also in possession of the baronetcy awarded to the Prime Minister's father in 1846. Sir William Gladstone was an assiduous patron whose involvement in the parish went far beyond the infrequent duty of appointing a rector. From his home at Hawarden Castle, Gladstone befriended and supported successive rectors, as well as visiting Liverpool to attend events at the parish church, including delivering Lent Talks.

In a letter to Gladstone in 2007, James Jones, Bishop of Liverpool, proposed that in the latest restructuring of the parish there might be a change: "As we both know the appointment to Liverpool Parish Church is of the utmost importance and significance in the City... Given the strategic importance of this living do you think there is any merit in it having the joint Patronage of yourself and the Bishop of Liverpool?"[25] Gladstone's reply three weeks' later was characteristic in its elegant management of the tension between two positions: "In principle, unlike most of the English bishops of whose opinion I have over the course of years become aware, I am opposed to Private Patronage. And unlike most of the parish priests of whose opinion I have been aware, I think that the 'Parish System' has been the bane of the Church of England since the late seventeenth century. The combination of private patrons and parsons' freeholds has done more to weaken the Anglican church than any of the other multiple handicaps which have constrained or prejudiced its operations, and which now leave it in perhaps, alas, irreversible decline." But Gladstone went on to demonstrate the advantages of private patronage, both in casting the net wide in the search for a suitable appointment, and in thwarting the interests of a particular bishop: "A conscientious patron of an important living is bound to consult both No 10 and the Archbishop's adviser on patronage, and thus to get two authentic (or 'establishment') lists, to add to the Bishop's list, of the most promising candidates. And any Tom, Dick or Harry, however often rejected for good reasons or bad, feels they (for they may be female TDHs) can put their merits to an individual private patron without being ruled out by the spiritual equivalent of the Bush Telegraph or Old Boy Network." And in his polite refusal of the bishop's proposal, Gladstone stated, "I have every intention of leaving [the advowson] to my elder son, in whose conscientiousness and judgement I have full confidence, because I wish for sentimental reasons to maintain the Gladstonian connexion."[26]

Having appointed four rectors, Sir William Gladstone died on Maundy Thursday 2018. The current rector and Nicholas Frayling attended the funeral in Hawarden, representing not just the parish of Liverpool, but also all the rectors who had benefited from Gladstone's friendship over the years.

The staffing of the parish church reverted, at the end of the Team Ministry, to the rector with assistant curates in either their first or second appointment after ordination. There has continued to be an acknowledgement that the relationship with the city of Liverpool increases the need for clergy beyond the normal demands of a parish church. From an early stage, women have shared in the ministry of the Parish of Liverpool on the staff team. After the war the parish employed a succession of "Lady Workers" who undertook pastoral duties. The last of these, Thelma Tomlinson, served for five years before she was ordained 'deaconess' (a lay order within the Church of England) in 1967, and in 1969 she moved to the staff of Liverpool Cathedral.[27] In 2012 the Revd Michelle Montrose became the first woman priest to be licensed to the parish. Today the parish has four licensed clergy as well a number of honorary assistant clergy (including retired priests) who give their time to serve the parish in different ways.

Ecumenism

Edwyn Young repeated the line from a well-known Liverpool comedian that the city has two religions: the one anti-Catholic, the other anti-Protestant.[28] Despite, or perhaps because of this reputation, Liverpool became a clarion for the ecumenical movement from the 1970s. The arrival of David Sheppard as Bishop of Liverpool in 1975, and Derek Worlock as the Catholic Archbishop in 1976, meant not just rapprochement, but also active collaboration in many areas. One of the catalysts for the parish of Liverpool to engage in active ecumenism was the financial strain of the parish magazine, 'Headline', and it was members of the Rector's Advisory Committee who pressed for making this an ecumenical venture.[29] The edition of September 1977 had a

Ecumenism: the installation of Nicholas Frayling as Rector of Liverpool in September 1987, at which there were sermons from both the Anglican Bishop David Sheppard, and the Catholic Archbishop Derek Worlock. The third ecumenical representative was the Revd John Newton, Chair of the Methodist District. *Courtesy of Nicholas Frayling*

Ecumenism: The Archbishop of York in the pulpit with (below) the Chair of the Methodist District, the Bishop of Liverpool, and the Archbishop of Liverpool. Ash Wednesday 2019.
OLSN Archives

front-page letter signed jointly by the Bishop and Archbishop stating their support for a new ecumenical ministry to the city, of which a joint publication was just a part. Although they were less prominent, the Free Churches gave their support to a new form of ministry from the start.

Ecumenical ministry became both pastoral and liturgical, and there was genuine commitment to dialogue centred around the parish church. Bishop Anthony Hitchen, the Catholic Auxiliary Bishop, became a member of the Rector's Advisory Committee and influenced the work of the church. Clergy from the parish church and from St Mary's RC Church, Highfield Street, became close colleagues. In

addition, the Blessed Sacrament Shrine opened in a former cinema
in Clayton Square in 1972. After the square was redeveloped in the
1980s, the shrine moved to a modern brick chapel on Dawson Street.[30]
The other members of the city centre Ecumenical Team were the
Methodists and the United Reformed Church. For over twenty years
clergy and people from different churches worked and worshipped
together. For example, at St Paul's Eye Hospital (then on Old Hall
Street) a curate each from the parish church and from St Mary's
toured the wards together, conducting prayers jointly, and giving Holy
Communion at the same time.[31] By the 1990s a regular pattern had
developed of contact between the clergy: they would come together
every Wednesday morning, spending a month at a time meeting in
a different church building, and praying together using the liturgy of
that church. Chaplaincy to the different premises and institutions of the
city was done in an inclusive way: each minister would represent the
entire Ecumenical Team when they visited shops, department stores,
theatres, the police, and other places. Many organisations would have
services in church, and in particular carol services in December, which
were held under the banner of the Ecumenical Team. Although most

The City Centre Ecumenical Team leading a walk of witness through Liverpool in
Holy Week 1978.
OLSN Archives

of these took place at Liverpool Parish Church, the equality of role in the team meant that the Rector of Liverpool might take a peripheral part in a service.

Non-Eucharistic services for the city were easily arranged, such as carol services and harvest festivals, but there were liturgically adventurous experiments as well. The parish church had a covenant with St Mary's, Highfield Street which brought them together at different times in the year. Most significantly, they held 'simultaneous Eucharists' on Maundy Thursday and at the Easter Vigil on Holy Saturday. This was ground-breaking and pushed at the ecumenical limits of the reforms of the Second Vatican Council, whilst also utilising the convergence of language and liturgical heritage. At these services there would be a shared Liturgy of the Word (readings and sermon), but then the Eucharistic Prayer would be in parallel, with each Catholic and Anglican priests echoing each other in almost identical words. Although the intention was to respect the boundaries of churches which were not in communion with each other, in fact the opposite effect was achieved: Catholic worshippers, indignant at the discipline of their own denomination, would march to receive communion from the Anglican priest, whilst Anglican worshippers, embarrassed at the paucity of communicants from the Catholic sacrament, headed across to receive communion there. Although there was no objection locally, it was a complaint from the Vatican to Archbishop Worlock which brought an end to this practice. The complaint, though, was erroneous, as it accused the clergy of concelebrating the Eucharist together, which was never the intention.[32]

When St Mary's, Highfield Street closed in 2001 there was still a need for a regular Catholic Mass in the city centre for those working nearby. An agreement was drawn up as the church closed, and a weekly Catholic Mass began in the Maritime Chapel at the parish church every Friday lunchtime. The Mass continues today, served by a variety of bishops and priests who value the continuation of ecumenical cooperation as well as pastoral and liturgical provision for Catholic worshippers. However, the closure of St Mary's and the withdrawal of the free churches from the city centre effectively brought an end to the Ecumenical Team Ministry. It did not, though, bring an end to the ecumenical nature of the parish church, which regularly welcomes regional church leaders to events and services. In 2018 the Catholic Church of England and Wales held in the city its first Eucharistic Congress since the London Congress of 1908. Thousands of Catholics from across the country gathered at the Arena on the

An aerial view of the centre of Liverpool in 2016.
Courtesy of Peel Holdings

waterfront, but amongst the events across Liverpool, the only one not to take place in a Catholic church was an ecumenical discussion on the Eucharist at Liverpool Parish Church, between the Catholic Archbishop, the Anglican Bishop, and the chair of the Methodist District. Similarly, since 2016 the leaders of all the denominations in the city region walk together just before Easter from the Metropolitan Cathedral through the city centre to the parish church where they join in prayers together.

An adjunct to ecumenism is the growing multi-faith demographic of the city, in which the civic work of the parish church affords a convenient position from which to coordinate the relationships across different faith traditions. In 2018 the rector established a Faith Leaders' Group, drawing together leaders from non-Christian places of worship to meet with Christian leaders from different denominations. On some civic occasions, especially those celebrating the Commonwealth or the diversity of Liverpool's communities, it has become a familiar sight to see representatives from other faiths do readings in the parish church.

Music and the Arts

The rebuilding of the church in 1952 gave an opportunity for skill and artistic expression in a new building. The wooden screens and choir stalls were made at the Pyghtle Works, Bedford, which also produced woodwork for a wide range of prominent buildings across the country, including Westminster Abbey, St Paul's Cathedral, Cambridge Guildhall, Royal Shakespeare Theatre in Stratford, and the Savoy Hotel. The parish church has developed a place within the artistic and musical tradition of the city. As the new building became familiar with age and use, there was greater scope for innovation. Brian Burgess' sculpture of 'Christ upon the Ass' was installed on a plinth outside the church in the 1970s, and when the Maritime Chapel was created out of the North Chapel in 1993 Arthur Dooley's sculpture of St Mary del Quay became the first significant work within the church. More recently two icons (one of St Mary, and one of St Nicholas) were added within the church, and in 2019 a large icon of the crucifixion was installed behind the altar. Further works within the church include 'The Grail Boat' – a wooden carved sculpture by Greg Tricker, and a new font (2019) designed by David Wilson of Dovetailors in Leeds with stained glass by Katharine Bayes. In 1984 the Cattrall Screens were installed to separate the narthex from the nave. They were engraved to the designs of David Peace, whose work is also found in Westminster Abbey. The engravings are rich in symbols connected with the church, and are designed to give a striking view of the hanging rood through the plain glass chalice on the central doors.

The gardens were remodelled in 1984 when Liverpool hosted the Garden Festival and the paths were relaid. Tom Murphy's sculpture commemorating the Liverpool and Bootle Blitz was unveiled by the Duke of Edinburgh in 2000, and is surrounded by a number of other military and seafaring memorials. Two more bronze sculptures have since been installed in the gardens: a memorial by Tony Evans to the victims of the sinking of the MV *Derbyshire* (2018), and the Homeless Jesus by Timothy Schmalz (2019). Overlooking Chapel Street, Burgess' sculpture of Christ has gone, but the plinth is used for an annual sculpture installation.

Music has continued to be an important part of the ministry of the parish. The regular concerts which continued until the 1970s were never revived, and the old choir was disbanded by Donald Gray, but the church has become a regular concert venue, as well as music in liturgical contexts. In the 1990s a new choir was established, the St

Art and social justice combine in the unveiling of the Homeless Jesus sculpture in 2019 as part of a conference in the parish church for the business community to participate in addressing issues of homelessness. *Copyright The Diocese of Liverpool, 2019*

Nicholas' Singers, comprising a small but changing group of professional singers. Regular contributors to the music have also included the Liverpool Bach Collective, which was formed in 2013 to perform the works of J.S. Bach in a liturgical context. As well as cantatas, they have come to Liverpool Parish Church twice for an ecumenical performance of the St John Passion. In addition, from 2018 there has been an early music 'orchestra in residence' made up of young people from across the region. Occasional lunchtime and evening concerts from other soloists and ensembles help to animate the commercial district of the city.

Epilogue

A history of the parish since the war can be no more than a survey, with many details omitted and perhaps some unduly emphasised. The significant narrative here is the focus of the entire book, that the parish continues to have an unusual but symbiotic relationship with the city of Liverpool, just as it has since the thirteenth century. The nature of the relationship has changed over the years and now rests not on legislation or compulsion, but on the service which each can give to the other. The interweaving of histories has meant that the Parish Church of Liverpool has remained a key institution in the city far longer than is the case in other towns and cities. The modern age is witnessing the decline in the influence of the church, but the parish of Liverpool will remain relevant to the city for as long as it can offer something to institutions as well as to individuals. The church can easily remain a place of celebration and of gathering, but she must also be a place where people are stimulated and given intellectual and cultural challenge. The church can also be a place to campaign and to name aloud the issues which the city is facing. The parish has seen myriad changes over the centuries, but it has usually managed to remain relevant to Liverpool, and this continues to be the formula which will ensure its survival.

Afterword

"A Christian presence in every community". With these words the Church of England in the twenty-first century defines itself. As this book makes clear, this is not a new aim. In central Liverpool through the centuries a Christian presence, visible through the Parish Church, has been constant – and constantly changing.

In the light of this rich history we may look to the future with real confidence. The Church of England has two poles of existence – God, who never changes, and England, which changes all the time. Thus a wise Christian presence will point to the unchanging God, and will love the world God loves, the world for which God freely gave Jesus Christ (John 3:16). This love demands an openness, a lightness, and a clarity of faith, all held together by a readiness to be available, and to relate to people as they are, just as Jesus did. Our Parish Church meets this demand with exuberant joy.

In Chapter 4 Crispin writes: "It has been suggested that the majority of the townspeople of Liverpool were Puritan, but it is difficult to see any evidence for this." What was true in the seventeenth century certainly remains true today. And the present-day ministry of the Parish Church makes it clear that the people of the city – extravert, courageous, funny, outspoken, warm, contrarian – still have room in their multi-textured lives for the Church and for the rumour of God that the Church keeps alive.

City centre ministry demands a faithful presence, at home among the homeless poor, at home in the food bank, equally at home in the Athenaeum, in the municipal grandeur of the Town Hall, in the law courts. Liverpool Parish Church, the Church of Our Lady and St Nicholas, sustains that presence in our own day and will do so into the future.

I pay tribute here to the ministry of the Parish Church across the centuries, but in particular to its ministry today. In the civic institutions and in the lives of everyday Scousers, this church retains an honoured place. Its convening power remains, whether in calling together those working to care for the homeless, or in providing a space and a voice for the leaders of the many faiths that enrich the city to meet and to express their mutual respect and commitment to the common good.

All this flows from a beautiful and ancient building with a history of radical change, as these pages show. Yet deeper even than the foundations of the building is its purpose; an unchanged and therefore wholly contemporary mission which catches us up in our own generation, just as it caught up all our predecessors in theirs. So we are called to be where the Church has always been; to be there for England as it is, for Liverpool as it is. In the heart of this great city we are called to point beyond the soaring buildings and the feisty people to a still greater hope - the Christian hope; that because of Jesus Christ love will conquer hate and that life will conquer death eternally.

The Rt Revd Paul Bayes
Bishop of Liverpool

Appendix

List of Clergy

	Date of evidence of existence or appointment
Richard	1250s
Thomas Rowley (Chantry of St John)	1326
Ralph Haworth (Chantry of St Katherine)	1361
Thomas of Caton	1416
Henry of Bretherton	1416
William Amot	1466
Richard Twathes	1476
Thomas Raynford	1512/3
Humphrey Crosse (Chantry of St Katherine)	1515
Richard Frodsham	1537
John Hurde (Chantry of St John)	1548
Evan Nicholasson	1555
James Milner	1572
James Seddon	1574
Hugh Janion	1590
Ralph Bentley	1596
Thomas Wainwright	1598
Edward Lappage	1626
Henry Shaw	1634

Joseph Tompson	1643
John Fogg	1645
Peter Stanynough	1651
Michael Briscowe	1651
James Rigbie	1651
John Fogg	1651
John Leigh	1662
Robert Hunter	1670
Samuel Smalhorne	1674
William Atherton	1688
Robert Stythe	1688

List of Rectors

	Inducted	Resigned/Died
Robert Styth (*c.* 1657–1713)	1699	1713
William Atherton (*c.* 1656–1706)	1699	1706
Henry Richmond (*c.* 1677–1721)	1706	1721
Thomas Bell (167?–1725)	1717	1725
Thomas Baldwin (*c.* 1681–1753)	1721	1753
John Stanley (1692–1781)	1726	1750
Afterwards Rector of Halsall		
Henry Wolstenholme (????–1771)	1753	1771
Robert Brereton (1716–1784)	1750	1784
Thomas Maddock (*c.* 1713–1783)	1772	1783
George Hodson (*c.* 1740–1794)	1784	1794
Thomas Dannett (*c.* 1742–1796)	1783	1796
Samuel Renshaw (1752–1829)	1794	1829
Robert Hankinson Roughsedge (1745–1829)	1796	1829
Jonathan Brooks (1775–1855)	1829	1855
Augustus Campbell (1786–1870)	1829	1870
Became sole Rector on Brooks' death in 1855		
Alexander Stewart (1826–1916)	1870	1904
John Augustine Kempthorne (1864–1946)	1904	1910
Afterwards Bishop of Hull and Bishop of Lichfield		
Harold Ernest Bilbrough (1867–1950)	1910	1916
Afterwards Bishop of Dover and Bishop of Newcastle		
Guy Wittenoom Hockley (1869–1946)	1916	1925
Afterwards Archdeacon of Cornwall		

John Charles Halland How (1881–1961)   1926   1935
Afterwards Vicar of Brighton and Bishop of Glasgow and Galloway
David Railton (1884–1955)   1935   1942
Afterwards Industrial Christian Fellowship
Richard Ambrose Reeves (1899–1980)   1942   1949
Afterwards Bishop of Johannesburg
Robert Nelson (1913–1959)   1949   1958
Afterwards Bishop of Middleton
George Christopher Cutts Pepys (1914–1974) 1958   1964
Afterwards Bishop of Buckingham
Cecil Edwyn Young (1913–1988)   1964   1973
Afterwards Queen's Chapel of the Savoy
Donald Clifford Gray (b. 1930)   1974   1987
Afterwards Canon of Westminster, Rector of St Margaret's Westminster, and Chaplain to the Speaker
Nicholas Arthur Frayling (b. 1944)   1987   2002
Afterwards Dean of Chichester
Steven David Brookes (b. 1960)   2003   2013
Afterwards Chaplain of the Royal Hospital, Chelsea
Crispin Alexander Pailing (b. 1975)   2014

Notes

Chapter One: A Medieval Chapel

1 'Liuerpul', meaning 'muddy pool'. John Belchem (ed.), *Liverpool 800*, Liverpool (2006), p. 59.

2 There is evidence of a chapel by the time of a survey of the castle in 1476. E.W. Cox, *An Attempt to Recover the Plans of the Castle of Liverpool from Authentic Records*, THSLC Vol. 42 (1890), p. 201.

3 Belchem, *Liverpool 800*, p. 65.

4 Moore MS 412 held in Liverpool Records Office.

5 Moore MS 414.

6 J. Elton, *The Chapel of St Mary del Key, Liverpool*, THSLC Vol. 54 (1902), pp. 76ff.

7 Church Council Minutes, 10 May 1956.

8 Moore MS 415. The anonymous comment on the agreement was probably made by John Brownbill, editor of *A Calendar of the Papers of the Moore Family*, Liverpool (1913).

9 Moore MSS 477 and 493.

10 Elton, *The Chapel of St Mary del Key*, p. 76.

11 F.R. Raines (ed.), *History of the Chantries*, Chetham Society (1862), pp. 82ff.

12 Elton, *The Chapel of St Mary del Key*, p. 79 cites a reference from 1395.

13 Raines (ed.), *History of the Chantries*, p. 86.

14 The translation given in Appendix VI of R. Brooke, *Liverpool As It Was in the Last Quarter of the Eighteenth Century*, Liverpool (1853), p. 501. The original

is in the *Patent Rolls* from 1355, quoted in Elton, *The Chapel of St Mary del Key*, p. 80.

15   This is claimed by Elton, *The Chapel of St Mary del Key*, p. 79, but without evidence.

16   J. Brownbill, *Old St Nicholas', Liverpool*, THSLC Vol. 66 (1914), p. 250.

17   Details of the King's command to fetch the Earl of Ulster (later Duke of Clarence) to Ireland in May 1361 are given in H. Peet, *St. Nicholas's Church, Liverpool: Its Architectural History*, THSLC Vol. 65 (1913), p. 14.

18   *Bishop Stretton's Register* in Staffordshire Records Office, B/A/1/5 Folio 44a; Rowland A. Hill, Staffordshire Historical Collections VIII (1905), p. 99.

19   Note that until 1752 the new year began on 25 March, and so February fell after September in 1361.

20   *Bishop Stretton's Register*, B/A/1/5 Folio 45b.

21   Held by National Museums Liverpool, Accession Number: 31.211.2.

22   Peet, *St. Nicholas's Church, Liverpool*, p. 18.

23   Moore MS 175.

24   H. Peel, *Liverpool Vestry Books Vol. 1*, Liverpool (1912) p. 161

25   V. Oakden, *Building Recording at Liverpool Parish Church (Our Lady and St Nicholas), Liverpool*, National Museums Liverpool (2018) [Unpublished], pp. 8–10.

26   Cited in Peet, *St. Nicholas's Church, Liverpool*, p. 17.

27   Raines (ed.), *History of the Chantries*, p. 89.

28   DDM 39/31 held in Lancashire Records Office.

29   Moore MSS 191, 192 and 194.

30   DDSH 1/118 held in Lancashire Records Office.

31   Cited in Cox, *Plans of the Castle of Liverpool*, p. 196.

32   *Vatican Regesta 457: 1455–1456* in J.A. Twemlow (ed.), *Calendar of Papal Registers Relating to Great Britain and Ireland: Volume 11, 1455–1464*, HMSO (1921), pp. 103–15.

33   The text from the Lichfield *Ecclesiastical Register* is reproduced in Elton, *The Chapel of St Mary del Key*, p. 87.

34   W. Enfield, *An essay towards the history of Liverpool*, London (1774), p. 41; Peet, *St. Nicholas's Church, Liverpool*, p. 42.

35   H. Melville, *Redburn*. First published in 1849. Edition consulted Penguin (1976), p. 249; A. Brown, *Smith's Strangers Guide to Liverpool for 1843*, Liverpool (1843), p. 115.

36   Okill MS, xiv, 117, quoted in Elton, *The Chapel of St Mary del Key*, p. 88.

37   Raines (ed.), *History of the Chantries*, p. 85.

38   Gregson's *Fragments* 1817 and 1824, quoted in J. Twemlow, *Liverpool Town Books, Vol. 2*, Liverpool (1935) [hereafter *LTB2*], p. 1049.

39   So concluded Twemlow in *LTB2*, p. 1049.

40   J. Twemlow, *Liverpool Town Books, Vol. 1*, Liverpool (1918) [hereafter *LTB1*], pp. 296ff.

41   *LTB2*, p. 175.

42 M. Power (ed.), *Liverpool Town Books 1649–1671*, The Record Society (1999), p. 69.

Chapter Two: The Reformation

1 T. Heywood (ed.), *Moore Rental*, Chetham Society Series (1847), p. 36.

2 *Old Bylaws Codified 1540–1541*, in *LTB1*, p. 3.

3 Debts owing to St Nicholas' Church, 29 September 1524 and 10 December 1526, printed in Appendix IV of *LTB1*.

4 F.A. Bailey, *Some Memoranda by William Moore, Esq., Concerning Liverpool and Walton 1510–12*, THSLC Vol. 100 (1948), pp. 33–44.

5 The will of William More is reproduced in F.N. Moreton (ed.), *Selections from the Ancient Papers of the Moore Family*, THSLC Vol. 40 (1888), pp. 180–2.

6 *Old Bylaws Codified 1540–1541*, in *LTB1*, p. 2.

7 *LTB1*, pp. 39ff, p. 99.

8 Moore MSS 552 and 553.

9 The will of John Crosse is reproduced in the *Liverpool Vestry Books Vol. 1* (ed. Henry Peet), pp. 450ff. The identity of the various members of the Crosse family is discussed in R. Stewart-Brown and F.C. Beazley, *The Crosse Family of Wigan, Chorley and Liverpool*, THSLC Vol. 23 (1921). pp. 153–86.

10 F.R. Raines (ed.), *History of the Chantries*, Chetham Society (1862), p. 154.

11 *Bylaws 1541–1542*, in *LTB1*, p. 23.

12 Diarmaid MacCulloch, *The Later Reformation in England, 1547–1603* Basingstoke (2001), pp. 18ff.

13 Three leases appear in the Duchy papers at the National Archives (DL 14/5/18) and further leases in the Lancashire Archives (DDM 39/71). Each lease lists the burgesses and other property separately.

14 Chantry Rentals printed in Appendix I of *LTB1*.

15 Elton, *The Chapel of St Mary del Key, Liverpool*, THSLC Vol. 54 (1902), p. 98.

16 J. Picton, *Municipal Archives and Records from 1700 to 1835* Vol. 2, Liverpool (1886), p. 227.

17 Raines (ed.), *History of the Chantries*, p. 83.

18 Elton, *The Chapel of St Mary del Key*, p. 97.

19 Raines (ed.), *History of the Chantries*, p. 21.

20 Printed in Appendix XI of *LTB1*.

21 *Duchy Depositions*, recorded in Elton, *The Chapel of St Mary del Key, Liverpool*, THSLC Vol. 54 (1902) p. 103.

22 Raines (ed.), *History of the Chantries*, p. 89; Chantry Rentals printed in Appendix I of *LTB1*; Speke MS text first transcribed and published by Gregson in 1817, but described by Twemlow in Appendix I of *LTB1*, p. 410, n. 3.

23 Elton, *The Chapel of St Mary del Key*, p. 90.

24 *LTB1*, p. 286.

25 *LTB1*, p. 32a.

26 *LTB1*, p. 125, n. 12. Elton, *The Chapel of St Mary del Key*, p. 100.

27 *LTB1*, p. 125.
28 *LTB1*, p. 48 and p. 63.
29 MacCulloch, *The Later Reformation in England*, pp. 18ff.
30 *LTB1*, p. 50.
31 *LTB1*, p. 51 and n. 10.
32 J.E. Bailey (ed.), *Inventory of Goods in the Churches and Chapels of Lancashire taken in the year 1552*, Chetham Society (1888), pp. 96ff.
33 *LTB1*, p. 32a.
34 Joseph Ketley (ed.), *The Two Liturgies, AD 1549 and AD 1552*, Parker Society (1844), p. 76.
35 *LTB2*, pp. 73ff.
36 *LTB1*, p. 120.
37 *LTB1*, p. 129.
38 *LTB2*, p. 468.
39 This is the assumption of Twemlow, *LTB2*, p. 1049.
40 *LTB2*, p. 145.

Chapter Three: Liverpool Chapel 1559–1642

1   *LTB1*, pp. 336ff.
2   *LTB1*, p. 141. If they were unable to attend then a selection of other venues was given including Wigan, Prescot, Ormskirk, Sefton and Childwall. For the meeting about Toxteth Park p. 169.
3   *LTB2*, p. 429.
4   *LTB2*, p. 44.
5   Burial Plans held in OLSN Archives.
6   *LTB2*, pp. 529ff.
7   G. Chandler, *Liverpool Under Charles I*, Liverpool (1965), p. 146.
8   *LTB2*, pp. 242ff.
9   H. Melville, *Redburn*. First published in 1849. Edition consulted Penguin (1976), p. 250.
10 H. Peet, *St. Nicholas's Church, Liverpool: Its Architectural History*, THSLC Vol. 65 (1913) p. 18.
11 *LTB1*, p. 196.
12 *LTB2*, pp. 68ff.
13 G. Chandler, *Liverpool Under James I*, Liverpool (1960), p. 227.
14 Chandler, *Charles I*, p. 138.
15 Chandler, *Charles I*, pp. 154ff.
16 *LTB2*, pp. 521, 577, 808.
17 Chandler, *James I*, pp. 281ff.
18 Chandler, *James I*, p. 130.
19 Canons XXI and XXII, published in H.A. Wilson, *Constitutions and Canons Ecclesiastical 1604*, Clarendon Press (1923).
20 Canon XLIX, in Wilson, *Constitutions and Canons*.
21 Cal. Stat. Papers, Spanish, Vol. IV p. 185, quoted in *LTB2*, p. xxviii.

22 H. Bowler, *Recusant Roll No. 2 (1593–1594)*, Catholic Record Society (1965), pp. 55, 59, 82.

23 J. Hollinshead, *Liverpool in the Sixteenth Century*, Carnegie (2007), p. 146.

24 Chandler, *Charles I*, p. 158.

25 *LTB1*, p. 275; *LTB2*, pp. 9, 162 *passim*.

26 *LTB2*, pp. 441ff.

27 *LTB2*, p. 243.

28 Hollinshead, *Liverpool in the Sixteenth Century*, p. 147; *LTB2*, p. 753.

29 *LTB2*, pp. 73ff.

30 *LTB2*, p. 728.

31 Chandler, *James I*, p. 109.

32 Chandler, *James I*, p. 132.

33 *LTB1*, pp. 51.

34 *LTB1*, p. 275. The list of taxes is listed in *LTB1*, Appendix 5, pp. 436–40.

35 *LTB2*, pp. 143, 152, 175.

36 Chandler, *James I*, p. 173.

37 Chandler, *Charles I*, p. 158.

38 DDSH 1/195 in the Lancashire Archives.

39 *LTB2*, p. 73.

40 *LTB1*, p. 107.

41 *LTB1*, pp. 325, 346, 385.

42 DDX 597/1 in the Lancashire Archives.

43 M. Power (ed.), *Liverpool Town Books 1649–1671*, The Record Society (1999), p. 54.

44 *LTB2*, p. 310.

45 The Grant, and a note on its date, is given in Appendix N of *Liverpool Vestry Books Vol. 1* (ed. Henry Peet), pp. 466ff.

46 Power (ed.), *Town Books 1649–1671*, pp. 238ff.

47 *LTB1*, pp. 124ff.

48 *LTB1*, p. 374.

49 *LTB2*, pp. 409, 548.

50 Chandler, *Charles I*, p. 131.

51 *LTB2*, p. 114.

52 *LTB2*, p. 184.

53 *LTB2*, pp. 221, 524, 635, 654, 672.

54 *LTB2*, pp. 672, 654.

55 *LTB2*, pp. 485ff.

56 *LTB2*, p. 572.

57 *LTB2*, pp. 675, 703.

58 *LTB2*, pp. 675, 703.

59 Chandler, *James I*, p. 166.

60 Canon XLVI, in Wilson, *Constitutions and Canons*.

61 Chandler, *James I*, p. 268.

62 Chandler, *James I*, pp. 181, 256, 261ff.

63 *LTB1*, p. 396.
64 *LTB1*, pp. 235, 249, 257.
65 Chandler, *James* I, p. 247.
66 *LTB2*, pp. 304, 321.
67 *LTB1*, pp. 291–4.
68 *LTB1*, pp. 294–8.
69 *LTB1*, p. 310.
70 *LTB2*, p. 550.
71 *LTB2*, p. 180.

Chapter Four: Civil War and Restoration

 1 *LTB2*, p. 231.
 2 John Belchem (ed.), *Liverpool 800*, Liverpool (2006), p. 101.
 3 M. Power (ed.), *Liverpool Town Books 1649–1671*, Liverpool (1999), p. 210.
 4 G. Chandler, *Liverpool Under Charles I*, Liverpool (1965), p. 106.
 5 R. Parkinson (ed.), *The Life of Adam Martindale*, Cheetham Society (1845), pp. 31ff.
 6 The most recent study of note is S. Bull, *A General Plague of Madness: The Civil Wars in Lancashire 1640–1660*, Lancaster (2009).
 7 G. Ormerod, *Tracts relating to Military Proceedings in Lancashire during the Great Civil War*, Cheetham Society (1844), p. 104.
 8 Bull, *A General Plague of Madness*, p. 40.
 9 Chandler, *Charles I*, p. 311.
10 Parkinson (ed.), *The Life of Adam Martindale*, p. 41.
11 H. Melville, *Redburn*. First published in 1849. Edition consulted Penguin (1976), p. 250.
12 E.M. Platt, Liverpool during the Civil War, THSLC Vol. 61 (1909), p. 184.
13 Power (ed.), *Town Books 1649–1671*, p. 65.
14 Chandler, *Charles I*, pp. 158ff.
15 R.C. Richardson, *Puritanism in North-West England: A Regional Study of the Diocese of Chester to 1642*, Manchester (1972), p. 88.
16 Chandler, *Charles I*, p. 288.
17 Parkinson (ed.), *The Life of Adam Martindale*, p. 36.
18 Chandler, *Charles I*, pp. 301, 295.
19 Moore MS 319.
20 Chandler, *Charles I*, pp. 321ff.
21 Belchem, *Liverpool 800*, p. 102; T. Heywood (ed.), *Moore Rental*, Chetham Society Series (1847), p. xii.
22 Parkinson (ed.), *The Life of Adam Martindale*, p. 37.
23 Chandler, *Charles I*, p. 373.
24 Chandler, *Charles I*, p. 412.
25 Chandler, *Charles I*, p. 337.
26 Chandler, *Charles I*, pp. 351ff.
27 Power (ed.), *Town Books 1649–1671*, p. 84.

28 Power (ed.), *Town Books 1649–1671*, pp. 17, 31.

29 Bull, *A General Plague of Madness*, pp. 297ff.

30 H. Fishwick, *Lancashire and Cheshire Church Surveys*, Record Society Vol. 1 (1879), p. 84.

31 Chandler, *Charles I*, p. 376.

32 Power (ed.), *Town Books 1649–1671*, pp. 22, 26.

33 Power (ed.), *Town Books 1649–1671*, p. 58.

34 Chandler, *Charles I*, pp. 352, 411, 412.

35 Power (ed.), *Town Books 1649–1671*, pp. 92, 107, 118.

36 Power (ed.), *Town Books 1649–1671*, pp. 140, 144, 157.

37 Power (ed.), *Town Books 1649–1671*, pp. 151, 233, 250.

38 Moore MS 384.

39 Heywood, *Moore Rental*, pp. 12ff.

40 H. Peet, *An Inventory of the Plate, Register Books, and other Removeables in the Parish Churches of Liverpool*, Liverpool (1893), pp. 102ff.

41 D. Ascott, F. Lewis and M. Power, *Liverpool 1660–1750: People, Prosperity and Power*, Liverpool University Press (2006), p. 166.

42 Heywood, *Moore Rental*, pp. 54, 15.

43 Heywood, *Moore Rental*, p. 2.

44 Heywood, *Moore Rental*, pp. 3ff.

45 J. Hunter (ed.), *The Diary of Thomas Cartwright, Bishop of Chester, 1686–1687*, Camden Society (1843), p. 79.

46 Moore MS 304.

47 Moore MS 1136.

48 Heywood, *Moore Rental*, p. 13.

49 Burial Plans held in OLSN Archives.

50 *Liverpool Vestry Books Vol. 1*, p. 20.

51 H. Peet, *St. Nicholas's Church, Liverpool: Its Architectural History*, THSLC Vol. 65 (1913) p. 18.

52 Both are reproduced in Bull, *A General Plague of Madness*, pp. 226.

53 *Liverpool Vestry Books Vol. 1*, p. 51.

54 H. Peet, *The Ancient Chest of St. Nicholas's Church, Liverpool.*, THSLC Vol. 79 (1927).

55 *Liverpool Vestry Books Vol. 1*, pp. 1ff.

56 Peet, *St. Nicholas's Church, Liverpool*, pp. 19ff.

57 *Liverpool Vestry Books Vol. 1*, p. 3.

58 Hunter, *Diary of Thomas Cartwright*, p. 24.

59 *Liverpool Vestry Books Vol. 1*, p. 8.

60 Pew Deeds in OLSN Archives.

61 Peet, *St. Nicholas's Church, Liverpool*, p. 23.

62 Belchem, *Liverpool 800*, p. 118.

63 The Faculty is printed as Appendix L in *Liverpool Vestry Books Vol. 1*.

64 Power (ed.), *Town Books 1649–1671*, p. 92.

65 Power (ed.), *Town Books 1649–1671*, pp. 70, 85ff.

66 Power (ed.), *Town Books 1649–1671*, pp. 95, 105.

67 Power (ed.), *Town Books 1649–1671*, p. 104.

68 Power (ed.), *Town Books 1649–1671*, pp. 109ff, 119, 121.

69 Power (ed.), *Town Books 1649–1671*, p. 143.

70 Power (ed.), *Town Books 1649–1671*, p. 239.

71 Power (ed.), *Town Books 1649–1671*, pp. 247, 256.

72 J. Touzeau, *The Rise and Progress of Liverpool Vol. 1*, Liverpool (1910), pp. 342ff.

73 10 and 11 Will III, cap. 36.

Chapter Five: The Georgian Parish

1 10 and 11 Will III, cap. 36: s. 3, 4.

 2 *Liverpool Vestry Books Vol. 1*, pp. 66, 75.

 3 J. Wallace, *A general and descriptive history of the ancient and present state, of the town of Liverpool*, Liverpool (?1796), p. 131.

 4 *Liverpool Vestry Books Vol. 1*, p. 63.

 5 An album of photographs of St Peter's, taken before its demolition, is held in the OLSN Archives.

 6 *Liverpool Vestry Books Vol. 1*, pp. 75ff.

 7 *Liverpool Vestry Books Vol. 1*, pp. 112, 158; H. Peet, *An Inventory of the Plate, Register Books, and other Removeables in the Parish Churches of Liverpool*, Liverpool (1893), pp. 25ff.

 8 *Liverpool Vestry Books Vol. 1*, p. 202.

 9 J. Addy, et al. (eds), *The Diary of Henry Prescott LLB, Deputy Registrar of Chester Diocese Vol. 1*, Gloucester (1987), p. 14.

10 *Liverpool Vestry Books Vol. 1*, pp. 73.

11 Appendix C of the *Liverpool Vestry Books Vol. 1*.

12 D. Ascott, F. Lewis and M. Power, *Liverpool 1660–1750: People, Prosperity and Power*, Liverpool (2006), pp. 32ff.

13 *Liverpool Vestry Books Vol. 1*, p. 73.

14 H. Peet, *Brief Historical Notes on the Churches of St. George and St. John, Liverpool*, THSLC Vol. 51 (1899), pp. 30ff.

15 E.W. Cox, *An Attempt to Recover the Plans of the Castle of Liverpool from Authentic Records*, THSLC Vol. 42 (1890), p. 203.

16 *Liverpool Vestry Books Vol. 1*, p. 51; pew plans held in OLSN archives.

17 *Vide* Plate III in Peet, *Brief Historical Notes*, THSLC Vol. 51 opposite p. 32.

18 Anon., *Liverpool a Few Years Since by an Old Stager*, Liverpool (3rd edn 1885), p. 134.

19 *Liverpool Vestry Books Vol. 2*, pp. 210, 261, 265.

20 *Commonplace Book of John Jones* in the Library of the Liverpool Athenaeum.

21 *Gore's Directory 1829*, pp. 87ff.

22 A. Brown, *Smith's Strangers Guide to Liverpool for 1843*, Liverpool (1843), pp. 134ff; R.E. Scoresby-Jackson, *The Life of William Scoresby*, London (1861), pp. 214ff.

23 *Liverpool Vestry Books Vol. 1*, p. 111.

24 *Williamson's Liverpool Advertiser and Mercantile Register*, 18 March 1757; J. Picton, *Municipal Archives and Records from 1700 to 1835* Vol. 2, Liverpool (1886), p. 170.

25 Faculty in OLSN Archives.

26 *Liverpool Vestry Books Vol. 1*, pp. 150, 313.

27 Wallace, *A general and descriptive history of the ancient and present state, of the town of Liverpool*, p. 169; H. Melville, *Redburn*. First published in 1849. Edition consulted Penguin (1976), p. 250.

28 I am grateful to Laurence Westgaph for bringing this to my attention.

29 J. Touzeau, *The Rise and Progress of Liverpool Vol. 1*, Liverpool (1910), pp. 437ff.

30 *Gore's Directory 1829*, p. 88; Peet, *Brief Historical Notes*, THSLC Vol. 51, p. 33; Picton, *Municipal Archives and Records*, Vol. 2, p. 166.

31 *Liverpool Vestry Books Vol. 1*, p. 251.

32 *Liverpool Vestry Books Vol. 1*, p. 61.

33 *Liverpool Vestry Books Vol. 1*, pp. 116, 160, 161, 208ff, 313.

34 *Liverpool Vestry Books Vol. 2*, pp. 53ff.

35 *Gore's General Advertiser*, 25 June 1795.

36 OLSN Archives.

37 *An Act for Exempting their Majestyes Protestant Subjects dissenting from the Church of England from the Penalties of certaine Lawes* in. Touzeau, *The Rise and Progress of Liverpool Vol. 1*, p. 377.

38 *Liverpool Vestry Books Vol. 1*, pp. 116, 165.

39 *Gore's Directory 1766*, p. 75.

40 D. Lewis, *The Churches of Liverpool*, Liverpool (2001), p. 10.

41 K. Hipper, *The Johnsonian Baptists in Norwich*, Baptist Quarterly Vol. 38 (1999), pp. 19ff.

42 Lewis, *The Churches of Liverpool*, pp. 17ff; T. Burke, *Catholic History of Liverpool*, Liverpool (1910), pp. 9ff.

43 *Liverpool Vestry Books Vol. 1*, pp. 91ff.

44 *Liverpool Vestry Books Vol. 1*, pp. 108ff.

45 Addy, et al. (eds), *The Diary of Henry Prescott LLB Vol. 2*, p. 331.

46 Picton, *Municipal Archives and Records*, Vol. 2, p. 167.

47 Joseph Mayer, MS on St Thomas' Church in Liverpool City Archives (920MAY Box 10) p. 58.

48 *Liverpool Vestry Books Vol. 1*, pp. 198, 202ff.

49 *Liverpool Vestry Books Vol. 1*, p. 245.

50 *Liverpool Vestry Books Vol. 2*, p. 4.

51 Addy, et al. (eds), *The Diary of Henry Prescott LLB Vol. 2*, p. 333.

52 Picton, *Municipal Archives and Records*, Vol. 2, p. 164.

53 *Liverpool Vestry Books Vol. 1*, p. 160.

54 Wallace, *A general and descriptive history of the ancient and present state, of the town of Liverpool*, p. 110. This book was undoubtedly a principle source for R. Brooke, *Liverpool As It Was in the Last Quarter of the Eighteenth Century*, Liverpool (1853).

55 *Liverpool Vestry Books Vol. 1*, p. 47.

56 *Liverpool Vestry Books Vol. 1*, p. 75.

57 *Liverpool Vestry Books Vol. 1*, pp. 89, 174.

58 *Liverpool Vestry Books Vol. 1*, pp. 134ff.

59 V. Oakden, *Building Recording at Liverpool Parish Church (Our Lady and St Nicholas), Liverpool*, National Museums Liverpool (2018) [Unpublished], p. 11.

60 *Liverpool Vestry Books Vol. 1*, pp. 180, 231; R. Brooke, *Liverpool As It Was in the Last Quarter of the Eighteenth Century*, p. 43.

61 *Liverpool Vestry Books Vol. 2*, p. 27.

62 W. Enfield, *An essay towards the history of Liverpool*, London (1774), pp. 41ff.

63 *Liverpool Vestry Books Vol. 1*, pp. 238ff.

64 *Liverpool Vestry Books Vol. 1*, pp. 295ff.

65 H. Peet, *St. Nicholas's Church, Liverpool: Its Architectural History*, THSLC Vol. 65 (1913) pp. 31ff.

66 *Liverpool Vestry Books Vol. 2*, pp. 65, 69ff; faculty held in OLSN Archives.

67 *Liverpool Vestry Books Vol. 2*, p. 264.

68 Enfield, *An essay towards the history of Liverpool*, p. 48. Touzeau, *The Rise and Progress of Liverpool Vol. 1*, p. 407.

69 *Liverpool Vestry Books Vol. 1*, p. 77.

70 P. Healey (ed.), *The Liverpool Blue Coat School Past & Present 1708–2008*, Liverpool (2008), p. 6.

71 Picton, *Municipal Archives and Records*, Vol. 2, p. 172.

72 G. McLoughlin, *A Short History of the First Liverpool Infirmary 1749–1824*, Chichester (1978), pp. 13, 94.

73 Addy, et al. (eds), *The Diary of Henry Prescott LLB Vol. 1*, p. 241.

74 *Liverpool Vestry Books Vol. 1*, pp. 165ff.

75 *Liverpool Vestry Books Vol. 2*, pp. 14, 21.

76 *Liverpool Vestry Books Vol. 2*, pp. 73, 247ff, 253.

77 Anon., *Liverpool a Few Years Since by an Old Stager*, Liverpool (3rd edn 1885), pp. 122ff.

78 Anon., *Liverpool a Few Years Since by an Old Stager*, p. 130.

79 *Liverpool Vestry Books Vol. 1*, p. 96.

80 *Liverpool Vestry Books Vol. 2*, pp. 92ff.

81 *Liverpool Vestry Books Vol. 2*, pp. 95ff.

82 A. Hewitson, *History (from A.D. 705 to 1883) of Preston in the County of Lancaster*, Preston (1883), p. 268.

83 *Liverpool Vestry Books Vol. 2*, pp. 162ff.

84 D. Thom, *Liverpool Churches and Chapels*, THSLC Vol. 4 (1851), p. 186.

Chapter Six: Vestry and Politics 1681–1834

1 J. Hollinshead, *Liverpool in the Sixteenth Century*, Lancaster (2007), p. 130.

2 *LTB2* p. 43.

3 *LTB2* pp. 751ff.

4 G. Chandler, *Liverpool Under Charles I*, Liverpool (1965), p. 210.

5 M. Power (ed.), *Liverpool Town Books 1649–1671*, Liverpool (1999), pp. 71, 73.

6 Power (ed.), *Town Books 1649–1671*, p. 92.

7 *Liverpool Vestry Books Vol. 1*, Appendix A pp. 385, 389, 394.

8 Power (ed.), *Town Books 1649–1671*, p. 193.

9 *LTB1*, pp. 405ff.

10 *Liverpool Vestry Books Vol. 1*, Appendix A, p. 393.

11 *Liverpool Vestry Books Vol. 1*, p. 89.

12 *Liverpool Vestry Books Vol. 1*, p. 114.

13 *Liverpool Vestry Books Vol. 1*, pp. 68, 78, 176; *Vol. 2*, p. 166.

14 *Liverpool Vestry Books Vol. 1*, pp. 350ff; *Vol. 2*, p. 21.

15 E.g. *Liverpool Vestry Books Vol. 1*, pp. 185, 303.

16 *Liverpool Vestry Books Vol. 1*, pp. 105ff.

17 *Liverpool Vestry Books Vol. 1*, pp. 113, 115ff.

18 *Liverpool Vestry Books Vol. 1*, pp. 173, 216ff.

19 J. Picton, *Municipal Archives and Records from 1700 to 1835* Vol. 2, Liverpool (1886), p. 227.

20 G. McLoughlin, *A Short History of the First Liverpool Infirmary 1749–1824*, Chichester (1978), p. 73.

21 *Liverpool Vestry Books Vol. 1*, pp. 254, 261ff.

22 *Liverpool Vestry Books Vol. 2*, p. 39.

23 *Liverpool Vestry Books Vol. 1*, pp. 189, 203.

24 A. Brown, *Smith's Strangers Guide to Liverpool for 1843*, Liverpool (1843), p. 93.

25 F. Eden, *The State of the Poor Vol. 2*, London (1797), p. 329.

26 OLSN Archives.

27 *Liverpool Vestry Books Vol. 2*, pp. 327ff.

28 *Liverpool Vestry Books Vol. 1*, p. lxxxvi.

29 *Liverpool Vestry Books Vol. 2*, pp. 61, 64ff, 208, 241.

30 *Liverpool Vestry Books Vol. 2*, pp. 119, 171.

31 *Liverpool Vestry Books Vol. 2*, p. 90.

32 *Liverpool Vestry Books Vol. 1*, p. lxxvii.

33 Eden, *The State of the Poor Vol. 2*, p. 329.

34 *Liverpool Vestry Books Vol. 2*, pp. 85, 134, 152.

35 *Liverpool Vestry Books Vol. 2*, p. 209.

36 *Select Vestry Minutes*, 7 April 1829.

37 *Liverpool Vestry Books Vol. 1*, pp. 103, 109.

38 *Liverpool Vestry Books Vol. 1*, pp. 144, 190.

39 *Liverpool Vestry Books Vol. 1*, p. 269.

40 *Liverpool Vestry Books Vol. 2*, pp. 227ff.

41 *Liverpool Vestry Books Vol. 1*, pp. 150, 170, 233.

42 *Liverpool Vestry Books Vol. 1*, p. 245; *Vol. 2*, p. 42; Picton, *Municipal Archives and Records*, Vol. 2, p. 227.

43 *Liverpool Vestry Books Vol. 2*, p. 83.

44 *Liverpool Vestry Books Vol. 1*, pp. 119, 291.

45 The minutes are held in Liverpool City Archives Ref. 353 PAR/3/1; reprinted in Appendix A of *Liverpool Vestry Books Vol. 2*.

46 J. Touzeau, *The Rise and Progress of Liverpool Vol. 2*, Liverpool (1910), pp. 847ff.

47 *Liverpool Vestry Books Vol. 1*, pp. 361ff; *Liverpool Vestry Books Vol. 2*, p. 19.

48 *Liverpool Vestry Books Vol. 1*, Appendix A §IX; plans in OLSN Archives.

49 *Liverpool Vestry Books Vol. 2*, pp. 135ff.

50 *Liverpool Vestry Books Vol. 2*, pp. 275, 286ff.

51 *Liverpool Vestry Books Vol. 1*, pp. 8, 10, 17, 23.

52 *Liverpool Vestry Books Vol. 2*, p. 89.

53 *Liverpool Vestry Books Vol. 1*, p. 97.

54 *Liverpool Vestry Books Vol. 2*, pp. 141, 174, 265ff.

55 Picton, *Municipal Archives and Records*, Vol. 2, p. 228.

56 *Liverpool Vestry Books Vol. 2*, pp. 3, 20.

57 *Liverpool Vestry Books Vol. 2*, pp. 2ff, 6, 9ff, 32.

58 *Liverpool Vestry Books Vol. 2*, pp. 127ff.

59 *Liverpool Mercury* 27 April 1832 2e–3a.

60 *Liverpool Vestry Books Vol. 1*, pp. 162, 166, 263.

61 *Liverpool Vestry Books Vol. 1*, p. 233.

62 *Liverpool Vestry Books Vol. 2*, pp. 211ff.

63 OLSN Archives.

64 M. Power, *Creating a Port: Liverpool 1695–1715*, THSLC Vol. 149 (1999), p. 53; J. Touzeau, *The Rise and Progress of Liverpool Vol. 1*, Liverpool (1910), pp. 337ff.

65 Power, *Creating a Port*, p. 54.

66 Picton, *Municipal Archives and Records*, Vol. 2, pp. 66ff; D. Ascott, F. Lewis and M. Power, *Liverpool 1660–1750: People, Prosperity and Power*, Liverpool (2006), p. 179.

67 *Liverpool Vestry Books Vol. 1*, p. 83.

68 Touzeau, *The Rise and Progress of Liverpool Vol. 2*, pp. 795ff.

69 *Liverpool Vestry Books Vol. 2*, p. 45.

70 Petition and Rate Assessment in OLSN Archives.

71 *Liverpool Vestry Books Vol. 2*, pp. 298ff, 364.

Chapter Seven: The Victorian Church

1 H. Peet, *An Inventory of the Plate, Register Books, and other Removeables in the Parish Churches of Liverpool*, Liverpool (1893), p. 127.

2 *Liverpool Parish Magazine*, May 1916, p. 45.

3 Table of expenditure in *An Act for the Administration of the Laws Relating to the Poor in the Parish of Liverpool*, Liverpool (1883).

4 OLSN Archives.

5 Hansard, *House of Commons Debates*, 22 May 1835, Vol. 28, col. 14f.

6 *Liverpool Vestry Minutes* in LCC Archives, 25 March 1835.

7 Licence in OLSN Archives.

8   A. Wilcox, *The Church and the Slums: the Victorian Anglican Church and its Mission to Liverpool's Poor*, Newcastle (2014), p. 9.

9   *Liverpool Mercury*, 10 February 1843, p. 50.

10 *Liverpool Daily Post*, 9 September 1862, p. 5.

11 A. Miller, *Poverty Deserved? Relieving the Poor in Victorian Liverpool*, Birkenhead (1988), pp. 8ff.

12 Miller, *Poverty Deserved?*, pp. 11ff.

13 Miller, *Poverty Deserved?*, pp. 30ff.

14 For example, *Liverpool Daily Post*, 10 January 1867, p. 5; 28 July 1887, p. 6.

15 *Liverpool Daily Post*, 2 February 1869, p. 5.

16 A. Hume, *Condition of Liverpool Religious and Social*, Liverpool (1858), p. 16.

17 The document is on display in the Parish Centre of Our Lady & St Nicholas.

18 H. Mann, *Religious Worship in England and Wales*, London (1854), p. 122.

19 Wilcox, *The Church and the Slums*, p. 42.

20 OLSN Archives.

21 Hume, *Condition of Liverpool*, p. 10.

22 Hume, *Condition of Liverpool*, p. 8.

23 Wilcox, *The Church and the Slums*, p. 51.

24 Wilcox, *The Church and the Slums*, p. 1.

25 Wilcox, *The Church and the Slums*, p. 14.

26 Wilcox, *The Church and the Slums*, p. 15.

27 Wilcox, *The Church and the Slums*, p. 47.

28 Wilcox, *The Church and the Slums*, pp. 117ff.

29 Wilcox, *The Church and the Slums*, p. 121.

30 Hansard, *House of Commons Debates*, 28 April 1893, Vol. 11, col. 1452.

31 *Liverpool Daily Post*, 22 January 1889, p. 7.

32 *Liverpool Daily Post*, 14 April 1898, p. 3.

33 *Liverpool Mercury*, 13 May 1869, p. 6; 11 March 1870, p. 6; 30 July 1864, p. 6; 30 January 1865, p. 6.

34 OLSN Archives.

35 H. Peet, *Brief Historical Notes on the Churches of St George and St John, Liverpool*, THSLC Vol. 53 (1899) p. 40.

36 T.H. Bankier, *History of St Luke's Church Liverpool*, Liverpool (1900), p. 28.

37 *Liverpool Courier*, 8 January 1916.

38 Wilcox, *The Church and the Slums*, p. 91.

39 *Liverpool Vestry Minutes*, 29 March 1842.

40 D. Lewis, *The Churches of Liverpool*, Liverpool (2001), p. 50.

41 *Liverpool Vestry Minutes*, 1841.

42 *Liverpool Mercury*, 22 December 1854, p. 12.

43 *Liverpool Vestry Minutes*, 1849.

44 R. Crawford, et al., *The Hidden Cemetery of Walton*, Walton-on-the-Hill History Group (2013), pp. 6ff, 45ff.

45 Plans in OLSN Archives.

46 Papers of J. Hargreaves in the Peet Collection (8/1/1), Liverpool University Archives.

47 *Liverpool Gazette*, 26 April 1862, p. 6.

48 *Sheffield Daily Telegraph*, 2 July 1875, p. 4.

49 Wilcox, *The Church and the Slums*, pp. 15ff.

50 A. Brown, *Smith's Strangers Guide to Liverpool for 1843*, Liverpool (1843), p. 249; *Parish Registers of St George's, Liverpool* at Liverpool Records' Office.

51 *Liverpool Vestry Minutes*, April 1879.

52 Wilcox, *The Church and the Slums*, pp. 94ff.

53 *Liverpool Daily* Post, 26 November 1863, p. 7; *Liverpool Mercury*, 3 December 1864, p. 3; *Liverpool Courier*, 3 March 1892, p. 4.

54 *Liverpool Mercury*, 14 November 1864, p. 6.

55 Hume, *Condition of Liverpool*, pp. 18ff.

56 *Liverpool Echo*, 14 June 1967 p. 9.

57 Correspondence in OLSN Archives.

58 *Liverpool Weekly Albion*, 26 March 1881, p. 3.

59 Registers of Services in OLSN Archives.

60 *Liverpool Daily Post*, 29 October 1862.

61 *Liverpool Mercury*, 17 June 1895; 26 June 1905, p. 4.

62 *Liverpool Vestry Books Vol. 2*, p. xxvii.

63 *Liverpool Vestry Books Vol. 2*, p. xliii.

64 Fuller details of the battle over endowments are given in J. Touzeau, *The Rise and Progress of Liverpool Vol. 2*, Liverpool (1910), pp. 872ff and *Liverpool Vestry Books Vol. 2*, pp. liiiff.

65 *Liverpool Vestry Books Vol. 2*, p. lxix.

66 *Crockford's Clerical Directory 1868*, p. 111.

67 W. Gibson, *Church, State and Society, 1760–1850*, Basingstoke (1994), pp. 122ff.

68 Bankier, *History of St Luke's*, p. 30.

69 *Liverpool Parish Magazine*, May 1916, p. 45.

70 H.C.G. Matthew (ed.), *The Gladstone Diaries Vol. 12*, Oxford (1994), pp. 255, 259.

71 H.C.G. Matthew (ed.), *The Gladstone Diaries Vol. 13*, Oxford (2003), p. 216.

72 *Gore's Directory* (1900) p. 1979.

73 Compulsory Church Rate Abolition Act, 1868, s7.

74 *Liverpool Vestry Minutes*, March and April 1853.

75 P. Toon and M. Smout, *John Charles Ryle Evangelical Bishop*, Cambridge (1976), pp. 71ff.

76 *Liverpool Parish Magazine*, May 1916, p. 44.

77 P. Kennerley, *The Building of Liverpool Cathedral*, Lancaster (1991), Ch. 1.

78 Hansard, *House of Commons Debates*, 9 August 1884, Vol. 292, col. 360.

79 Toon and Smout, *John Charles Ryle*, pp. 84ff.

80 *Liverpool Review*, 15 November 1884, p. 10.

81 *Liverpool Review*, 13 December 1884, p. 9.

82 Peet, *An Inventory of Parish Churches of Liverpool*, p. 127; H. Peet, *St. Nicholas's Church, Liverpool: Its Architectural History*, THSLC Vol. 65 (1913), pp. 36ff.

83 *Liverpool Mercury*, 6 February 1868, p. 6.

84 *Liverpool Mercury*, 6 February 1868, p. 6.

85 *Liverpool Daily Post*, 28 September 1868, p. 7.

86 Registers and plans in OLSN Archives.

87 *Liverpool Mercury*, 16 September 1876, p. 8.

88 OLSN Archives; Peet, *An Inventory of Parish Churches of Liverpool*, p. 7.

Chapter Eight: The Great War and its aftermath

1 *Liverpool Daily Post*, 12 January 1918, p. 3.

2 *London Gazette*, 3 March 1916, p. 2340.

3 Register of Services in OLSN Archives; *Liverpool Daily Post*, 22 October 1914, p. 3.

4 *Liverpool Echo*, 11 December 1915, p. 1.

5 *Liverpool Parish Magazine*, June 1918, p. 47.

6 Register of Services in OLSN Archives.

7 *Liverpool Parish Magazine*, August 1916, p. 78.

8 Register of Service in OLSN Archives; *Liverpool Daily Post*, 12 January 1918, p. 3.

9 *Liverpool Echo*, 7 June 1916, p. 2.

10 A. Clayton, *Chavasse: Double VC*, London (1992), pp. 104ff.

11 *Liverpool Echo*, 25 August 1917, p. 2.

12 From a contemporary newspaper cutting in the Dunt Album held by the Liverpool Scottish Museum Trust.

13 *Liverpool Daily Post*, 12 November 1918, p. 3; *Liverpool Echo*, 12 November 1918, p. 4.

14 *Liverpool Parish Magazine*, December 1918, p. 94.

15 *Liverpool Echo*, 11 November 1918, p. 3; Music Register in OLSN Archives.

16 *Liverpool Parish Magazine*, August 1917, p. 74.

17 *Liverpool Echo*, 11 November 1926, p. 9.

18 Church Council Minutes, 20 October 1932, in OLSN Archives.

19 *Liverpool Parish Magazine*, November 1930, p. 4.

20 *Liverpool Parish Magazine*, July 1930, p. 4; November 1930, pp. 4ff.

21 *Liverpool Parish Magazine*, October 1922, p. 2.

22 Papers held in OLSN Archives.

23 Church Council Minutes, 1 May 1934.

24 Plans in OLSN Archives.

25 *Liverpool Echo*, 17 August 1931, p. 9.

26 *Liverpool Parish Magazine*, December 1925, p. 3; January 1926, p. 1.

27 G. Tibbatts, *John How: Cambridge Don, Parish Priest, Scottish Primus*, Oxford (1983), p. 56.

28 G. Tibbatts, *The Oratory of the Good Shepherd*, Windsor (1988), p. 7.

29 Licence in OLSN Archives; Tibbatts, *John How*, pp. 56ff; O. Chadwick,

Michael Ramsey, A Life, Oxford (1990), pp. 37ff; Church Council Minutes 1935 *et passim*.

30 Tibbatts, *The Oratory of the Good Shepherd*, pp. 9, 27ff.

31 Tibbatts, *The Oratory of the Good Shepherd*, p. 36.

32 Church Council Minutes, 20 October 1932.

33 *Liverpool Daily Post*, 5 October 1940, p. 3.

34 A. Mason, *History of the Society of the Sacred Mission*, Norwich (1993), p. 270.

35 Church Council Minutes, 2 February 1934.

36 Church Council Minutes, 8 February 1935.

37 Church Council Minutes, 31 October 1946.

38 Church Council Minutes, 8 February 1935; *Liverpool Echo*, 6 May 1935, p. 2.

39 A. Richards, *The Flag: The Story of the Revd David Railton MC*, Oxford (2017), pp. 234ff.

40 *Liverpool Daily Post*, 23 February 1942, p. 3.

41 Church Council Minutes, 10 March and 2 April 1936; 25 May 1939, in OLSN Archives.

42 Richards, *The Flag: The Story of the Revd David Railton*, p. 236.

43 *Liverpool Echo*, Monday 12 June 1939, p. 9; Church Council Minutes, 12 December 1939.

44 *Liverpool Parish Magazine*, May 1916, p. 42.

45 Registers in OLSN Archives.

46 H. Peet, *Reliquiae of St. Peter's Church, Liverpool*, THSLC Vol. 74 (1922), p. 74.

47 Peet, *Reliquiae of St. Peter's Church, Liverpool*, pp. 76ff.

48 Unknown, *The Story of the Church of Our Lady and St Nicholas Liverpool*, Gloucester & London (*c.* 1932), p. 21.

49 Peet, *Reliquiae of St. Peter's Church, Liverpool*, p. 79.

50 Hansard, *House of Lords Debates*, 22 June 1938, Vol. 110, col. 127ff.

Chapter Nine: The Blitz and Rebuilding

1 A. Richards, *The Flag: The Story of the Revd David Railton MC*, Oxford (2017), pp. 237ff.

2 Church Council Minutes, 19 October 1940 in OLSN Archives.

3 R. Whitworth, *Merseyside at War*, Liverpool (1988), p. 51.

4 Church Council Minutes, 2 December 1943.

5 Diary in OLSN Archives.

6 *Liverpool Evening Express*, 21 December 1940, p. 1.

7 Church Council Minutes, 1 March 1941.

8 D. Lewis, *The Churches of Liverpool*, Liverpool (2001), p. 14.

9 Lewis, *The Churches of Liverpool*, p. 45.

10 Whitworth, *Merseyside at War*, pp. 72ff.

11 Lewis, *The Churches of Liverpool*, pp. 16, 18.

12 Whitworth, *Merseyside at War*, p. 78.

13 Church Council Minutes, 1 March 1941; *Liverpool Daily Post*, 23 August 1941, p. 4.

14 Richards, *The Flag: The Story of the Revd David Railton*, p. 240.

15 *Liverpool Echo*, 23 July 1941, p. 6.

16 Church Council Minutes, 10 March 1942.

17 Receipt in OLSN Archives; Church Council Minutes, 9 April 1942.

18 *Liverpool Echo*, 6 June 1942, p. 4; *Liverpool Daily Post*, 8 June 1942, p. 4.

19 Church Council Minutes, 20 March 1942.

20 A. Mason, *History of the Society of the Sacred Mission*, Norwich (1993), p. 271.

21 Church Council Minutes, 20 April 1944, 24 January 1946, *passim*; J. Peart-Binns, *Ambrose Reeves*, London (1973), p. 49.

22 Church Council Minutes, 4 September 1942; 5 March 1943.

23 Church Council Minutes, 4 July 1943; *Liverpool Daily Post*, 12 July 1943, p. 4.

24 Church Council Minutes, 19 October 1944.

25 *Liverpool Daily Post*, 5 May 1945, p. 3.

26 *Liverpool Echo*, 31 January 1944, p. 4

27 *Yorkshire Evening Post*, 5 October 1945, p. 12.

28 Peart-Binns, *Ambrose Reeves*, pp. 57ff.

29 Peart-Binns, *Ambrose Reeves*, p. 63.

30 Church Council Minutes, 18 October 1945.

31 Church Council Minutes, 17 March 1946.

32 Church Council Minutes, 18 March 1948.

33 Newspaper cutting in Diary in OLSN Archives, p. 63.

34 *Policy of the New Parish of Liverpool*, pasted in the Church Council Minute Book for 1947.

35 Church Council Minutes, 22 January 1948.

36 Church Council Minutes, 27 November 1947; 16 April 1952.

37 *Liverpool Echo*, 26 September 1949, p. 3.

38 Diary in OLSN Archives, p. 79.

39 *Liverpool Echo*, 13 February 1952, p. 1.

40 Diary in OLSN Archives, p. 85.

41 *Liverpool Evening Express*, 21 December 1940, p. 1.

42 Church Council Minutes, 24 March 1944.

43 Church Council Minutes, 5 April 1945.

44 Church Council Minutes, 18 October 1945.

45 Church Council Minutes, 31 October 1946.

46 Church Council Minutes, 5 June 1947.

47 Church Council Minutes, 25 September 1947; *Festival of Consecration*, Liverpool (1952), p. 18.

48 Church Council Minutes, 27 November 1947; 19 July 1951.

49 *Daily Post*, 17 May 1949, p. 3.

50 Church Council Minutes, 27 January 1949.

51 *Festival of Consecration*, pp. 19ff; Church Council Minutes, 21 February 1952.

52 Church Council Minutes, 4 September 1952.

53 *Liverpool Parish Church Review*, January 1950, p. 3.

54 *Church Times*, 21 April 1950, p. 303.

55 Church Council Minutes, 8 May 1952.

56 Diary in OLSN Archives, p. 94.

57 *Festival of Consecration*, pp. 21ff; Diary in OLSN Archives, pp. 99ff.

58 Church Council Minutes, 24 November 1955.

59 Church Council Minutes, 19 July 1951.

60 Diary in OLSN Archives, p. 112.

Chapter Ten: The Church since the War

1 *Daily Post*, 2 November 1953, p. 5; *Radio Times*, 30 October 1953, p. 14.

2 *Radio Times*, 27 September 1957, p. 32.

3 Author's interview with Frank Telfer, 25 July 2018.

4 Diary in OLSN Archives, p. 185.

5 Church Council Minutes, 9 October 1961.

6 *Daily Mirror*, 27 September 1960, p. 22.

7 Author's interview with Alan Woodhouse, 18 July 2018.

8 Liverpool Samaritans Log Book, 13 and 14 December 1962.

9 Author's interview with Alan Woodhouse, 18 July 2018.

10 G. Whalley (ed.), *Christopher Pepys: A Remembrance by his Friends*, Oxford (1980), p. 41.

11 Diary in OLSN Archives, p. 124.

12 *Liverpool Echo*, 25 June 1964, p. 3.

13 E. Young, *No Fun Like Work*, London (1970), pp. 141ff.

14 Church Council Minutes, 14 May 1970.

15 Church Council Minutes, 17 June 1970.

16 Young, *No Fun Like Work*, pp. 138ff.

17 *Daily Post*, 13 October 1982, p. 17.

18 Rector's Advisory Committee, 15 December 1975, from the papers of Nicholas Frayling.

19 *Daily Post*, 29 March 1965, p. 8.

20 Lent programmes in OLSN Archives.

21 *Liverpool Echo*, 9 March 1982, p. 1.

22 *Liverpool Echo*, 11 March 1982, p. 1; 12 March 1982, p. 1.

23 *Liverpool Echo*, 9 December 1970, p. 2; 16 February 1971, p. 2.

24 Author's interview with Nicholas Frayling, 3 May 2019.

25 Bishop of Liverpool to Sir William Gladstone, 16 February 2007, in OLSN Archives.

26 Sir William Gladstone to the Bishop of Liverpool, 7 March 2007, in OLSN Archives.

27 *Liverpool Echo*, 3 October 1967, p. 3; 14 November 1968, p. 17.

28 Young, *No Fun Like Work*, p. 135.

29 Rector's Advisory Committee, 14 February 1977.

30 D. Lewis, *The Churches of Liverpool*, Liverpool (2001), p. 13.

31 Rector's Advisory Committee, 23 June 1980.

32 Author's interview with Nicholas Frayling, 3 May 2019.

Bibliography

Primary Sources

Addy, J., et al. (eds), *The Diary of Henry Prescott LLB, Deputy Registrar of Chester Diocese (3 Volumes)*, Gloucester (1987)

Bailey, J. E. (ed.), *Inventory of Goods in the Churches and Chapels of Lancashire taken in the year 1552*, Chetham Society (1888)

Bishop Stretton's Register in Staffordshire Records Office, B/A/1/5 Folio 44a.

Chandler, G., *Liverpool Under James I*, Liverpool (1960)

Chandler, G., *Liverpool Under Charles I*, Brown, Liverpool (1965)

Fishwick, H., *Lancashire and Cheshire Church Surveys*, Record Society Vol. 1 (1879)

Heywood, T. (ed.), *Moore Rental*, Chetham Society Series (1847)

Hill, Rowland A., Staffordshire Historical Collections VIII (1905)

Hunter, J. (ed.), *The Diary of Thomas Cartwright, Bishop of Chester, 1686–1687*, Camden Society (1843)

Liverpool Vestry Minutes (untranscribed) in LCC Archives

Moore MSS in Liverpool City Archives, cf J. Brownbill, *A Calendar of the Papers of the Moore Family*, The Record Society (1913)

Ormerod, G., *Tracts relating to Military Proceedings in Lancashire during the Great Civil War*, Cheetham Society (1844)

Our Lady and St Nicholas (OLSN) Archives

Parkinson, R. (ed.), *The Life of Adam* Martindale, Cheetham Society (1845)

Peet, H., *An Inventory of the Plate, Register Books, and other Removeables in the Parish Churches of Liverpool*, Liverpool (1893)

Peet Collection, Liverpool University Archives

Peet, Henry (ed.), *Liverpool Vestry Books Volume 1*, Liverpool (1912)

Peet, Henry (ed.), *Liverpool Vestry Books Volume 2*, Liverpool (1915)

Power, M. (ed.), *Liverpool Town Books 1649–1671*, The Record Society (1999)

Raines, F. R. (ed.), *History of the Chantries*, Chetham Society (1862)

Twemlow, J. A. (ed.), *Calendar of Papal Registers Relating to Great Britain and Ireland: Volume 11, 1455–1464*, HMSO (1921)

Twemlow, J., *Liverpool Town Books* Volume 1, Liverpool (1918)

Twemlow, J., *Liverpool Town Books* Volume 2, Liverpool (1935)

Secondary Reading

Anon., *Liverpool a Few Years Since by an Old Stager*, Liverpool (3rd edn 1885)

Ascott, D., F. Lewis, M. Power, *Liverpool 1660–1750: People, Prosperity and Power*, Liverpool (2006)

Bailey, F. A., *Some Memoranda by William Moore, Esq., Concerning Liverpool and Walton 1510–12*, THSLC Vol 100 (1948)

Bankier, T. H., *History of St Luke's Church Liverpool*, Liverpool (1900)

Beazley, F. C., *A Legacy To S. Mary Del Key, 1509*, THSLC 82 (1930)

Belchem, John (ed.), *Liverpool 800*, Liverpool (2006)

Blease, W. Lyon, *The Poor Law In Liverpool 1681–1834*, THSLC 61 (1909)

Brazendale, D. (ed.), *Georgian Liverpool, a Guide to the City in 1797 by Dr William Moss*, Lancaster (2007)

Brooke, R., *Liverpool As It Was in the Last Quarter of the Eighteenth Century*, Liverpool (1853)

Brown, A., *Smith's Strangers Guide to Liverpool for 1843*, Liverpool (1843)

Brownbill, J., *Old St Nicholas', Liverpool*, THSLC 66 (1914)

Broxap, E., *The Great Civil War in Lancashire* Manchester (1910), 2nd edn Dore (1973)

Bull, S., *A General Plague of Madness: The Civil Wars in Lancashire 1640–1660*, Lancaster (2009)

Burke, T., *Catholic History of Liverpool*, Liverpool (1910)

Chadwick, O., *Michael Ramsey, A Life*, Oxford (1990)

Clayton, A., *Chavasse: Double VC*, London (1992)

Cox, E. W., *An Attempt to Recover the Plans of the Castle of Liverpool from Authentic Records*, THSLC Vol. 42 (1890)

Crawford, R., et al., *The Hidden Cemetery of Walton*, Walton-on-the-Hill History Group (2013)

Denny, W. H., *Cure and Regimen of the Soul: Lenten Sermons Preached in the Parish Church of Liverpool* (1858)

Eden, F., *The State of the Poor* Vol. 2, London (1797)

Elton, J., *The Chapel of St Mary del Key, Liverpool*, THSLC Vol. 54 (1902)

Enfield, W., *An essay towards the history of Liverpool*, London (1774)

Farley, I. D., *J. C. Ryle – Episcopal evangelist a study in late Victorian evangelicalism*, Durham theses, Durham University (1988)

Gibson, W., *Church, State and Society, 1760–1850*, Basingstoke (1994)

Gratton, M., *Liverpool under parliament: the anatomy of a civil war garrison, May 1643 to June 1644*, THSLC 156 (1997)

Healey, P., (ed.), *The Liverpool Blue Coat School Past & Present 1708–2008*, Liverpool (2008)

Herdman, W. G., *Pictorial Relics of Ancient Liverpool*, Liverpool (1878)

Hewitson, A., *History (from A.D. 705 to 1883) of Preston in the County of Lancaster*, Preston (1883)

Hipper, K., *The Johnsonian Baptists in Norwich*, Baptist Quarterly Vol. 38 (1999)

Hollinshead, Janet, *Liverpool in the Sixteenth Century*, Lancaster (2007)

Hume, A., *Condition of Liverpool Religious and Social*, Liverpool (1858)

Kennerley, P., *The Building of Liverpool Cathedral*, Lancaster (1991)

Ketley, J. (ed.), *The Two Liturgies, AD 1549 and AD 1552*, Parker Society (1844)

Lewis, D., *The Churches of Liverpool*, Liverpool (2001)

MacCulloch, D., *The Later Reformation in England 1547–1603*, Basingstoke (2001)

Mann, H., *Religious Worship in England and Wales*, London (1854)

Mason, A., *History of the Society of the Sacred Mission*, Norwich (1993)

McLoughlin, G., *A Short History of the First Liverpool Infirmary 1749–1824*, Chichester (1978)

Melville, H., *Redburn*. First published in 1849. Edition consulted by Penguin (1976)

Miller, A., *Poverty Deserved? Relieving the Poor in Victorian Liverpool*, Birkenhead (1988)

Moreton, F. N. (ed.), *Selections from the Ancient Papers of the Moore Family*, THSLC Vol. 40 (1888)

Oakden, V., *Building Recording at Liverpool Parish Church (Our Lady and St Nicholas), Liverpool*, National Museums Liverpool (2018) [Unpublished]

Peart-Binns, J., *Ambrose Reeves*, London (1973)

Peet, H., *Brief Historical Notes on the Churches of St. George and St. John, Liverpool*, THSLC Vol. 51 (1899),

Peet, H., *Brief Historical Notes on the Churches of St George and St John, Liverpool*, Transactions of the HSLC Vol. 53 (1899)

Peet, H., *Liverpool In The Reign Of Queen Anne, 1705 And 1708*, THSLC 59 (1907)

Peet, H., *St. Nicholas's Church, Liverpool: Its Architectural History*, THSLC Vol. 65 (1913)

Peet, H., *The Recently Recovered Plans Of Old St. Nicholas's Church, Liverpool*, THSLC Vol. 71 (1920)

Peet, H., *Reliquiae Of St. Peter's Church, Liverpool*, THSLC Vol. 74 (1922)

Peet, H., *The Ancient Chest Of St. Nicholas's Church, Liverpool*, THSLC Vol. 79 (1927)

Picton, J. A. *Memorials of Liverpool*, Liverpool (1873)

Picton, J., *Municipal Archives and Records from 1700 to 1835*, Liverpool (1886)

Platt, E. M., *Liverpool during the Civil War*, THSLC 61 (1909)

Power, M., *Creating a Port: Liverpool 1695–1715*, THSLC Vol. 149 (1999)

Richards, A., *The Flag: the Story of the Revd David Railton MC*, Oxford (2017)

Richardson, R. C., *Puritanism in North-West England: A Regional Study of the Diocese of Chester to 1642*, Manchester (1972)

Saxton, E. B., *Losses of the Inhabitants of Liverpool on the Taking of the Town 1644*, THSLC 91 (1939)

Scoresby-Jackson, R. E., *The Life of William Scoresby*, London (1861)

Stewart-Brown, R. and F. C. Beazley, *The Crosse Family of Wigan, Chorley and Liverpool*, THSLC Vol. 23 (1921)

Thom, D., *Liverpool Churches and Chapels*, THSLC Vol. 4 (1851)

Tibbatts, G., *John How: Cambridge Don, Parish Priest, Scottish Primus*, Oxford (1983)

Tibbatts, G., *The Oratory of the Good Shepherd*, Windsor (1988)

Toon, P., and M. Smout, *John Charles Ryle Evangelical Bishop*, Cambridge (1976)

Touzeau, J., *The Rise and Progress of Liverpool* Vol. 1 and Vol. 2, Liverpool (1910)

Wallace, J., *A general and descriptive history of the ancient and present state, of the town of Liverpool*, Liverpool (?1796)

Whalley, G. (ed.), *Christopher Pepys: A Remembrance by his Friends*, Oxford (1980)

Whitworth, R., *Merseyside at War*, Liverpool (1988)

Wilcox, A., *The Church and the Slums: the Victorian Anglican Church and its Mission to Liverpool's Poor*, Newcastle (2014)

Wilson, H. A., *Constitutions and Canons Ecclesiastical 1604*, Clarendon Press (1923)

Young, E., *No Fun Like Work*, London (1970)

Index